THE CHILD'S POLITICAL WORLD

THE CHILD'S POLITICAL WORLD

A Longitudinal Perspective

by Stanley W. Moore,
James Lare,
Kenneth A. Wagner

PRAEGER

PRAEGER SPECIAL STUDIES • PRAEGER SCIENTIFIC

New York • Philadelphia • Eastbourne, UK
Toronto • Hong Kong • Tokyo • Sydney

Library of Congress Cataloging in Publication Data

Moore, Stanley W.
  The child's political world.

  Includes index.
  1. Children and politics—Longitudinal studies.
  2. Political socialization—Longitudinal studies.
  3. Civics.   4. School children—Attitudes—Longitudinal
  studies.   I. Lare, James.   II. Wagner, Kenneth A.
  III. Title.
  HQ784.P5M66   1985   305.2'3   84-15975
  ISBN 0–03–001529–4 (alk. paper)

Published in 1985 by Praeger Publishers
CBS Educational and Professional Publishing, a Division of CBS Inc.
521 Fifth Avenue, New York, NY 10175 USA

Printed in the United States of America on acid-free paper

INTERNATIONAL OFFICES

Orders from outside the United States should be sent to the appropriate address listed below. Orders from areas not
listed below should be placed through CBS International Publishing, 383 Madison Ave., New York, NY 10175 USA

Australia, New Zealand
Holt Saunders, Pty. Ltd., 9 Waltham St., Artarmon, N.S.W. 2064, Sydney, Australia

Canada
Holt, Rinehart & Winston of Canada, 55 Horner Ave., Toronto, Ontario, Canada M8Z 4X6

Europe, the Middle East, & Africa
Holt Saunders, Ltd., 1 St. Anne's Road, Eastbourne, East Sussex, England BN21 3UN

Japan
Holt Saunders, Ltd., Ichibancho Central Building, 22-1 Ichibancho, 3rd Floor, Chiyodaku, Tokyo, Japan

Hong Kong, Southeast Asia
Holt Saunders Asia, Ltd., 10 Fl, Intercontinental Plaza, 94 Granville Road, Tsim Sha Tsui East, Kowloon,
Hong Kong

**Manuscript submissions should be sent to the Editorial Director, Praeger Publishers, 521 Fifth Avenue,
New York, NY 10175 USA**

We dedicate this book to the young men and women who have patiently responded to our questions year after year.

Foreword *by Jack Dennis*

A quarter of a century has now passed since serious empirical study of the processes of political socialization was begun. The early investigators of the late fifties and early sixties—such as Hyman, Lane, Easton, Eulau, Almond, Greenstein, Sigel, and their associates[1]—developed a definition of the phenomenon and of the field of academic research that has continued to be applicable to this day. The early work has served to inspire new waves of scholarship, despite the inevitable criticisms, revisions, and expansions of the original findings, methods and theories.[2] While the science of political socialization is still far from the idea of a cumulative, fully codified body of knowledge, we have made considerable strides toward being able to give a systematic account of these processes and of their products since the late fifties.

A feature that stands out in the progress of this area of research is that some kinds of topics have been more fully addressed than others. In a broad sense, the first decade of empirical study was marked especially by an emphasis upon preadult political learning. Some would argue that serious inquiry was indeed limited to childhood and adolescence during that phase of inquiry. What changed was the advent of the Indochina War and then the era of Watergate, both of which had new socializing effects that went well beyond what had occurred for most people as they were growing up. In addition, a realization began to grow among researchers that adulthood could also be a period of significant, even far reaching changes in political attitudes and behaviors, if the conditions were right. Thus, some of the attention began to shift to the later years of the political life cycle, after early adulthood, as, for example, with the second wave of the high school seniors study of Jennings and Niemi.[3]

What the earlier studies had shown definitively, however, was that even relatively young persons in America and in other societies often develop a wide ranging set of political cognitions, feelings, commitments and standards of evaluation. Such political ideas and commitments typically spread and grow much before adolescence; and they are relatively well formed before the onset of political maturity in a formal-legal sense. Thus, despite a growing interest among scholars in adult political growth and development, the fascination with preadult political socialization has not waned. There continues to be new work on preadult political learning each year that is reported at professional conferences, in scholarly journals, and in new book lists. Some of this work follows along similar lines to that of the earliest empirical studies, yet makes improvements in our base of knowledge.[4] Other work extends the earlier types of inquiries on preadult political learning to other societies.[5]

The work of the present volume is one of the new studies that advance our cumulative knowledge of preadolescent political socialization in the United States. It is a unique investigation in a number of important respects. First, it takes its beginning well before most of the existing studies, in terms of initial age of the respondents. A problem of most prior research has been to get an early enough start, and thus to capture the first fleeting images that people learn with respect to the political system and their roles within it.

The few preschool and early grades studies done before this work do not cumulate well, either among themselves or with the studies of middle and later school years.[6] This lack of fit is due to several things. First and foremost has been our inability to use these studies to trace the course of early development for even of a few of the beginning school years. We have had only very provisional answers to most of the questions we need to ask about the course of early political attitude development.

A real advantage of the present study is that the authors began their observations with kindergartners, and they then followed them yearly through four subsequent grade levels. Thus, they provide unique evidence on the course of development of political orientations from a very early point—one which marks the beginning of school experience for most American children.

Aside from the early age with which they begin their observations and their charting of the changes, they have included another very uncommon attribute in their research design. That is the empanelization of their respondents. This initial volume covers the first five years of their repeated interviewing of these same young interviewees. By conducting year-to-year interviews with the same respondents, they are in a strong position to chart the course of development at the level of the individual. The usual cross-section study, by contrast, typically compares only sets of individuals of differing ages at one or two data points, and thus fails to provide the more fine-grained evidence that relates to individual shifts in political orientation and behavior.

An example of the advantage of these authors' approach is that they are able to show that some children (only about 5 percent) retrogress from one year to the next in their political awareness. This process of "political forgetting" is easily missed in the usual study of childhood socialization because of the extreme difficulty of documenting such effects with cross-sectional data. That such effects are observable here is due to the unique panel data collected over a substantial period that begins with very young children.

Another striking feature of this study is that the data have been collected by the authors themselves in face-to-face interviews over the whole period of the study. Thus, most of the usual problems about pencil and paper questionnaires, interviewer effects and group administrations of data collection instruments in classroom settings have been eliminated. These investigators have made an unusually strong effort to insure validity and reliability in their observations, especially through their extensive use of appropriate open-ended questions. Their approach demonstrates a strategy that establishes and maintains excellent rapport with respondents and maintains therefore a high reinterview rate.

Substantively, these authors make contributions of a variety of kinds. They are able to employ hypotheses that come out of several theoretical frameworks, especially systems-persistence, social learning and cognitive development theories. They place special emphasis upon the latter, given the nature of their subjects. They find a variety of intriguing things about how well Piagetian theory and its derivatives apply to political learning in the earliest school years. There is again demonstrated that a clear, cognitive progression over the early school years occurs for children's grasp of political objects and relationships. Thus, in a very broad sense the assumptions of cognitive development theory are not disconfirmed. Yet, when we turn to the particulars of Piagetian theory, such as the idea that children are not usually able to think about abstract matters before about fourth grade, or to the hypothesized geopolitical cognitive progression known as the "the proximo-distal hypothesis," there is suggestive evidence in this study that the theory is wrong.

This study also offers a number of useful comparisons with earlier studies and findings. For example, these investigators confirm for their young sample the continued socialization—even in the period of the feminist revolution—of gender differences in political awareness. This effect was found again and again in the early studies, if only in certain areas of the content of learning about politics. Studies done since that time have been more sporadic in showing male/female differences—in that these have varied from place to place, age of respondent and content of political learning.[7] From the present evidence, one would guess that young girls are still being affected by differential gender role socialization in this area. They evidently continue to receive less support for their involvement and attentiveness to politics than is the case for young boys.

There are also some important contrasts in these data relative to that of earlier times. The children being studied here show extremely low partisan awareness or commitment relative to their counterparts in the studies of the nineteen sixties. This is no doubt part of the wider trend toward a departisanized public political consciousness that has appeared in a number of recent American studies.[8] But for these young southern California children, the effect is very pronounced.

On the other hand, such declining partisanship may be counterbalanced by rising issue awareness, even among the very young. These authors, suspecting that there might be some rise of policy consciousness, included some questions which suggest, in their patterns of response, that such awareness does begin to arise earlier than one might have suspected. Clearly, the issue concerns of children are relatively simple and restricted. Yet, there is the strong suggestion that we may be running some danger in not including such content in surveys of this kind from this point forward. Again, this set of findings is not entirely consonant with the expectations one would usually derive from the dominant forms of stage theory of cognitive development.[9]

In general, Moore, Lare and Wagner have made an exceptional contribution to the literature on early childhood political socialization. They have laid down a more secure and relevant empirical basis for understanding what happens in these early years than was true previously. If we are to understand how political thought and motivations arise in the general population of Americans under present conditions, then we very much need this kind of persistent and technically proficient effort. Early childhood is, from this study and others, not known to be an intriguing span of years. It is one that exhibits a rapidly developing sense of political awareness for the average individual. Thus, this contribution to the literature on political socialization is especially important, especially given that the observations made are more than commonly pertinent and useful to our understanding. That these authors have continued to monitor these same children's political progress into the later school years holds great promise for an equally intriguing contribution in a subsequent volume.

NOTES

1. For some of these definitional efforts, see, for example, Herbert H. Hyman, *Political Socialization* (N.Y.: Free Press, 1959); Robert E. Lane, "Fathers and Sons: Foundations of Political Belief," *American Sociological Review*, Vol. 24 (1959), pp. 502–511; David Easton, "An Approach to the Analysis of Political Systems," *World Politics*, Vol. 9 (1957), pp. 383–400; David Easton and Jack Dennis, *Children in the Political System* (N.Y.: McGraw-Hill, 1969); Heinz Eulau, William Buchanan, LeRoy Ferguson and John C. Wahlke, "The Political Socialization of American State Legislators," *Midwest Journal of Political Science*, Vol. 3 (1959), pp. 188–206; Gabriel A. Almond, "A Functional Approach to Comparative Politics" in Gabriel A. Almond and James Coleman (eds.), *The Politics of Developing Areas* (Princeton: Princeton University Press, 1960), pp. 26–33; Fred Greenstein, *Children and Politics* (New Haven: Yale University Press, 1965); and Roberta Sigel "Assumptions about the Learning of Political Values," *Annals of the American Academy of Political and Social Science*, Vol. 361 (1965), pp. 1–9.

2. For some overviews of this literature see, for example, Jack Dennis, "Major Problems of Political Socialization Research," *Midwest Journal of Political Science*, Vol. 12 (1968), pp. 85–114; Fred Greenstein, "A Note on the Ambiguity of 'Political Socialization': Definitions, Criticisms and Strategies of Inquiry," *Journal of Politics*, Vol. 32 (1970), pp. 969–978; Roberta Sigel, "Political Socialization: Some Reactions on Current Approaches and Conceptualizations," paper delivered at the Annual Meeting of the American Political Science Association, New York, September 6–10, 1966; David O. Sears, "Political Socialization," in Fred Greenstein and Nelson Polsby (eds.), *Handbook of Political Science*, Vol. 2 (Reading, MA: Addison Wesley, 1975); Stanley Renshon, "Assumptive Frameworks in Political Socialization Theory," in Renshon (ed.), *Handbook of Political Socialization* (New York: Free Press 1977), pp. 3–44; and Richard G. Niemi, "Political Socialization", in Jeanne N. Knutson (ed.), *Handbook of Political Psychology* (San Francisco: Jassey-Bass, 1973), pp. 117–138.

3. M. Kent Jennings and Richard G. Niemi, *Generations and Politics* (Princeton: Princeton University Press, 1981).

4. A few recent examples are: Steven A. Peterson, "Biology and Political Socialization: A Cognitive Developmental Link?", *Political Psychology*, Vol. 4 (1983), pp. 265–288; Timothy J. Cook, "Another Perspective on Political Authority in Children's Literature: The Fallible Leader in L. Frank Baum and Dr. Seuss," *Western Political Quarterly*, Vol. 36 (1983), pp. 326–336; M. Kent Jennings, "Gender Roles and Inequalities in Political Participation: Results from an Eight-Nation Study" *Western Political Quarterly*, Vol. 36 (1983), pp. 364–385; Robert G. Meadow, "Information and Maturation in Children's Evaluation of Government Leadership

During Watergate," *Western Political Quarterly*, Vol. 35 (1982), pp. 539–553; and M. Margaret Conway, M.L. Wyckoff, E. Feldbaum and D. Ahern, "The News Media in Children's Political Socialization," *Public Opinion Quarterly* Vol. 45 (1981), pp. 164–178.

5. Some examples are Bernhard Claussen and Klaus Wasmund (eds.), *Handbuch der Politischen Sozialisation* (Braunschweig: Agentur Pedersen, 1982); and T.S. Farah, "Learning to Support the PLO: Political Socialization of Palestinian Children in Kuwait," *Comparative Political Studies*, Vol. 12 (1980), pp. 470–484.

6. See, for example, Mary Ellen Goodman, "Emergent Citizenship: A Study of Relevant Values in Four-Year Olds," *Childhood Education*, Vol. 35 (1958–59), pp. 248–251; Sandra Kenyon Schwartz, "Preschoolers and Politics," in David C. Schwartz and Sandra Kenyon Schwartz (eds.), *New Directions in Political Socialization* (New York: Free Press, 1975), pp. 229–253; and Freda Rebelsky, Cheryl Conover and Patricia Chafetz, "The Development of Political Attitudes in Young Children," *Journal of Psychology*, Vol. 73, second half (1969), pp. 141–146.

7. See, for example, the literature cited in Jennings, note 3 above.

8. See, for example, Martin P. Wattenberg, *The Decline of American Political Parties 1952–1980* (Cambridge, MA: Harvard University Press, 1984), and the works cited therein, pp. 147–154.

9. See, for example, the work of Richard Merelman, such as "The Development of Policy Thinking in Adolescence," *American Political Science Review*, Vol. 65 (1971), pp. 1033–1047; or Norah Rosenau, "The Sources of Children's Political Concepts: An Application of Piaget's Theory," in David C. Schwartz and Sandra Kenyon Schwartz (eds.), *New Directions in Political Socialization* (New York: Free Press, 1975), pp. 163–187.

Preface

Credit for the initial concerns motivating this study belongs with the several graduate faculty mentors who stimulated our initial interest in the study of political socialization. It was Jack Dennis, however, who—under the auspices of the National Science Foundation and the American Association for the Advancement of Science—conducted the Chautaqua-style seminar where the authors met and conceived of this project. Each of the researchers had a five- or six-year-old child; this, plus the interest in understanding what, how, when, and why young children learn about politics and government provided a bond of commitment that moved the authors to pursue this project.

Longitudinal research requires sustained effort over an extended period of time. In 1974, when the study was designed, four researchers anticipated a commitment that would extend through at least five years of interviews—following the panel members through the end of fourth grade. Thus, the study was designed to fill the void on the political socialization of children younger than second grade and would carry the panel forward to the point where comparison with the pioneering socialization studies conducted in the late 1950s and early 1960s would be possible. At the end of the second year, Steve McHargue decided that earning a law degree should take precedence over remaining a part of the research team. Thus, the weekly meetings where drafts of conference papers were reviewed moved from his home, which was located at a midpoint between the researchers' residences, to alternate locations. We are grateful for Steve's important contributions to the study during its formative stages.

Earlier empirical studies provided an important conceptual foundation for our research design. Thus, when new findings were reported in the literature after 1974, we found that, instead of requiring a revision of the original research design, we were able to incorporate new dimensions of inquiry by adding several new interview questions. When our findings were supported, or partially explained, by newly published material, this increased our resolve to see the project through the completion.

Gathering, processing, and analyzing the data for the five years of this study required the efforts of many people. We extend our thanks to those elementary school principals and teachers, who must remain unnamed, but whose cooperation made our task possible as well as pleasurable. Jeri Ann Steinberg, Bob Cendejas, Carla Ryhal, Kyle McDougal, Nancy Moore, and Joan Wagner made substantial contributions to the interviewing of students over several years. Paul Blakely of the California State University, Los Angeles Political Science Data Laboratory and Penny Gerritsen, John Vannoy, and Ken Coley from the Pepperdine University Academic Computing Lab provided essential technical assistance. Kathleen Geer and Helen Kilday of the Pepperdine University Word Processing Center invested many hours typing and retyping the manuscripts, as did Ann Manning of Occidental College.

We wish to acknowledge the insightful comments provided by M. Kent Jennings and Charles Andrain while serving as commentators on conference panels where segments of this analysis were presented, while the latter, along with Jack Dennis, read an earlier draft of this manuscript and provided many helpful suggestions. Timothy Cook provided a major insight concerning our use of alternative learning theories. To the Cleveland Foundation and the Spencer Foundation of Chicago we express our appreciation for funding that supported significant portions of this study. All of the foregoing individuals and organizations are absolved of any errors of omission or commission that may remain.

We especially want to thank the children who looked forward to our annual interviews, who provided the data for our analysis, and who made this project so enjoyable. We owe them our deepest gratitude.

An earlier version of Chapter 3 appeared in the *Western Political Quarterly* and an earlier version of Chapter 6 appeared in the *Proceedings of the Eighth Annual International Interdisciplinary UAP Conference on Piagetian Theory and Its Implications for the Helping Professions: Emphasis Moral Development.*

Contents

— List of Tables and Figures

Tables		Page

Figures   **Page**

— PART I
INTRODUCTION

1

Missing Links in the Study of Early Political Awareness

Regardless of their ideological orientation or political persuasion, most students of politics have an underlying concern with the vitality and stability of national political communities. Taking these characteristics of a political system as dependent variables, this study examines some of the independent variables appearing early in the lives of young citizens, with the dual purpose of assessing their impact on the political community and determining how educators might optimize that influence in constructive ways. Identification with political parties, ability to distinguish between public and private sector roles, awareness of the fallibility of governments, and a sense of themselves as political subjects or participants are just four of a myriad of politically relevant cognitions that are beginning to emerge in the political world of the young child. What influence are these perceptions likely to have on the vitality and stability of the U.S. polity during the next generation? What might those who are responsible for civic education in elementary school classrooms do to enhance the process by which these cognitions emerge and become part of the young citizen's political orientation? These are among the central issues to be addressed in the pages that follow.

Many behavioral scientists believe that adult mental structures are at least in part the outgrowth of the individual's early cognitive and affective development.[1] Consequently, over the last two decades considerable political socialization research has focused on the study of political awareness among children. However, previously it has been difficult to address the issues enumerated above in part because of the absence of essential information concerning not only what young children know about government and politics but even more importantly how they learn what they do know.

Although it may not be surprising that we lack extensive knowledge about the level of political awareness among preschool children,[2] we find that the storehouse of information concerning the development of political knowledge and values among elementary school-aged children contains lacunas as well. This continues to be the case in spite of the observations by Easton and Hess in the early 1960s that

> every piece of evidence indicates that the child's political world begins to take shape well before he even enters elementary school and the it undergoes the most rapid change during these years. . . . The truly formative years of the maturing member of a political system would seem to be in the years between the ages of three and thirteen.[3]

Thus, we are still seeking answers to such questions as: What does a kindergarten child know about government and politics? How rapidly do primary school children acquire political information? What do they understand about law? about fairness in society? about major public controversies like the Vietnam War or Watergate? How knowledgeable are young children about such issues as inflation? the energy crisis? taxation? What accounts for variations in the knowledge of different children about the political world? Are these variations explained by a child's sex? race? parental occupations? academic performance? sibling order? exposure to television?

Can some political concepts be understood at an earlier age than others? If so, which ones? Do all individuals progress through a series of identical stages in their growing political awareness, or is political learning episodic and primarily a reflection of environmental stimuli? Does early political learning affect adult orientations toward government and politics?

There are social scientists, of course, who are not convinced that the experiences during the early years of life have substantial influence on one's later adult behavior.[4] It is important to recognize that early childhood socialization may not be fully determinative; rather, it is enough that it has a significant impact on the developing citizen. Nevertheless, the importance of childhood socialization is supported by several longitudinal studies. Windmiller, Lambert, and Turiel assume that a child's basic moral value system is formed between ages five to eight.[5] Burton L. White of Harvard has found that his measurements of children as young as three years of age are very predictive of their academic achievements years later.[6] Evidence seems to indicate that intelligence quotients are fairly stable after the age of eight.[7] And, Lefkowitz, Eron, Walder, and Huesmann have found in a 22-year longitudinal study that levels of aggression in eight-year-old boys have predicted their levels of aggression when they are 30 years old.[8]

At present the discipline of political socialization has nothing comparable to the White and Lefkowitz, et al., studies. It is important to recognize that early childhood political socialization may not be fully determinative of adult behavior, but nevertheless, it may provide a basepoint and foundation that shapes the amount of change that may occur in later life as the maturing individual interacts with his or her political environment. It is hoped by these researchers that this continuing study will help in time to clarify the relationship between early childhood and adult political behavior.

To be sure, our knowledge of what children learn about the areas cited above has expanded significantly during the past 25 years.[9] However, in spite of these advances, several notable gaps exist in our understanding of political socialization. In the first place very little is known about the growth of civic awareness among children under the ages of eight or nine. The most significant investigations to date have involved children old enough to use the researcher's most efficient data-gathering instrument—the written questionnaire: Fred Greenstein used fourth-graders as his youngest subjects, while the youngest in the Dennis, Easton, Hess, and Torney eight-city sample were second-graders. The youngest children in Charles Andrain's study were in fifth grade.

In part our lack of knowledge about the political awareness of younger children exists because individual interviewing is necessary when seeking information about them. Even with older children who have improved reading and writing skills, however, the use of a written questionnaire has limitations, especially in obtaining data on affective and evaluative orientations toward political authorities, processes, and issues. Oral interviews not only permit the study of children younger than eight or nine but also allow the researcher to ask open-ended questions and to use probing techniques when confronted with incomplete or unclear responses.

A second major weakness in political socialization research is that few of the completed studies are longitudinal. With the exception of Jennings and Niemi's use of a panel of high school seniors and their parents interviewed in 1965 and again in 1973, all the major studies employ the cross-sectional, one-shot approach to data gathering in which several grades are surveyed simultaneously.[10] This procedure forces the researcher to make the unwarranted assumption that there really is a panel of subjects rather than a series of separate sets of data, one for each grade level. The analyst therefore is tempted to assume that a "pattern" of increasing political awareness across age or grade levels represents purely maturational changes rather than being the product of differing life experiences among distinct cohort groups. Longitudinal panel studies are difficult to design and time-consuming to administer, but they are the only means of assuring that perceived changes do, in fact, represent genuine developmental patterns.[11] Dean Jaros[12] and Stanley Renshon emphasize the importance of obtaining longitudinal data in seeking a clearer understanding of political learning. As Renshon wrote in his introduction to the *Handbook of Political Socialization*:

> As one examines current assessment procedures in political socialization research, at least three glaring omissions . . . are discernible. The first concerns the lack of a major longitudinal study, begun with a sufficiently young age group, to trace the processes of political socialization . . . as we approach the third decade of research in this area, the lack of a major longitudinal study is a cause for action as well as concern.[13]

Third, students of political awareness must confront the possibility that different periods in history may produce different patterns of political socialization. There was very little systematic investigation of childhood political socialization prior to 1960. How did children in the 1920s or 1930s view the presidency? How did they come to identify with a political party? We lack empirical data with which to answer these questions. The pioneering studies of the late 1950s and early 1960s are without systematic empirical precursors and therefore lack a basis for comparison and validation. This void leads us to a crucial question: are findings from the socialization research conducted in the early 1960s still valid today? Or, is it necessary to repeat such studies periodically in order to review and perhaps to revise our understanding of both the content and the process of political socialization?

Since the early 1960s U.S. society has undergone shattering political experiences such as the soul-searching over Vietnam, the assassinations of Martin Luther King and two Kennedys, greatly increased use of the media (especially television) to popularize campaigns and issues, the resignation of a Vice-President, as well as the traumatic series of events known as Watergate that culminated in the first resignation of a President. With these events in mind and with the knowledge that significant changes do occur (however slowly), we hypothesize that a child's posture toward the political realm in the late 1970s may be dramatically different from a predecessor who was in grade school during the late 1950s and early 1960s.

A fourth lacuna in political socialization research is the dearth of systematic exploration of alternative learning theories. Several learning models have been proposed, and some have been partially tested. These models presuppose differing conditions as prerequisites for political learning. They range from a simple identification model that is almost devoid of any requisite learning conditions to a more complex series of social learning theories to a sophisticated cognitive-developmental theory that embodies a series of conditions that are required for political learning to occur.[14]

A complex social learning model such as that advanced by Albert Bandura acknowledges the important influence personal factors like endowed potentialities, acquired competencies, and other expressions of individual initiative have on human learning, but he stresses the reciprocal relationship between these "internal" forces and the social environment. He does not view the learning process as one of either personal maturation or environmental causation but emphasizes that both are involved in an interaction he calls "reciprocal determinism."[15]

The cognitive-developmental model assumes that a child's mental capabilities develop through a series of clearly identifiable stages. Based on the research of Jean Piaget, this theory postulates that these stages are sequential and that a child must attain a particular maturational level in order to comprehend more complex and abstract phenomena.[16] For example, the cognitive-developmental theory of political learning would assert that a child is incapable of truly understanding the relationship among cities, states, and nations until he or she has mastered the notion of spatial inclusiveness, that is, that a city is contained within a state and a state within a nation.

It is important to recognize that Piaget's cognitive-developmental model, as a comprehensive theory of learning, does not rely exclusively on the influence of cognitive maturation in explaining why learning takes place. Piaget, in fact, acknowledges the role of four distinguishable factors in explaining how children learn: (1) heredity (internal maturation), (2) physical experience with the world of objects, (3) social transmission (education), and (4) equilibrium—representing a balancing of the first three.[17]

No single model has been advanced by analysts of political behavior as capable of explaining all political learning, but it is clear that the more intricate models, especially the cognitive-developmental, need to be investigated with greater precision than has heretofore been attempted.

Given these missing links in the study of political socialization, students in this field are divided over (1) what period of life is most critical in the acquisition of both cognitive information and affective orientations, (2) how active or passive the "learning" individual is, (3) which learning model(s) best explains the process, and (4) the permanency of the cognitive and affective outcomes. In an effort to understand these issues, some synthetic integration of theories surrounding the socialization process and its consequences has been developed. For example, Dawson, Prewitt, and Dawson, relying very heavily on Weissberg,[18] have suggested certain connections relating three periods of life (early childhood, adolescence, and adulthood) with three methods of learning (psychodynamic, cognitive-developmental, and social learning) to produce three different outcomes (basic attachments, an understanding of processes, and policy preferences). First, they suggest that the *primacy model*, describing the development of basic regime support and attachment to the national community, can be best explained by psychodynamic theories. Second, they refer to an *intermediate model*, encompassing approximately ages 12 to 18 when the young person attains the capacity to think abstractly and understand the workings of the political realm, as best described by the Piagetian cognitive-developmental approach. Finally, the *recency model* stresses the importance of personal responses to environmental stimuli, which are seen as determining adult attitudes and choices regarding current political issues.[19]

Jennings and Niemi, using very recent work by David O. Sears, posit four basic models of life-span persistence to explain variations in patterns of continuity and change evident in political attitudes and orientations over time. While their results offer considerable evidence for the stability suggested by a *lifelong persistence model* that stresses the critical influence of early socialization processes, they also find support for a *lifelong openness model* suggesting the susceptibility most individuals have to changes in political orientation throughout their life spans. Two intermediate models between these polar opposites are advanced: a *life-cycle model* that "holds that while persistence is the rule, certain orientations are very amenable to alteration at given life stages," and a *generational model* that assumes that substantial remolding of political orientations can occur as a result of powerful social and political forces. This remolding at a particular time in history will produce a sharp break—a discontinuity—between the generation in question and those preceding or following it.[20] Thus, while certain major patterns of political socialization may remain stable, other learning trends, such as the propensity for early attachment to a political party or ideology, for example, may change from one time to another. This might be particularly true after a major foreign policy controversy such as Vietnam or a domestic upheaval such as Watergate. For example, a cohort separation might result between children affected by the trauma of Watergate and those a few years younger who were not so affected by this national scandal.

These two differing synthetic integrations of theories surrounding the socialization process and its consequences are promising. But, they are largely intuitive and therefore systematic longitudinal testing is required to determine their validity.

The present study is designed to fill these four significant gaps in our knowledge of the political socialization process. First, it generates much needed empirical data on young school-aged children. In the first year those in our panel were at least two years, and in some cases four or five years, younger than those questioned in any of the major studies of early political socialization. The children were interviewed individually, and open-ended questions were used extensively to encourage clear and complete responses.

The findings of developmental psychology indicate that attitudes and learning behavior appear to be a product of interaction with an individual's environment and that early influences on the developing personality are likely to affect both the style and the content of later interactions.[21] Therefore, we will be especially attentive to the kindergarten child's view of laws and authority figures in an effort to determine whether these early perceptions are important determinants of an emerging view of government and of the President.

Second, this study is also longitudinal; the same children were interviewed near the end of each school year from kindergarten through fourth grade. This feature not only enables us to measure changes in cognitive knowledge and affective orientations toward government and politics, but it also permits us to address the third lacuna and thereby explore the usefulness of a cognitive-developmental perspective as well as the social learning model in explaining growth of civic awareness among young children. The ultimate goal of this latter effort is eventually to build a unified theory that satisfactorily explains the significant products of the political socialization process.

Finally, since the children were interviewed during the years 1974 through 1978, and because many of the questions and themes used in earlier studies were included in the interview schedules, these data provide bases for comparison with the findings reported in the pioneering socialization studies of the early 1960s. In particular we want to determine whether these children evidence a decline in their identification with political parties compared with their counterparts in the 1960s, which would parallel a similar decline among the adult population during this period. We also want to know whether youngsters growing up in the mid- to late 1970s believe that government is more pervasive and more trustworthy than did their counterparts of a similar age in the early 1960s.

We seek to understand how and why changes occur in political information and attitudes over the five years of this study. This effort to examine what and how children think about government and politics involves an attempt to operationalize some notions about the learning process based upon the work of Jean Piaget and Lawrence Kohlberg. Specifically, we have designed *two stage-related schemata*: one illuminating growth in political understanding and the other measuring the child's developing conception of law. As explained in Chapter 2, we seek to identify levels and stages of understanding that characterize the child's ability to comprehend political phenomena beginning with a very general understanding and moving to a more differentiated and integrated perception until finally a comprehensive understanding of the realm of government and law is achieved. The usefulness of this cognitive-developmental theory of political learning will be examined in conjunction with a social learning perspective that emphasizes modeling, reinforcement, and observation of others as modes that describe the way people learn.[22]

The method that we will use to test whether the cognitive-developmental model applies to political learning involves identifying levels of knowledge that represent thresholds that a child must surmount before going on to an understanding of more complex political phenomena. If, for example, it could be demonstrated that children with a clear grasp of what governments do also understand the legislative and judicial processes, while those who do not understand the functions of government are not familiar with the legislative and judicial processes, this would suggest that an understanding of governmental funtions precedes an ability to explain particular political processes. If a series of increasingly more specialized threshold structuring concepts can be identified, they could serve to delineate the developmental stages through which an individual's political awareness would pass on the way to a mature understanding of the government system.[23]

We begin our examination of the political world of a young child at a critical time of life. In Western society, until children enroll in school, they are normally exposed to a limited group of parental and other adult authorities. This often results in their developing a view of laws as absolute and unchanging and a perception of authorities as all-powerful and omniscient.[24] When children enter school, however, they are introduced to the divergent viewpoints of other adult authority figures. This broadened exposure leads to changes in their attitudes toward rules, laws, and authority. We are concerned about identifying the initial orientation toward laws and authority held by each child and comparing this measuremnt with that child's orientation four years later. We hypothesize that these initial cognitive and affective orientations provide a base point or foundation that determines, at least in part, the character of development during the early elementary years. For example, if those kindergarten children who believe that religious authorities govern in the political realm feel more positively about government and politics than their classmates, this would lend support for the view that early orientations toward political authorities and processes may be influential in later life as well.

Before moving to a discussion of the research findings that begin in Chapter 3, it is necessary to explain (1) the strategies used to obtain information from these young children and (2) the procedures used to develop operational indexes for measuring the degree of political and legal knowledge possessed by these children.

NOTES

1. Jean Piaget and Barbel Inhelder, *The Psychology of the Child*, translated by Helen Weaver (New York: Basic Books, 1969), is just one of the many sources for this concept. The concept underlies much of the work being done in developmental psychology. For a cogent argument stressing the importance of studying early childhood political socialization, see David Easton and Jack Dennis, *Children in the Political System* (New York: McGraw-Hill, 1969), Chapter 1, and Robert Weissberg, *Political Learning, Political Choice, and Democratic Citizenship* (Englewood Cliffs, NJ: Prentice-Hall, 1974), Chapter 2.

2. Only a handful of these studies involved an effort to learn about preschool children's political orientations and their awareness of the political environment. One pilot study involving 79 children three to six years old investigated the children's emerging conception of the political world. The conclusions were that many preschool children perceive the church as political and that few children have a sense of their national identity, that is, of being Americans. See Sandra Kenyon Schwartz, "Preschoolers and Politics," in *New Directions in Political Socialization*, eds. David C. Schwartz and Sandra Kenyon Schwartz (New York: The Free Press, 1975), Chapter 9. Another study involved 92 four-year-old nursery school children in the northeastern United States. The investigator, Mary Ellen Goodman, observed and interviewed the children, their parents, and their teachers in the late 1950s. She was primarily interested in the children's orientation to authority figures (mother, father, teacher, and policeman), their developing concept of "standards and limits, rules concerning behavior, interpersonal rights and obligations," and their concept of what is "good and bad." See Mary Ellen Goodman, "Emergent Citizenship: A Study of Relevant Values in Four-Year-Olds," *Childhood Education* 35 (February 1959): 248.

3. David Easton and Robert D. Hess, "The Child's Political World," *Midwest Journal of Political Science* 6 (August 1962): 235–36.

4. Jerome Kagan, who with Howard Moss wrote *Birth to Maturity*, originally emphasized the crucial relationship between early experiences and adult characteristics. However, Kagan has now begun to place more emphasis on the possibility of change in later life. See Jerome Kagan and Howard Moss, *Birth to Maturity*, reprint with new preface by Kagan (New Haven: Yale University Press, 1983). See also, Richard E. Dawson, Kenneth Prewitt, and Karen S. Dawson, *Political Socialization* (Boston: Little, Brown, 1977), pp. 74–78, 85–92.

5. M. Windmiller, N. Lambert, and E. Turiel, *Moral Development and Socialization* (Boston: Allyn and Bacon, Inc., 1980), p. 27f.

6. Burton L. White, *Experience and Environment: Major Influences on the Development of the Young Child: I* (Englewood Cliffs, NJ: Prentice-Hall, 1973), and "Critical Influences in the Origins of Competence," *Merrill-Palmer Quarterly 1975*

21 (Oct.): 243–66. See also, White's *Human Infants: Experience and Psychological Development* (Englewood Cliffs, NJ: Prentice-Hall, 1971).

7. Henry L. Minton and Frank W. Schneider, *Differential Psychology* (Monterey, CA: Brooks/Cole Publishing Co., 1980), pp. 120–22, and Anne Anastasi, *Psychological Testing*, 5th edition (New York: Macmillan Publishing Co., 1982), pp. 324–26.

8. The researchers found that they could predict with significant success the future psychopathology of the boys at ages 19 and 30, but not of girls. Monroe M. Lefkowitz, Leonard D. Eron, Leopold O. Walder, and L. Rowel Huesmann, *Growing Up to be Violent: A Longitudinal Study of the Development of Aggression* (New York: Pergamon, 1977); Lefkowitz, Huesmann, and Eron, "Parental Punishment: A Longitudinal Analysis of Effects," *Archives of General Psychiatry* 35 (Feb. 1978): 186–91; Eron, Lefkowitz, Walder, and Huesmann, "Relation of Learning in Childhood to Psychopathology and Aggression in Young Adulthood," in A. Davids, *Child Personality and Psychopathology: Current Topics* (New York: J. Wiley and Sons, 1974), p. 239f., and many other articles. In their conclusion to *Growing Up*, they state: "The most dramatic and consistent finding of this study was that many of the behaviors exhibited by the child during the period of 6 to 10 years of age, and a few during the age period of 3 to 6, were moderately good predictors of theoretically related behaviors during early adulthood." (p. 266) They conclude Chapter 9, "Summary and Conclusions," by stating "We need more standard measures, more rigorous theory, and the initiation of limited longitudinal studies (i.e., 5 to 10 years) aimed at specific developmental hypotheses." (p. 284)

9. A major stimulus for a systematic study of political socialization was provided by Herbert Hyman. His volume, published in 1959, catalogued extant knowledge about political behavior and emphasized the need to view political learning in terms of process: *Political Socialization* (New York: The Free Press, 1959). At the time Hyman's volume appeared, data for a major empirical exploration of children's political awareness had been collected in New Haven by Fred Greenstein. His findings were reported in *Children and Politics* (New Haven: Yale University Press, 1965). The most complete mapping of a grade school child's political world was the eight-city study reported in two volumes: Robert Hess and Judith Torney, *The Development of Political Attitudes in Children* (Garden City, New York: Doubleday, 1967), and David Easton and Jack Dennis, *Children in the Political System*. Charles Andrain, *Children and Civic Awareness* (Columbus, Ohio: Merrill, 1971), supplied a major stimulus for the emphasis of the present study on cognitive-developmental learning theory. For a recent bibliography of political socialization studies see Stanley Renshon, ed., *Handbook of Political Socialization* (New York: The Free Press, 1977), pp. 468–528. For a commentary on these empirical studies, see Richard E. Dawson, Kenneth Prewitt, and Karen S. Dawson, *Political Socialization*, 2nd ed. (Boston: Little, Brown, 1977).

10. M. Kent Jennings and Richard G. Niemi, *Generations and Politics: A Panel Study of Young Adults and Their Parents* (Princeton: Princeton University Press, 1981). Two additional exceptions to the cross-sectional design pattern are studies reported in Richard Niemi and Associates, *The Politics of Future Citizens* (San Francisco: Jossey-Bass, 1974); see Roberta Sigel and Marilyn Brookes, "Becoming Critical About Politics," and Pauline Vaillancourt and Richard Niemi, "Children's Party Choices." Kenneth Bailey of the University of Arkansas has a report in preparation that involves parallel longitudinal samples of third- through twelfth-grade children.

11. A longitudinal time-series design may also permit the analyst to use patterns of change in the past to predict future patterns or developments. In sum, the longitudinal design controls for virtually all internal invalidities except history, and even in that case provides some measure for the effect of events that occur during the course of the research. See Donald T. Campbell and Julian C. Stanley, *Experimental and Quasi-Experimental Designs for Research* (Chicago: Rand McNally and Company, 1963), pp. 37–43.

12. Dean Jaros, *Socialization to Politics* (New York: Praeger, 1973), p. 153.

13. Stanley A. Renshon, ed., *Handbook of Political Socialization*, p. 14.

14. Several models are summarized in Hess and Torney, *The Development of Political Attitudes in Children*, pp. 22–26, and in Dennis Ippolito, Thomas Walker, and Kenneth Kolson, *Public Opinion and Responsible Democracy* (Englewood Cliffs, NJ: Prentice-Hall, 1976), pp. 48–53. The *Identification* model suggests that some political learning occurs randomly, simply because a child imitates the behavior or attitudes of another person. Many students of socialization maintain, for example, that young children acquire a political party identification from their parents when they become aware, by whatever means, of their parents' party preference. This process of simple acceptance of an attitude or value orientation from an older role model by a younger imitator may occur with strongly held opinions concerning prominent politicians or intense feelings about taxes or other public issues. A second model emphasizes a process commonly referred to as *Conditioning*. A "stimulus-response" approach may condition children into a desired pattern of thinking or behavior by rewarding approved actions and by expressing disapproval or imposing sanctions for unwanted behavior. This procedure can provide a general orientation toward rules and authorities that may affect a child's view regarding governmental regulations as well. A classroom teacher's "good citizen" award for cooperatively following the rules of the classroom conditions primary school children to view citizenship as an exercise in *passivity and obedience to authority*. The *Interpersonal Transfer* model explains political learning as a product of identifying remote political objects, such as a President or a vote, with those that are a part of the child's immediate environment. Very young children may transfer the benevolence and omniscience they see in their own fathers to their perception of the President or other prominent authority figures. By contrast, a harsh teacher or parent may prompt a child to view more remote political authorities as similarly intimidating and unresponsive. A fourth model, *Accumulation*, suggests that specific increments of knowledge can be assimilated as a result of purposeful and goal-oriented instruction. The teaching procedure need not be systematic, and the capability of the child and the type of information are not essential considerations; what is critical is to make the instruction simple enough so the child can comprehend the material. This model assumes that a hierarchy of governmental levels or of more inclusive jurisdictions, for example, city-state-nation, can be taught to a young child even though he or she has not yet learned the concept of spatial inclusiveness.

15. Albert Bandura, *Social Learning Theory* (Englewood Cliffs, NJ: Prentice-Hall, 1977), Chapter 6.

16. See Jean Piaget, *The Psychology of Intelligence* (London: Routledge and Kegan Paul, 1947). For an excellent discussion of the applicability of this model for

political socialization, see Charles F. Andrain, *Children and Civic Awareness*, Chapters 7 and 8.

17. R. Murray Thomas, *Comparing Theories of Child Development* (Belmont, CA: Wadsworth, 1979), pp. 300–302.

18. Robert Weissberg, *Political Learning, Political Choice, and Democratic Citizenship* (Englewood Cliffs, NJ: Prentice-Hall, 1974), Chapter 2.

19. Dawson, Prewitt, and Dawson, *Political Socialization*, pp. 68–86.

20. Jennings and Niemi, *Generations and Politics*, pp. 19–22. See also Roberta S. Sigel and Marilyn Brookes Hoskin, "Perspectives on Adult Political Socialization—Areas of Research," in Renshon, ed., *Handbook*, pp. 262–71.

21. See Herbert Ginsburg and Sylvia Opper, *Piaget's Theory of Intellectual Development: An Introduction* (Englewood Cliffs, NJ: Prentice-Hall, 1969), Chapter 4. See also Jean Piaget and Barbel Inhelder, *The Psychology of the Child*, translated by Helen Weaver (New York: Basic Books, 1969); and Jean Piaget, *The Moral Judgment of the Child* (New York: The Free Press, 1965).

22. For an explication of this learning perspective see Albert Bandura, *Social Learning Theory* (Englewood Cliffs, NJ: Prentice-Hall, 1977). For an application of this theory for the purpose of explaining the causes of homicide, see Charles F. Andrain, *Foundations of Comparative Politics: A Policy Perspective* (Monterey, CA: Brooks/Cole, 1983), pp. 10–15.

23. This is demonstrated by Hyman's 1959 summary of the state of our knowledge in this field. See Hyman, *Political Socialization*.

24. For a discussion of this patterning, see Herbert Ginsburg and Sylvia Opper, *Piaget's Theory of Intellectual Development*, Chapter 4.

2

Research Strategy

A number of crucial procedural questions quickly come to the fore at the beginning of a survey research project. How should the target population—kindergartners—be approached? How many questions can be asked of children this age? What vocabulary is appropriate in presenting questions? Researchers are forced to weigh the advantages and disadvantages of alternative strategies. Precision, realism, and generalizability are all desirable, yet all three cannot be maximized at the same time.[1] Should this study adopt the clinical method of Piaget and utilize an open, basically unstructured interview that permits the respondents a great deal of freedom but limits statistical precision and is heavily dependent on the subjective interpretation of the analyst? This strategy attepts to capture as fully as possible the child's actual ideas and expression on the interview topics—it attempts to maximize realism.[2] Or, should this study develop a structured interview schedule that would ask the children to address specific questions and offer them a limited number of fixed responses, a verbal equivalent of the fixed-response questionnaire? This strategy maximizes precision of analysis, but may sacrifice both realism and generalizability.[3] Should open-ended questions be used? If they are used, would we be able to record verbatim the children's responses? After completing a pilot study, a strategy combining these two approaches was adopted: a structured interview schedule was designed that permits statistical analysis but also contains many open-ended questions that encourage children to express themselves freely. This strategy seemed an appropriate compromise, although it was necessary to accept the limitations of the approach as well as the additional time required by open-ended questions and the increased difficulty in coding them.

16

How intrusive would the presence of the researchers be in kindergarten classrooms? Would five- and six-year-old children be intimidated by unfamiliar adults asking them questions? Should middle-aged professors do the interviewing, or should college students be trained? Or, should we attempt to find teachers who would be willing to interview their pupils for us? Campbell and Stanley argue that educational researchers often have such poor rapport with their subjects that they are "gradually coming to the view that experimentation within schools must be conducted by regular staff of the schools concerned, whenever possible...."[4]

To answer a number of these procedural questions, a pilot study was conducted by one of the researchers in a nontargeted school district. A day of interviewing by this researcher and five university students demonstrated that the age and sex of the interviewer did not significantly affect the responses of kindergarten children. There was some indication, however, that formal attire and the dropping of academic titles such as "professor" or "doctor" helped the kind of rapport essential for satisfactory interviews. It was also found to be desirable to remove interviewees from the classroom setting so that they would not be distracted by curious peers observing the interview process. Further, the researchers decided to conduct most of the interviews for this five-year longitudinal study themselves because the use of multiple and changing interviewers would increase the likelihood of errors. The possibility of using the teachers to conduct the interviews was rejected because of the great imposition on their time and the likelihood that their teaching would be influenced by their knowl-edge of questions to be asked of their pupils in subsequent years. Teaching to prepare students for future interview questions would obviously affect the rate of the children's growth in civic awareness as measured by our interview schedule. It was also assumed that each researcher would take great care to establish rapport with the children prior to beginning the kindergarten interviews. If these efforts to establish rapport were successful, the children would accept, and indeed welcome, the return of the increasingly familiar interviewer.*

---

*For example, one researcher spent three days in each kindergarten classroom before interviewing any of the children. Efforts such as this have been rewarded with good interviewer-interviewee rapport as evidenced by the relaxed demeanor of the children, their friendliness in greeting the interviewers each year, and their continuing responsiveness to the open-ended questions in the interview sched-ule.

TABLE 2.1
Number and Type of Questions by Grade Level for Five Annual Interviews

Types of Questions	Grade Level and Year of Interview				
	K 1974	1 1975	2 1976	3 1977	4 1978
Maximum Possible Questions					
(Total)	57	91	115	162	177
Fixed-Choice[a]	39	46	53	76	83
Open-Ended	18	45	62	86	94
Cognitive Questions (Total)	41	50	59	82	92
National political community	7	7	11	12	12
Regime	16	20	24	31	36
Authorities	5	9	9	19	23
Political geography	3	3	4	5	5
Public/private sector role	6	7	7	9	10
Public-policy issues	4	4	4	6	6
Affective Questions (Total)	6	10	12	22	23
Regime	4	6	8	13	14
Authorities	—	—	—	1	1
Public-policy issues	2	4	4	8	8
Evaluative Questions (Total)	2	19	31	40	44
National political community	—	3	6	6	6
Regime	1	6	14	16	19
Authorities	—	—	1	2	2
Public/private sector roles	—	—	—	2	2
Public-policy issues	1	10	10	14	15
Self-report Questions (Total)	8	12	13	18	18
National political community	—	2	2	2	2
Regime	2	1	2	4	4
Authorities	3	3	3	4	4
Public-policy issues	3	6	6	8	8
Totals by Political Object					
National political community	7	12	19	20	20
Regime	23	33	48	64	73
Authorities	8	12	13	26	30

Types of Questions	Grade Level and Year of Interview				
	K 1974	1 1975	2 1976	3 1977	4 1978
Political geography	3	3	4	5	5
Public/private sector roles	6	7	7	11	12
Public-policy issues	10	24	24	36	37
Total Questions	57	91	115	162	177

[a]Fixed-choice questions implied either a "Yes" or "No" response or a single correct answer.

QUESTIONNAIRE DESIGN AND ADMINISTRATION

The interviews were conducted annually during the last four to eight weeks of the school year. A major constraint was the need to accommodate ourselves to each child's attention span. In kindergarten the children were asked 57 questions in one interview session that lasted about 10 to 15 minutes. Starting in first grade the interviews were frequently conducted in two parts because the number of questions had increased to 91 (see Table 2.1). Before conducting the third grade interviews, an experiment with pencil and paper responses to a limited number of fixed-choice items was attempted with third graders who were not in the panel. Because we found these children were more likely to indicate the "Don't know" (DK) response when it appeared on the paper in front of them than was the case when they were asked the same questions orally, we elected to continue utilizing oral interviews exclusively. By fourth grade the interview schedule contained 177 questions and required approximately 50 to 60 minutes to administer.

Related to our concern about the children's limited attention span was the further need to avoid demoralizing these young children by compelling them to respond "I don't know" to a large number of questions. For that reason kindergartners and first-graders were not asked all of the questions that might appropriately be asked of third- and fourth-grade children. Even in the relatively shorter kindergarten and first-grade interview schedules, special care was taken in the sequencing of the questions to offer the children regular opportunities to give some kind of affirmative response. In addition, Table 2.1 indicates the increasingly heavy reliance on open-ended as opposed to fixed-choice questions in each year of the study. Open-ended questions are defined as those eliciting more than a simple "yes" or "no" response ("Do we have a king in our country?") or implying a single correct answer ("Who is the President now?"). Very few questions were either deleted or modified once they were introduced into the questionnaire (see Appendix A for a full listing of all questions used in this study).

The wording of questions was another major concern. We wanted to test what the children really knew and felt about the political process, not the scope and limits of their vocabulary. In developing a vocabulary for the interview schedule, we wished to avoid ambiguity, loaded words, and, above all, misunderstanding between researchers and respondents.* We faced a typical research trade-off: if we used only language that the children could be expected to understand in kindergarten, our questions would be limited in subject matter, yet if we waited until most children understood more complex political terminology, we would not be able to ascertain the trend as the first few children, and then more, came to hear about and comprehend a particular political pheno-menon. In addition, if we were to use one term intelligible to the kindergartner, and a different term when the children were older, we would create a comparability problem. The Educational Develop-mental Laboratory's *A Revised Core Vocabulary: A Basic Vocabulary for Grades 1–8* was used in selecting key terms.[5] For example, "Who rules the country?" would be too difficult for many primary school children and certainly for five- or six-year-olds. Therefore, as the first question we asked, "Who is the boss of our country?" "Boss" has the advantage of being in the vocabulary of most kindergartners whereas alternatives like "leader" or "ruler" might not. We also purposefully introduced terms, such as "politician," that would not be in the kindergartner's vocabulary. One reason for using "ad-vanced vocabulary" was to check on the child's truthfulness in

*One problem that research on children always poses and that is never completely resolved is that of equivalence of meaning; terms and phrases of a query may not have the same meaning for the researcher and his or her young respondents, and their response may also not be perceived accurately. See Renshon, *Handbook of Political Socialization*, pp. 10, 48.

telling whether or not he or she knew what the word meant, but more importantly it enabled us to determine the level of maturity and other circumstances required for an understanding of complex political phenomena to emerge.

What is the effect of repeatedly interviewing the same children year after year? Will they be sensitized to government and politics and become more knowledgeable simply because of the stimulation of being repeatedly interviewed? A longitudinal design controls most internal validities, but it is vulnerable to the problem of sensitization, the possibility that repeated testing will affect the results.[6] Researchers want to be able to generalize their findings beyond their sample, indeed to the entire target population, in this case, primary school children. In order to check on the possibility that children in the panel were being sensitized and thus no longer typical of primary school children, the researchers incorporated two control features into the research design. The responses of first-grade children who were members of the kindergarten sample were compared with the responses of first-grade classmates who were not interviewed during the kindergarten year. Secondly, in third grade the researchers again made a check against the possibility of testing sensitization (while simultaneously checking the effects of a written questionnaire vis-à-vis an oral one) by presenting a 21-item sub-section of the oral interview schedule as a *written* questionnaire to seven intact third-grade classrooms, a population containing a sizeable proportion of the original panel. Analysis indicated that responses of the first grade panel and nonpanel children were similar; and even by the third grade, children in the panel were not sensitized to the point of becoming more knowledgeable in responding to cognitive questions than third-graders not in the panel.[7]

CATEGORIZATION OF QUESTIONNAIRE CONTENT

Most of the political objects the children were asked about may be classified according to the triad of Eastonian categories: the *national political community*, the *regime*, and the *authorities* of government.[8] In addition, the interview schedule raises questions similar to those used in earlier studies concerning *political geography* (for example, "What city do you live in?"[9]) and *public vs. private sector roles* (for example, "Does a mailman, milkman, policeman, and so on, work for the government?").[10] A category of questions unique to this study concerns a series of *contemporary public policy issues*: Vietnam, Watergate, crime, the energy crisis, inflation, and unemployment. Another way of classifying these same interview questions is according to those that are *cognitive*, *affective*, *evaluative*, and *self-reporting*. "What is inflation?" is a cognitive query; "Is inflation good or bad?" calls for an affective response; "Why is it good or bad?" calls for an evaluative judgment; and whether the child has ever heard the word "inflation" asks for a self-report.

NATIONAL POLITICAL COMMUNITY

In this study the number of cognitive questions used to measure the child's awareness of the national political community increased from seven in the kindergarten and first-grade interviews to 12 for the third- and fourth-grade children (see Table 2.1). The seven questions used in the kindergarten and first-grade interviews focused primarily on the recognition of national symbols: the flag, Statue of Liberty, Liberty Bell, and the national Capitol, as well as pictures of George Washington and Abraham Lincoln. The seventh question asked directly: "What country do you live in?" Because the U.S. flag had been identified correctly from among four national flags by 99 percent of the kindergarten children, it was not repeated in first grade, but a picture of the White House was added to the symbols of the national community and its major institutions. Four additional questions were asked in the second-grade interviews: "What is the Star Spangled Banner?", "What do we celebrate on the Fourth of July?", "What is a nation?", and "What is the Bicentennial?" Earlier studies have indicated that kindergarten children might be expected to recognize national symbols, such as the flag, before they are aware of elements in the regime and of political authorities.[11] In addition to testing this hypothesis, we also expected to find that children who can correctly identify national symbols are more likely than other children to know the name of their country. Moreover, we hypothesized that symbol recognition is associated with more *positive feelings* toward a variety of political objects and processes.

REGIME

The largest single category of questions, increasing from 16 in kindergarten to 36 in fourth grade, was used to measure the children's awareness of certain features of the democratic constitution regime in which they live. Following the lead of earlier socialization research, we focused primarily on the executive branch and the electoral process. Although earlier studies included a limited number of law-related questions, we have made this area a central focus of our study. We sought to determine a child's conception of the role of law in society by asking such questions as: What is a law? Who makes the laws? Why do we have them? Are laws fair? What would happen if there were no laws? Why do they like (or not like) them? How are they enforced? Would a President be treated differently from the child's parents if he were caught violating the law? We also queried the children on political ideals (freedom), governmental operations, and special functions in the public sector (police, defense, education, and taxation).

Based on earlier research, we expected the children to be most familiar with the President and perhaps the electoral process, while their understanding of the legislative and judicial branches would be much more limited. Our measure of their information concerning the legislative branch came from a question asked all five years: "Who makes the laws?" and by the later addition of such questions as "What is the Congress?" (second grade), "What is a senator?" (third grade), and "What does Congress do?" (fourth grade). A question concerning the Supreme Court was appropriately introduced in second grade, but we found it was clearly a mistake not to ask additional questions concerning the courts and judges before third grade. Courtroom dramas on television and the high level of interest evoked by a child's concern for what happens to people who are arrested appear to give those in the early primary grades an impressive level of awareness concerning the role of judges and the functioning of courts. By contrast these California children had very limited knowledge about the regime-related topic of political parties. Because Greenstein found that a majority of children identify with their parent's party preference by fourth grade,[12] we began in kindergarten to ask the children whether they had ever heard of a "Republican" or a "Democrat." By the third grade the interview schedule contained such questions as: "Can you think of a difference between the Republican party and the Democratic party?" and "Which party do you like better?"

AUTHORITIES

The category of political authorities included queries about contemporary Presidents, governors, mayors, and United States senators as well as the names of parties. This series of questions increased rapidly, in part, because the study spanned the terms of three Presidents and two governors of California. By the fourth interview there were cross-checking questions concerning the governor and the mayor, which paralleled the kindergarten sequence of queries concerning the President: "Who is the President?", recognition of the incumbent President's picture, and "Who is _____ (incumbent's first and last names)?" Our expectation was that young children would be most likely to know the incumbent President. Contrary to Greenstein's finding in his New Haven study,[13] involving an extraordinarily visible mayor, we expected that the governor of California would be more salient among young children than either the mayor of Los Angeles or the part-time mayors of smaller suburban communities. We did not, however, anticipate how many kindergarten children would identify religious authorities (God or Jesus) as having political roles.

POLITICAL GEOGRAPHY, PUBLIC-PRIVATE SECTOR, AND POLICY ISSUES

Cognitive questions concerning political geography, contemporary political issues, and the distinction between public-sector occupations and those in the private sector were asked in all five years of the study. Previous research concerning the young child's awareness of political jurisdictions offers conflicting evidence as to which levels of government are identified first.[14] Gustave Jahoda found that Scottish children became aware first of their local jurisdiction, subsequently about the province, and still later, the nation. On the other hand, Fred Greenstein concluded that his New Haven subjects became first aware of authorities governing national and local jurisdictions (the President and the mayor of New Haven) before recognizing the governor of Connecticut.[15] The standard queries about "What city (state, country) do you live in?" were included in an effort to resolve this conflict. To determine how consistently a child was able to distinguish among geo-political entities, beginning in the third grade we began asking "Can you tell me the name of another state? . . . and another country?"

In all five years the interview schedule contained the series of six occupational-role questions used by the eight-city study to measure a child's ability to distinguish private- from public-sector occupations.[16] The limited ability of our panel to distinguish those occupations normally associated with government (policeman, soldier, judge, mailman, and teacher) from an occupation in the private sector (milkman) was in striking contrast with the earlier study. In successive annual interviews we added other private-sector occupations (gas station man, candy store person, and the person who gives the news on television) in an effort to probe the causes of this confusion. In fourth grade we specifically asked the question "How do you tell whether a person works for the government or not?" Responses to this query enabled us to distinguish those who were guessing from those who had developed a basis for deciding who works for the government and who does not.

Studies of early political socialization did not include references to major public controversies. This seemed to be a major omission; clearly, young children are exposed to the most salient issues of the day, both through adult conversations and electronic media. We identified four major public issues receiving extensive media attention throughout the five years of our study: Vietnam, Watergate, the energy crisis, and the state of the economy. We assumed that young children in the spring of 1974 would be most likely to recognize terms like "Watergate" and the "energy crisis" because everyday experiences provided constant references to these issues; the Watergate hearings preempted television programming during much of the spring and the Arab oil boycott created long lines at the many Southern California gas stations. Even though the state of the economy was a matter of widespread public anxiety during the mid-1970s, it was difficult to find appropriate vocabulary for framing questions to elicit relevant responses from these very young children. In first grade we simply asked "Tell me something about the economy," but the word "economy" was clearly not yet in the working vocabulary of most children. In second grade we asked

"Tell me something about prices," but found that it was perceived as a purely cognitive question about commercial transactions—about going shopping with their mother or father—rather than evoking an association with economic problems such as inflation. Finally, beginning in third grade, we simply asked "Tell me something about unemployment" and "Tell me something about inflation." The insights gained from these questions concerning how young children become aware of public-policy issues represent one of the distinctive contributions of this study.

AFFECTIVE, EVALUATIVE, AND SELF-REPORT

Slightly more than one-tenth of the questions in all five interview schedules were designed to elicit affective responses and thereby measure positive and negative feelings toward various political objects. Our ultimate objective was to determine whether there is any relationship between cognitive awareness of the polity and a child's affective orientation toward it. To measure this relationship a five-question Affect Index was constructed. In turn, this index is used to measure the extent to which increased knowledge of the political system tends to make a child's orientation toward government more supportive or more cynical. More than half of the affective items concerned regime-related matters, for example, "Would you like to vote?", "Are policemen your friends?", and "Does the government listen to what your mom or day say?" Beginning in the first grade we asked, "Do you like the government?" and "Do you like the laws?" as well as asking whether each child perceived the four policy concerns (Watergate, Vietnam, the energy crisis, and the economy) as "good" or "bad." In third grade a series of personal efficacy/governmental responsiveness questions was added: for example, "If the government makes a mistake, should you write a letter or just forget about it?" and "Would the government want to help you if you needed help?" This enabled us to develop a five-question Political Efficacy/Governmental Responsiveness Index.

We were particularly curious as to whether some five- to ten-year-old children had begun to develop the capacity to go beyond the simple expression of positive or negative reactions to politics and give rational explanations for their feelings. If their affective responses were based on a growing evaluative capacity,[17] then their later relationship to the political process might have a different quality than if their feelings were not supported by reasoned analyses. Those questions that have been classified as evaluative require that the pupil combine a cognitive awareness with some feelings about a governmental object in the process of making a judgment. We anticipated that most children at this age would not be very adept at verbalizing their political judgments, but we expected that their responses would begin to suggest an emerging evaluative skill.

Only two questions in the kindergarten interview were intended to elicit an evaluative response: "Tell me something that isn't fair" and "If you wre the boss of the whole country, what would you do to help people?" The number of these queries increased dramatically in the first-grade interview, primarily because we began to explore in greater depth the reasons why children had certain feelings about political objects, for example, why did they like or not like "government," "laws," or "America." In the same fashion we asked them to explain why they felt Watergate, Vietnam, the energy crisis, and the economy were either "good" or "bad." By the second grade this category included: Why are laws fair (or unfair)? Why would you like to vote (or not vote)? Why are taxes good (or bad)? Why do you like (or not like) other countries better than ours? How often does the President (and government) make mistakes? What is the most important problem facing America? Why is it so important? In the third-grade interview a further type of evaluative question relating to the public-private-sector distinction was asked: "Who is more important, a judge or a famous athlete like Mohammed Ali or Dorothy Hamill?" and "Who is more important, a police chief or a TV person like the six-million-dollar man or bionic woman?"

A final category designated as "self-report" contains a number of queries concerning whether a child has *heard* of a word, for example, "Republican," "Democrat," "political party," "impeachment," "energy crisis," "Watergate," or "Vietnam." Also included in this category were questions bordering on affect, for example, "What do you think of when you see our flag?", "What makes you most proud to be an American?", "What would you like to do when you grow up?" and "Name a famous person you want to be like." In some instances these self-report responses gave an indication of the child's cognitive awareness (whether he or she had heard a word), while in other cases the self-report suggested certain positive or negative feelings about political objects such as our country or the flag.

DESCRIPTION OF THE PANEL

The panel of 243 children used in this study may be described as an "availability sample." Each of the principal researchers approached the school authorities in his local district and requested permission to interview from one to three complete kindergarten classes during May and June of 1974. The conditions for interviewing the children varied from district to district. One school board required that the parents return a signed permission slip before a child could be interviewed, and this only after one member of the board publicly vouched for the researcher. Another simply asked that a notice be sent home with each child, and parents who did not wish their child interviewed could contact either the school or the researcher with that request. In one district the approval of the Committee on Research was all that was necessary. Although only about one-third of the parents returned the permission slips where they were required, in the districts where only notification was required, not one parent raised a complaint about the study in the initial year. In the following four years, only one parent raised an objection to the study.

The children comprising the original kindergarten sample resided in five school districts located in four communities separated by as many as 60 miles: two inner suburbs within ten miles of Los Angeles' civic center and two outlying suburbs located almost 50 miles from the central city. The first interviews with 218 kindergartners were conducted in late May and early June of 1974.[18] One year later, 186 (85.3 percent) of these children were re-interviewed and 135 of their first-grade classmates were questioned for the first time. In the spring of 1978, when most of these children were completing fourth grade, 148 of the 218 interviewed first in kindergarten and 95 of the 135 initially interviewed in first grade remained to provide the panel of 243 children on which this longitudinal analysis is based. They represent 69 percent of all the children interviewed during the course of this study.[19]

The original panel of 218 pupils consisted of six intact kindergarten classes and portions of three other classes in the district requiring permission slips.* Assignment to these classes at each school was random in that no criterion, other than equal distribution of sexes, was employed. Given the random assignment of pupils to the kindergarten classes, it was decided to interview all the children in the first-grade classes at the schools used for the kindergarten interviews. The researchers assumed that the cognitive and affective responses of the newly interviewed and the re-interviewed first-grade pupils would be similar. This assumption was confirmed when analysis showed that there were no significant differences in the responses of the children interviewed for the first time in 1975 when compared with those given by pupils in the original sample for any of the variables used in this analysis.[20] The addition of the new students and the comparison of their responses with those provided by members of the original panel served two functions: first, it permitted enlarging the panel without impairing validity, and second, the analysis provided a check on the test-retest influence of the original questioning.

An analysis of the demographic characteristics of the 243 children interviewed over the period of this study (see Table 2.2) shows an almost even split between boys and girls (119 and 124, respectively) along with an 81.5 percent Anglo and an 18.5 percent non-Anglo population. A majority of the 45 non-Anglo children in the panel were Spanish surnamed, while the remainder included Asian, black, and Near Eastern children. Almost 90 percent of the sample attended public schools, while most of the private school youngsters (21 out of 25) attended parochial schools.

Just 6 percent of the 243 respondents were "only" children, while 45 percent were the youngest siblings in their families. About one-quarter were the oldest sibling, while another quarter had both older and younger siblings. We appear to have a higher percentage of youngest siblings and perhaps a slightly lower percentage of only children than is likely to be found in a truly random sample of youngsters in the five- to ten-year age range. However, the trend

---

*Those interviewed did not usually include all kindergarten children in their respective schools: two researchers selected two of the four available classes—one used the two morning sessions from two schools, while the other used one morning and one afternoon class from the same school. A third interviewed all children in two kindergarten classes at one school, and the fourth was permitted to interview one-third of the three kindergarten classes at one school.

TABLE 2.2.
Demographic Profile of the Panel

Sex[a]		_Race_	
Male	49.0	Anglo	81.5
Female	51.0	Non-Anglo	18.5

Grade in School		_School Type_[b]	
Fourth	91.4	Public	89.7
Third	8.6	Parochial	8.6
		Private non-parochial	1.6

Mobility by 1978		_Estimated Academic Rank_[c]	
Same school all years	65.8	Upper quarter	35.4
Two schools	26.7	Middle half	29.6
Three schools	6.2	Lower quarter	27.2
Four schools	1.2	Not available	7.8

Sibling Order		_Frequency of TV News Viewing_[d]	
Only child	5.8	Often	22.2
Oldest child	24.3	Sometimes	35.4
Middle child	25.1	Rarely	38.7
Youngest child	44.9	Never	3.7

	Father's Occupation[e]	_Mother's Occupation_[e]
Professional or business	38.3	11.5
Clerical	14.4	29.2
Homemaker	—	40.3
Law enforcement	4.5	—
Government (nonlaw)	4.9	2.9
Labor	25.1	10.3
Other	8.2	2.9
Not available	4.5	2.9

[a]All figures represent percentages based on the panel of 243 children.

[b]The kindergarten sample was taken from five public schools; by fourth grade the children were dispersed into 47 different schools.

[c]Twenty-seven different third-grade teachers were asked to rank the panel children in their rooms in comparison with all the third-grade children they had ever taught.

[d]Based on a response to the question "How often do you watch the evening news with your parents or by yourself?" "Often" was four or more times per week, "sometimes" was 2 or 3 times a week, "rarely" is once a week or less.

[e]Obtained by categorizing the responses of the children when they were asked in fourth grade "What does your father do when he goes to work?" and "What does your mother do when she goes to work?"

toward fewer children in many middle-class families in the United States may account for the higher percentage of primary school children without younger brothers or sisters.

The extent of school mobility on the part of these 243 children seems quite consistent with the general pattern for Southern California. One-third of the children have attended more than one school during their first five years of formal education, with 10 percent moving from a public to a private school, the majority of these transferring to parochial schools that did not offer kindergarten programs. The 18 children who have attended three to five schools in five years are usually youngsters from broken homes or else from upwardly mobile families who move with each change of employment or rise in family income.*

We relied on the queries "What does your dad do when he goes to work?" and "What does your mom do when she goes to work?" as the best available means of ascertaining parental occupations. When these questions were posed at the end of fourth grade, most youngsters were able to give a response that enabled the researchers to group the parents into the broad occupational categories found in Table 2.2. Because of the predominantly suburban, as opposed to central city or rural character of this panel, it is not surprising to find almost two-fifths of the fathers in business or the professions with another 10 percent in law enforcement or other governmental occupations. The one-quarter of the fathers working as blue-collar laborers and the one-seventh in clerical positions also seem consistent with the occupational profile of this suburban population. The distribution of the mothers' occupations (two-fifths as homemakers, almost one-third in clerical positions, and just over 10 percent each in blue-collar or in business or professional pursuits) seems representative of the communities in which the respondents lived.

The demographic item having the least objective basis in Table 2.2 involves the child's estimated academic rank. At the end of third grade the researchers asked each child's teacher whether the youngster's academic performance was in the top quartile, middle half, or bottom quartile for all children they had taught at that grade level. The teachers appear to have rated somewhat more of the youngsters in the top quartile than is probably in fact the case. It

---

*The number of children attending 3 or more schools is diminished by not including those children who returned to a school attended earlier.

may be that these fairly stable families—insofar as their residence is concerned—are more likely to have children who do somewhat better in their school work than those who moved away from Southern California and could therefore not be followed for all five years. It is also possible that the halo effect surrounding the most recently taught youngsters may have prompted some teachers to rank these children more highly than they would if they were randomly distributed throughout their years of teaching. In any case the slightly more than 27 percent rated in the lowest quartile would appear to be a valid reflection of which pupils in the panel were the weakest academically. Since other more precise records of academic achievement are confidential, and therefore unavailable to us, we have relied on these estimates of the third-grade teachers in our analysis of the relationship between academic performance and civic awareness.

These nine factors represent the most widely used demographic variables in the analysis of evolving civic awareness among young children. We hypothesize that there may be significant correlations between certain demographic traits and both higher and lower levels of knowledgeability and more positive or more negative feelings about political phenomena. Among the correlations we would expect to find are those between greater civic awareness, on one hand, and boys,[21] Anglos,[22] higher academic performance,[23] and children from higher socioeconomic families, on the other.[24] Cognitive-developmental theory has suggested to us that certain cognitive independent variables may be more powerful than these traditional demographic characteristics in explaining why some children are more knowledgeable about government than others.[25] This possibility has led us to posit certain key threshold understandings* as possible explanations for varying rates of growth in civic awareness among primary school children.

_____

*Dawson, Prewitt, and Dawson refer to "reference points or conceptual filters for the individual's perceptions of the political world." We will discuss the fuller meaning of "threshold understandings" later; however, we see these understandings providing a structure that makes meaningful references to the political domain. See *Political Socialization*, p. 176.

STAGES OF COGNITIVE AND MORAL DEVELOPMENT

The work of Jean Piaget and Lawrence Kohlberg suggests that as children mature they progress through a series of stages of cognitive as well as moral development. These stages imply qualitative differences in a child's mode of thinking or problem solving at different ages and are posited to be sequential—a child moves from one stage to another in a prescribed pattern. Each of these distinctive and sequential modes of thought forms a "structured whole," or an integrated system of thought, which involves more than just a certain level of knowledge or familiarity with a subject matter, such as politics and government. In addition, it involves an underlying pattern or structuring of thought as, for example, "the level of concrete operations," or, at a higher level, a pattern of "formal operations." Furthermore, these cognitive stages, according to Piaget and his disciples, represented hierarchical integrations; that is, each stage represents an increasingly differentiated and integrated structure of thought that helps individuals better adapt to their environment. Any theoretical set of structural stages, like stages of political or legal understanding, must be formulated so that a higher stage is more differentiated (diverse and complex) and more integrated (structured and interrelated) than a lower stage.[26] If this cognitive-developmental sequence is valid, children must be able to understand basic and more concrete elements of the political process before they can comprehend more complex and abstract phenomena. For example, children need to know what it means to vote before they can understand the electoral process, and prior to understanding how the judicial process functions, they must be aware of what a police officer does and what laws are.

In order to explore the applicability of the Piagetian model to the area of politics and government, this study poses a series of research questions: Do stages of political knowledgeability exist? Are they empirically identifiable? Are they sequential? That is, do they occur in a fixed and predetermined order? What are the key landmarks along the pathway a child follows toward greater awareness of the political world? Are there certain key political concepts that must be grasped before a child can move on to more advanced levels of political awareness? Are they empirically identifiable? If such "threshold" understandings do exist, then they may be useful as independent variables to help identify levels of knowledge-ability among the children in our panel.

The six-stage, three-level framework posited by Lawrence Kohlberg for describing stages of moral sensitivity suggested to us the utility of developing a hierarchy of stages and levels of cognitive political awareness and a similar hierarchy involving sensitivity to law and morality.[27] The stages of cognitive political awareness begin at the lowest *prepolitical level* (Level I) with two stages, an initial symbol recognition stage and then in Stage 2 an accurate but very general identification of a public process or function. Responses to the query "What does the President do when he goes to work?" will suggest the distinction between Stages 1 and 2. He "signs papers," "makes speeches," and "has meetings" are Stage 1 responses. "Makes laws," "runs the country," and "solves problems" illustrate Stage 2 responses. At Level I there is no clear perception of the President as having distinctive functions that are different from those of other political notables such as members of Congress. There is an amorphous task pool of public functions with which the President is associated.[28] This inability to recognize a division of labor among key political actors suggests that this initial level comprising Stages 1 and 2 is "prepolitical." Awareness at this lowest level is limited to symbol recognition and a rudimentary understanding of a pool of governmental functions carried on by important persons who help others in various ways.

The second or *quasi-political level* (Level II) involves the recognition of at least one critical function that is normally associated with a political actor or object. The distinction between Stages 3 and 4 in this second level turns on whether the respondent identifies one central function (Stage 3) or more than one central function (Stage 4). The researchers have specified a set of central functions for each of nine political actors or objects that we posit as key threshold variables. (See Appendix B for a listing of the criteria used in staging each threshold cognitive variable.) In responding to "What does the President do when he goes to work?", for example, children were assigned to Level II if they explained (1) the President's interactive role with Congress in lawmaking, (2) how the President governs or administers the country, (3) the role of the President in suggesting new legislation, or (4) the preeminence of the President in foreign affairs.

Although none of the children in our sample gave responses that could be characterized as beyond Level II (Stages 3 and 4), the researchers have posited a third *political level* (Level III) at which the respondent has a complete as well as factually accurate picture of a political system. We have tentatively characterized Stage 5 of this level as the senior high school or college textbook understanding of politics. The distinction between Stages 5 and 6 in this political level of civic awareness turns on whether the respondent has a sense of the possibility of varying interpretations for political objects or processes. It would seem to the researchers that the highest level of political cognition is one in which a person is aware that there is no one completely accurate view of a given political process or system and that differences in cognition are partly due to differing ideological assumptions concerning the purpose of political activity. At this highest stage of cognitive development (Stage 6) the individual recognizes that his or her own value assumptions may influence his or her view of the political world and appreciates that others will have their own assumptions or "biases" that account for their differing interpretations of political processes and outcomes.

Our three levels of political cognition (prepolitical, quasi-political, and political) represent differing modes or structures of thought about politics. The first level, which we characterize as prepolitical and corresponding to the Piagetian preoperational level, represents an undifferentiated view of society, authority, and governance. Political symbols are recognized as *important*, but they are not clearly differentiated from religious symbols or from other nongovernmental objects. In short, there is neither differentiation between the political and the nonpolitical nor any sense of integration or formally abstracting categories within the realm of the political. At the second, quasi-political level, which roughly corresponds with the Piagetian concrete operational level, we find children beginning to identify the critical features or functions of political objects—but they are not yet ready to articulate the interconnections between and among political authorities and institutions; they do not see politics as a fully integrated system. Furthermore, they are not yet ready to appreciate that perceptions of politics are affected by the underlying value assumptions of the observer. These latter features—understanding interconnections and integrative systems and appreciating cultural and ideologial bias—are characteristics of the political or formal operational level of cognitive development. It is at this level that the individual begins to understand causal connections between economic conditions and political outcomes or between ideological orientations and political behavior. The three levels then represent clearly distinguishable *modes of thought* concerning political phenomena.

The responses of each child to nine key threshold cognitive questions were scored according to this six-stage, three-level hierarchy. Each threshold query is used as an independent variable to predict the extent of the children's political knowledge. Then all nine variables were combined to form a composite Political Understanding Index. This index is also used as an independent variable to predict levels of political knowledgeability.

In describing cognitive political development, we borrowed the notion of levels and stages from Kohlberg's moral development framework, but his typology can be applied much more directly to children's notions concerning the purpose of law. Responses to the following six questions were also used to construct a composite Law Understanding Index: "What is a law?", "Who makes the laws?", "Why do we have laws?", "Why do you like (not like) laws?", "Why are laws fair (not fair)?", and "What would happen if there were no laws?" Individual scores of this index placed each child at a level and stage reflecting his or her conception of law. The initial preconventional *level* (Level I) is almost entirely self-centered. Stage 1 of this *level* represents an egocentric orientation toward law, and Stage 2 may be termed reciprocal. Stage 1 thinking conceives of law as protecting the respondent from harm and punishment, whereas at Stage 2 the child has begun to realize that the benefits of law may extend to others at the same time they apply to oneself.

According to Kohlberg, the children begin to move from the preconventional to the conventional *level* (Level II) at about age nine. In our schema Level II children first concern themselves with the society in which they live (Stage 3: System View). In the second stage of this *level* (Stage 4: Social Norm) they demonstrate an explicit concern for the expectations of others. This ordering represents a reversal of Stages 3 and 4 in Kohlberg's moral development typology. When using Kohlberg's model to identify stages with responses to law-related questions, we found that the higher Stage 2 responses were frequently closer to Stage 4 than they were to Stage 3. This repeated occurrence led us to reexamine the rationale for the ordering of Stages 3 and 4. We concluded that the social norms explain what maintains lawfulness and thus "the system." Therefore, it seems reasonable to infer that the identifiable political community, "the system," and its desirability must be recognized first, and only then will the legal norms that maintain it be fully appreciated. A complete explication of the rationale underlying the modification of Kohlberg's moral development typology is found in Chapter 6.

The postconventional *level* (Level III) of an individual's orientation to law is reached when the rationale for the law's existence is ascribed to abstract moral principles. Thus, people at Stage 5 (Social Contract) consider laws to be legitimate because they are formulated according to fair procedures by the entire community. At Stage 6 the legitimacy of law is acknowledged when it corresponds with standards such as justice or equality that are part of an individual's value system.

Using this typology we examined the hypothesis of Piaget and Kohlberg that movement through these stages is sequential and irreversible. We also sought to determine whether movement among stages of orientation toward law is related to an ethnocentric attitude about the "goodness" of the United States. If movement from a lower to a higher stage of orientation to law is accompanied by a less ethnocentric attitude toward the United States, a variety of practical implications are evident.

PLAN FOR PRESENTATION AND ANALYSIS

Part II reports an analysis of what children from kindergarten through fourth grade know and feel about politics and government and why these children understand and feel as they do.

Chapter 3 discusses the political world of the kindergarten child. This constitutes our base for measuring growth in civic awareness among primary school children. The analysis includes a mapping of the young child's cognitive awareness, his or her sensitivity to issues of law and morality, as well as his or her knowledge and feelings about public-policy issues. Differences among the responses of children are explained by using traditional independent variables as well as selected threshold cognitive variables.

Chapter 4 reports the changing cognitive political world of first-through fourth-graders. A 20-item cognitive map is used to measure the varying rates of increasing knowledge about six basic categories of political objects: the national community, the regime, authorities, political geography, distinguishing private- from public-sector occupations, and contemporary policy issues.

An analysis of how and why cognitive political awareness increases is presented in Chapter 5. Stages of political awareness are developed for each of nine threshold variables, and these in turn are used to predict the level of awareness that each child has of the cognitive map items. These threshold independent variables are then used to explain why the knowledge of some children increased while that of others did not. Special attention is given to whether increasing ability to distinguish between public- and private-sector occupations is related to a broader understanding of civic matters. Traditional demographic variables are also used to determine how effectively they explain differences in political awareness growth rates among children between kindergarten and the end of fourth grade.

Chapter 6 explores the developing perceptions of law and morality among primary school children. The stage of each child's orientation toward law is compared with answers to queries regarding national virtues and governmental responsiveness.

The first chapter of Part III (Chapter 7) examines linkages between cognitive, moral, and affective development. This discussion includes findings about sex-role stereotyping and increasing tolerance of sex-role diversity. An analysis of data concerning feelings about political efficacy and governmental responsiveness is also presented.

The final chapter discusses the key implications of this study for: (1) understanding the political learning process, (2) promoting regime support and political stability, (3) modifying curricula and teaching in the field of civic education, and (4) future political socialization research.

NOTES

1. Phillip J. Runkel and Joseph E. McGrath, *Research on Human Behavior: A Systematic Guide to Method* (New York: Holt, Rinehart and Winston, Inc., 1972), pp. 114–17.

2. Herbert Ginsburg and Sylvia Opper, *Piaget's Theory of Intellectual Development: An Introduction* (Englewood Cliffs, NJ: Prentice-Hall, 1969), pp. 3–4.

3. Runkel and McGrath, *Research on Human Behavior*, Chapter 4.

4. Donald T. Campbell and Julian C. Stanley, *Experimental and Quasi-Experimental Designs for Research* (Chicago: Rand McNally and Company, 1963), p. 21.

5. Stanford E. Taylor, Helen Frackenpohl, and Catherine E. White, *A Revised Core Vocabulary: A Basic Vocabulary for Grade 1–8*, Research and Information Bulletin No. 5, Revised (Huntington, NY: Educational Developmental Laboratories, Inc., A Division of McGraw-Hill, March, 1969).

6. Campbell and Stanley, *Experimental and Quasi-Experimental Designs for Research*, pp. 18, 37–42.

7. There is evidence, however, that by third grade children in our panel were more likely to view government as more pervasive and benevolent than third-graders not in this study. (See Appendix B.)

8. David Easton, *The Political System*, 2nd edition (New York: Knopf, 1971). See also, David Easton and Robert D. Hess, "The Child's Political World," *Midwest Journal of Political Science* 6 (August 1962): 235f.

9. Gustave Jahoda, "The Development of Children's Ideas About Country and Nationality. Part 1: The Conceptual Framework," *British Journal of Educational Psychology* 33: 47–60.

10. David Easton and Jack Dennis, *Children in the Political System* (New York: McGraw-Hill, 1969), Chapter 6.

11. R. W. Connell, *The Child's Construction of Politics* (Melbourne, Australia: Melbourne University Press, 1971), Chapter 1; and further confirmation of this tendency was presented by Sandra Schwartz in "Preschoolers and Politics" in David and Sandra Schwartz, eds., *New Directions in Political Socialization* (New York: The Free Press, 1975), p. 230f.

12. Fred I. Greenstein, *Children and Politics* (New Haven: Yale University Press, 1965), p. 71.

13. Greenstein, *Children and Politics*, Chapter 4.

14. Greenstein, *Children and Politics*, pp. 60–61; and Jahoda, *British Journal of Educational Psychology* 33: 47–60.

15. Jahoda found that Scottish children were first aware of the immediate locality, and then progressively their awareness extended outward in a series of concentric circles. Greenstein, in *Children and Politics*, pp. 60–61, on the other hand, notes that "first awareness" of government is of the national and local levels, not the state, and "full understanding" of the working of a government level occurs first with the national government. Greenstein's movement, however, relates to political authorities rather than political jurisdictions per se.

16. Easton and Dennis, *Children in the Political System*, pp. 121–23.

17. Gabriel A. Almond and Sidney Verba, *The Civic Culture*, (Boston: Little, Brown and Company, 1965), p. 14. By second grade children are moving from what Piaget calls the *preoperational* stage of cognitive growth to a *concrete-operational* stage. During this latter, middle childhood stage, several intellectual achievements take place. See John H. Flavell, *Cognitive Development* (Englewood Cliffs; NJ: Prentice-Hall, 1977), Chapter 3.

18. Stanley W. Moore, Kenneth A. Wagner, James Lare, and D. Stephen McHargue II, "The Civic Awareness of Five and Six Year Olds," *The Western Political Quarterly* 29, 3 (September 1976): 410–24.

19. The demographic characteristics of the 110 children who were lost from the sample closely resemble those of the 243 youngsters who comprise the panel used in this study.

		Panel Members (N=243)	Lost From Panel (N=110)
Sex	Male	49.0	55.4
	Female	51.0	44.5
Race	Anglo	80.7	87.3
	Non-Anglo	19.3	11.8
	NA	0.0	0.9
Sibling order	Only child	5.8	12.7
	Oldest child	24.3	25.5
	Middle child	25.1	25.5
	Youngest child	44.9	34.5
	NA	0.0	1.8

20. The responses to items on the first-grade questionnaire given by the 95 children interviewed for the first time in 1975 were compared with those of the 148 youngsters who were in the original kindergarten sample. In no instance did the percentage difference for any of the affective or cognitive items reach the .05 level of significance. See William Buchanan, *Understanding Political Variables* (New York: Scribner's, 1969), Chapter 5. Furthermore, those instances when the percentage differences were closest to statistical significance were nearly equally divided between times when those in the original kindergarten sample were more knowledgeable and instances when the children added in the first grade were more knowledgeable.

21. Robert Hess and Judith Torney, *The Development of Political Attitudes in Children* (Garden City, NY: Doubleday, 1967), pp. 199–222; Greenstein, *Children and Politics*, Chapter 6.

22. A. Jay Stevens, "The Acquisition of Participatory Norms: The Case of Japanese and Mexican-American Children in a Suburban Environment," *Western Political Quarterly* 28 (June 1975): 281–95; and F. Chris Garcia, *The Chicano Political Experience* (North Scituate, MA: Duxbury Press, 1977); and *The Political Socialization of Chicano Children* (New York: Praeger Publishers, 1973).

23. Hess and Torney, *The Development of Political Attitudes in Children*, Chapter 7.

24. Kenneth P. Langton, *Political Socialization* (New York: Oxford University Press, 1969): 136–38, 163f.; Hess and Torney, Ibid., Greenstein, *Children and Politics*, Chapter 5.

25. A summarization of this literature is provided by Lawrence Kohlberg in "Stage and Sequence: The Cognitive Developmental Approach to Socialization," in D. A. Goslin, ed., *Handbook of Socialization Theory and Research* (Chicago: Rand McNally, 1969), pp. 347–480.

26. Stanley Allen Renshon, ed., *Handbook of Political Socialization* (New York: The Free Press, 1977), pp. 352–53.

27. Kohlberg's typology is outlined in his "Moral Stages and Moralization," in T. Lickona, ed., *Moral Development and Behavior* (New York: Holt, Rinehart and Winston, 1976), Chapter 2.

28. Connell in *The Child's Construction of Politics* discusses the existence of a task pooling perception among young children.

PART II
ANALYSIS

3

The Kindergartner's Political World

WHO RULES?

The focus of this chapter is on the political world of the five- and six-year-old kindergarten child. Findings from this first set of interviews conducted in 1974 will serve as a base for drawing comparisons with four subsequent annual interviews. Following the lead of David Easton, a principal area this study seeks to probe is the young child's awareness of and feelings about political authorities. Obviously "authority" and "ruler" would not be in the typical kindergarten child's vocabulary, and he wanted to refrain from introducing words such as "President" and "government" to the children before they had an opportunity to use these terms spontaneously. As a consequence, the first question on the interview schedule each of the five years was "Who is the *boss* of our country?" "Boss" has the advantage of being in the kindergartner's vocabulary.

When asked "Who is the boss of the country?" the kindergarten children provided a variety of responses:

"I don't know"

"God"

"Jesus"

"The President" "Nixon"

"George Washington"

"Abraham Lincoln"

"President Kimball" (leader of the Mormon Church)

One-third of the kindergartners responded that they did not know who "the boss" of our country is (see Table 3.1). But, when a substantive answer was ventured, nearly one-quarter (24 percent) said "God" or "Jesus." Furthermore, in confirmation of Schwartz's finding that many young children perceive the church as political,[1] this religious referent was not an isolated response; at least three other questions establish that many kindergarten-aged children see religious authorities as serving important public roles. For example, 30 percent of the kindergartners answered "God" or "Jesus" when responding to the question "Who does the most to run the country?" Three other children gave the name of the president of the Mormon Church. In families with a strong religious emphasis, young children tend to view the world from a predominantly religious perspective. A major finding of this study is that an early religious orientation predisposes children to have more positive feelings toward the President and other civil authorities.

The second most common substantive response to the "boss" query was "The President" or "Nixon." Given repeated findings concerning the salience of this office among school-aged children, we were surprised that these "correct" answers were given by only 16 percent of the panel. The frequency of this answer was matched by

TABLE 3.1
Perceptions of Who Governs (in percentages)

| | *Questions* | | |
Responses	Who is the boss of our country?	Who does the most to run the country?	Who makes the laws?
God or Jesus	24	30	15
President Nixon	16	15	12
Police	1	0.5	24
Government	5	6	7
Other political figures	16	0	9
D.K.	32	37	32
N.A. or other	6	12	1
	100	100.5	100
N (number of respondents)	(149)	(149)	(149)

the 24 children who believed that other political figures, notably our most famous Presidents, George Washington and Abraham Lincoln, were the boss. Washington and Lincoln seem very real to many young children; from their responses it is obvious that a number thought they were still alive. In spite of the massive Watergate-related publicity focused on President Nixon in the late spring of 1974, many more children could identify pictures of George Washington (52 percent) and Abraham Lincoln (41 percent) than could identify Richard Nixon (29 percent). (See Table 3.2)

Because the kindergarten interviews were conducted in May, several months after the birthdays of the two best-known Presidents, it seemed reasonable to believe there might be a school-promoted "February effect." In order to test this possibility, a follow-up survey was conducted using 56 entering kindergarten children during the third week of school in September 1974.[2] Forty-seven percent of the children could, at the start of kindergarten, identify a picture of George Washington. Abraham Lincoln was recognized by one-fifth of the children. The ability to identify Washington and Lincoln is acquired by many children prior to entering kindergarten, though the percentage able to recognize Lincoln's picture increases dramatically during the first year in school.

Although more than two-thirds of the kindergartners claimed that they had seen the President on television, three different indicators reveal that only about one-third could, in fact, recognize the incumbent President. Forty-one percent could respond correctly to "Who is Richard Nixon?"—34 percent knew the President's name

TABLE 3.2
Recognition of Pictures of Presidents (in percentages)

Response of child	Do You Know Who This Is? (Pictures of Presidents shown)		
	Washington	Lincoln	Nixon
Identified Correctly	52	44	29
No, or didn't know	23	41	62
Washington	—	3	0
Lincoln	12	—	0
President	9	5	0
Other	4	7	8
	100	100	99

when asked "Who is the President right now?"—and 29 percent recognized his picture. In contrast, the incumbent state and municipal chief executives were known by very few kindergartners; less than one percent recognized the name of Ronald Reagan, who was then completing his second term as Governor of California, or Tom Bradley, the Mayor of Los Angeles, who had been in office more than two years.

From our interview data it is clear that kindergarten children have a very confused perception of the executive in our national government. They are not yet able to distinguish clearly between the office and the incumbent. They sometimes assume that several Presidents hold office simultaneously; some even described Washington and Lincoln as picking new Presidents. These children tend to view political authorities as responsible for a "task pool"[3] of functions, and they generally see political and religious authorities as benevolent.

If kindergarten children are not particularly aware of who rules our society, it may be useful to inquire concerning their awareness of the national political community, the constitutional democratic regime, pressing public needs, and certain contemporary political issues.

AWARENESS OF THE NATIONAL POLITICAL COMMUNITY

Earlier studies have suggested that by the time a child in the United States is in second grade, a "we/they" distinction involving membership in the political community called the United States of America has joined a list of other distinctions such as boys/girls, blacks/whites, rich/poor, and perhaps Protestant/Catholic/Jew.[4] Two questions in our interview schedule provide a measure of national community awareness among kindergarten children: (1) identification of "our flag" in a grouping of four national flags and (2) responses to the query "What country do you live in?" When shown a chart with four national flags (Great Britain, Canada, Mexico, and the United States), only two of the children questioned, both girls, did not point to the flag of the United States in response to the questions "Which is our flag?" This suggests that kindergarten children almost universally recognize the most prominent symbol of our national political community. By contrast Jahoda found that only 42 percent of middle-class Glasgow children, ages 6 to 7 recognized the Union Jack.[5] The early stage at which children in the United States recognize the flag was further confirmed by the September 1974 interviews in which only one child failed to identify the U.S. flag at the beginning of kindergarten. This finding virtually eliminates an alternative hypothesis that nine months of flag salutes during the kindergarten year inculcates recognition of "our flag." The dramatic difference in flag recognition between our panel and Johoda's may be partially explained by the possibility that more U.S. children than Scottish children are exposed to public events or facilities or to advertising in which the national flag is used. It is possible that the place of the United States flag and the circumstances surrounding its creation are more central to the national folklore, indeed to a civil religion in the United States,[6] than is the case in the United Kingdom.

It seems, however, that recognition of the flag involves *symbol recognition only* and would appear to be the product of rote learning through repetition. This rudimentary awareness of the national flag is obviously shallow since only 21 percent answered "What country do you live in?" with "the United States" or "America" (see Table 3.3). Almost two-thirds indicated that they did not know what country they lived in. It should be noted, of course, that the open-ended question, "What country do you live in?", is a very conservative way of measuring awareness of the national political

TABLE 3.3
Political Community Awareness (in percentages)

	Questions			
Response	Where do you live?	What city do you live in?	What state do you live in?	What country do you live in?
Local (street, landmark)	66	0	0	0
City	14	42	4	5
California	2	10	17	0
U.S., America	3	9	17	21
D.K.	13	34	57	64
Other & N.A.	1	4	4	10
	99	99	99	100

community; it carries a rather strong bias against a young child's making the correct identification because many kindergarten-aged children do not understand the term "country."

When asked "Where do you live?", the kindergartner is most apt to respond with the name of his street or a local landmark. Only 14 percent respond with the name of their local community. Fifty-eight percent give their street address while 8 percent identify a local landmark such as a hill, a large house, or a winding road. These responses confirm the local focus of the young child's geographic orientation; the emphasis is clearly on the neighborhood in which he or she lives. This finding attests to the success of the family and the schools, two primary socializing agencies, in teaching youngsters their home addresses.

In kindergarten children are just beginning to sort out the names and relationships of geo-political jurisdictions.* A significant number of the kindergarten children (42 percent) are able to name correctly the city in which they live, but the percentage of correct answers falls off sharply in their responses to "What country do you live in?" (21 percent) and "What state do you live in?" (17 percent). This differs somewhat from the conclusions of Greenstein, who found elementary school children in New Haven became aware first of their country and their city.[7] The order of identification among our kindergarten children is strongly toward the local first, while the nation is a distant second and the state third. This also represents a deviation from the concentric circles sequence suggested by Jahoda. He found that Scottish children were first aware of the immediate locality and then progressively their awareness extended outward. Ninety percent of his six- and seven-year-olds had not yet progressed beyond a conception of "Glasgow."[8]

It is clear from our data that the attention of young children is focused primarily on their local community, and at best they are only vaguely aware of living in a country called "the United States" and even less familiar with the name of their state, "California." The

---

*Only six children (four girls and two boys—4 percent) can sort out all three tiers of government. Eleven children know both their city and state, and an identical number know both their city and country. Two children know the name of their state and country. Fifty-five know only the name of one jurisdiction. Finally, 64 pupils (45 percent) are unable to provide even one correct response to these three geo-political queries.

government authorities who visit their classrooms are representatives of such community agencies as the Police Department, the Fire Department, and perhaps the school board. It is rare for an elementary school child to have direct contact with representatives of either the state or national governments, and on the rare occasions when this occurs, those officials, usually elected representatives, are not in uniform. It would also appear that the flag, as a symbol of the national government, is not clearly identified in the mind of the kindergarten-aged child as representing the country in which he or she lives—despite a year of daily flag salutes.

AWARENESS OF THE REGIME

During the presidential campaign of 1972, these children were only three or four years old, and at the time of the California primary in the spring of 1974, they were five or six years old. What did they know about "politicians," "elections," "voting," and the choosing of a President? We wanted to query the children about these terms even though we knew they were not likely to be in their working vocabularies for at least several years. By constructing questions that can be used as the children progress through the elementary school grades, we expect to identify the precise grade levels at which most children first become familiar with a term and the grade level at which they are reasonably knowledgeable about a key political concept. When not one child answered "yes" to the self-report question, "Do you know what politicians do?", this provided a zero base from which to measure future growth in knowledge-ability.[9]

What then *do* kindergarten children know about the political regime? When asked "Do you know what an election is?", 7 percent answered "yes", and most of them explained their understanding of "election" in meaningful terms: "You go out voting." "Something if the president dies, they vote for another president." When asked if they had "ever *voted* in an election," 19 percent (28 children) said they had, and their teachers reported that most of the children had voted on various classroom options. But a number of those reporting that they had *not* voted in an election indicated that they had some awareness of the electoral process by referring to their parents having voted: "My mom voted for a government."

"Mommy and daddy did."* Some children indicated their confusion about the election/voting questions by responding: "I don't know who they are even" and "What does 'voted' mean?" But when asked whether they would "like to vote," 75 percent responded affirmatively. Since "What is a vote?" was not asked, this overwhelming response does not indicate knowledge of voting or elections, but rather the generally positive outlook characteristic of young children.

Because only a few children were knowledgeable about the electoral process, it is not surprising that 61 percent said they did not know "how the President was picked." Nineteen children (the largest single-response category) asserted that it was God or Jesus who picked the President. There were 13 percent who made references to "other governmental leaders," principally Washington, Lincoln, or "the other presidents." Occasionally a child would say "the government." Only 7 percent answered the question, "Who picks the President?", with "people," "us," or "the voters," indicating that they recognized participation by a broad constituency. One child declared: "People do. They all vote together at schools. People who want the most, vote him. The more vote. The president voted most wins."

As a further index of their regime awareness, the children were asked a series of questions relating to political parties, beginning with the query "Have you ever heard of the word 'Republican'?" Thirty-three children (22 percent) said they had; the identical question with the word "Democrat" received precisely the same number of affirmative responses. Only 14 children, however, claimed to recognize both labels. There is no correlation between recognizing the word "Democrat" and claiming to know about "government." But the correlation between asserted knowledge

---

*References to "mom" voting outnumber references to "dad" voting by about three to one. M. Kent Jennings and Richard G. Niemi's 1965 sample indicated that Mother-Son and Mother-Daughter political agreement correlations were slightly higher than Father-Son and Father-Daughter correlations, in spite of "the common lore . . . that the male is more dominant in political matters than the female." The preponderance of references to "mom voting" may result because single-parent homes are predominantly headed by females and many women are homemakers for their families. See Jennings and Niemi, "The Transmission of Political Values from Parent to Child," *American Political Science Review* 62 (1968):342–43 and *The Political Character of Adolescence: The Influence of Families and Schools* (Princeton: Princeton University Press, 1974), p. 167.

about the term "government" and having heard of the word "Republican" is significant at the .05 level. Since the researchers were asked not to query the children about their parents' party identification, it can only be hypothesized that children from "Republican" homes hear the terms "Republican" and "government" earlier and more frequently than children from "Democratic" homes hear either "Democrat" or "government." It is conceivable that this correlation may reflect the presence of a Republican administration in Washington, but we suspect that because Republicans are more likely to vote than Democrats, they may also be more likely to discuss government and politics in front of their children.[10]

What do kindergartners know about law? All societies seek cohesion by attempting to create a normative consensus. Robert Dahl in *A Preface to Democratic Theory* emphasizes the necessity for "social training" in the norms of a society as the prerequisite for social solidarity and the gaining of popular support for national policy.[11] Mary Ellen Goodman focuses attention upon the conceptualization of "standards and limits (rules) concerning behavior, interpersonal rights and obligations" among nursery school children;[12] Charles Andrain observes that public schools instruct "children in the proper rules (norms) of political behavior . . . stress obedience to law and respect for authority."[13] In this study we began to probe the kindergartner's conception of law by asking, "Can you tell me what a law is?" Forty-six percent gave reasonable answers. These ranged from references to specific laws, for example, "the policeman's law, that everyone can't go fast on the road," to very generalized conceptions of law such as "it is the things that you are supposed to do," "It's a thing that you do—you obey. You have to obey the law," and "a rule—tells you not to do things." In fact, these kindergarten children were as likely to give a very general definition of law as they were to mention a specific example. This appears to run counter to Piaget's cognitive-developmental model, which suggests that children grasp the concrete situation before they can articulate the general principle.[14] According to Piaget, five- and six-year-old children are in the "concrete operational stage" and would therefore be expected to refer to specific examples when attempting to explain what a law is.

Following the query, "Can you tell me what a law is?", kindergartners were next asked "Who makes the laws?" Fifty children, one-third of the panel, said they did not know. The largest substantive response, provided by 24 percent, was that the policeman makes the laws. It is noteworthy that while this lawmaking role was ascribed to the police, they were not among those mentioned as "boss of the country" or as one of those who "does the most to run the country." Again, we find a sizeable number of children, 15 percent, who believe that God or Jesus makes the laws. Nearly 19 percent of the children gave politically aware responses, referring either to the President (11 percent) or the government (8 percent). These children lead us to question Andrain's assertion that "before age nine the cognitive abilities of the child are not sufficiently well developed to comprehend the abstract processes of government."[15] Admittedly, Andrain's test for "comprehension" of the abstract processes of government, electoral or legislative, for example, is more rigorous than our queries concerning "Who picks the President?" or "Who makes the laws?" Nevertheless, it appears that at least one kindergarten child in ten, and perhaps as many as one in six is able to grasp key elements in these basic processes of democratic government.

Our questions concerning the regime refer not only to electoral and legislative processes, but also to the way in which the chief executive and his aides function. When the children were asked, "What do you think the President does when he goes to work?", 51 percent did not know; our efforts to categorize the 73 substantive responses were unproductive. They included, for example, "writes," "governs," "solves problems," "helps people," "makes speeches," and interestingly, for 1974, "tells his secretary to tape."

After the President, kindergartners view the policeman as the next most influential governmental figure. A question probing the kindergartner's perception of this highly visible local official was "What does a policeman do?" About 70 percent of the responses concerned law enforcement duties: "He catches robbers," "gives tickets," "sees if you do things wrong," and "chases people who are going too fast and puts them in jail." Another 20 percent were service-oriented responses: "He helps people," "finds lost children," and "saves the world." Sometimes the policeman is seen as serving both functions: "helps people when they get run over. When people go through red lights, he tells them not to." These replies closely resemble the distribution of *fourth-grade* responses reported by Easton and Dennis. Their questionnaire, administered in the early 1960s, contained a fixed-choice item that led them to conclude that 23 percent of the fourth-graders felt the most important job of the policeman was to "help people who are in trouble"; 38 percent chose "make people obey the law"; and 39 percent selected "catch people who break the law."[16] Clearly, the police, although they are generally regarded as friendly and helpful, may also be seen as a potential threat by some young children.

As a further measure of the child's awareness of the regime, the interviewers asked whether a milkman, policeman, soldier, judge, mailman, or teacher "works for the government." In addition to exploring the children's cognizance of the distinction between public and private employment, this series of questions also sought to measure their perception of the scope of government, which in turn would indicate whether they were attuned to the historic emphasis our political tradition places on preserving a limited role for government (see Table 3.4). The public role of a judge was by far the most visible governmental occupation, already known by three-quarters of the kindergartners. Surprisingly, the least accurately perceived was the uniformed mailman, an everyday figure in most neighborhoods, who was identified as working for the government by just 45 percent. Only two children were able to indicate the public/private affiliation correctly for all six roles.

When the children were asked "Do you know what the word 'government' means?", 24 percent reported that they did. The researchers proceeded to ask, "What does the government do?" Twelve percent were able to respond with some form of government activity, but these responses were quite diverse, ranging from "helps the President," and "He does the government sidewalk," to "makes

TABLE 3.4
Response to "Which of the Following Work for the Government?"

Role	Percent Correctly Identifying Role*
Judge	76
Policeman	67
Milkman	58
Soldier	49
Teacher	46
Mailman	45
Average	57

*The roles were presented to the children in the following order: milkman, policeman, soldier, judge, mailman, and teacher.

pennies," "makes rules," "judge of the people," and "tells you laws, what to do." Is this initial and quite limited political awareness correlated with evidence of knowledgeability on other questions in the interview schedule? In some cases it is. For example, in responding to the query, "Does a judge work for the government?" 16 of the 18 children who had some sense of "what the government does" also perceived a judge as working for the government. In fact, those children who reported that they knew what government means were on the average 18 percent more likely to identify correctly which occupational roles are associated with government. Indeed, the question, "Do you know what the word 'government' means?", was extraordinarily helpful in predicting knowledge of governmental activities. If a child claimed to know what "government" means, he or she was much more likely to identify a picture of the national Capitol correctly, know for whom a policeman works, and know what "laws" and "taxes" are.[17] It appears that some kindergarten children, like most of their parents, associate government with law and taxes.

ATTITUDES CONCERNING FAIRNESS, PUBLIC NEEDS, AND OCCUPATIONAL PREFERENCES

In addition to the kindergartners' views concerning our governmental regime, their perceptions of the political and interpersonal environment were examined in three additional questions relating to: (1) their notions of fairness or unfairness, (2) their identification of urgent public needs, and (3) the occupational role they wished to pursue as an adult. We sought to determine whether the kindergarten children have a notion of fairness either in interpersonal or public-policy terms. Indeed they do, though it is usually not presented in a political or legal context. Thirty percent of the 105 youngsters replying to "Tell me something that isn't fair" responded -with references to situations that implied either inequity or privilege. Sometimes the inequity is expressed in impersonal terms: "when someone has some food and the other person doesn't," or "one team has 100 people and the other has one. One hundred to 98 is almost fair." Sometimes the injustice is directed against the respondent: "when someone else gets something and you don't." Occasionally the inequity is pictured as benefiting the speaker: "If you get a lollipop and he doesn't." Some kindergarten children understand that, even when they are the privileged party, the principle of fairness is violated, but only 15 percent of the inequity-privilege answers depicted the respondent as the beneficiary of the unfairness. Even more infrequent is the response that has direct political or public-policy implications, such as one girl's comment that it "isn't fair to take money from such poor people." The next most common category of substantive responses, after those implying the inequity-privilege concept, involves explicit references to cheating or stealing (rule violations). Representative responses include: "it's not fair to cheat in games," "stealing someone else's money," and one reference that sounded as though it came from a poignant life experience— "telling them where the donkey's tail is at my birthday party." Finally, 11 percent of the children identified unfairness with experiencing violence or destruction, not sharing, disobedience, speeding, and their comments ranged from "when you say wrong things" to "if someone crashes on his bicycle and dies."

The children in schools and classrooms with greater socio-economic diversity appeared to be more attuned to the inequity-privilege dimension of unfairness, while those in more homo-geneous student populations were inclined to offer the rule violation (cheating-stealing) conception of unfairness. Perhaps when children have more firsthand opportunities to experience inequities, this becomes more central to their notion of unfairness. Children without such contrasts in their daily experience focus instead on such interpersonal conflicts as cheating and stealing.

The fact that a significant majority of the 149 kindergarten youngsters had some conception of fairness suggests that they are beginning to conceptualize about matters of direct relevance to political and legal processes. This again calls into question the assertion that children are not ready to begin comprehending abstract political processes until about the fourth grade.[18]

In order to get a sense of the kindergarten child's conception of public needs, we asked, "If you were the boss of the whole country, what would you do to help people?" Sixty-two percent of those interviewed gave a substantive response to this question. The interviewers found that kindergarten youngsters could identify an impressive array of public needs. The largest group (37 percent) of the 92 who responded mentioned humanitarian or specific assist-ance to individuals unable to help themselves, including assistance for people who are ill, disabled, or in some physical danger. The second strongest impulse, suggested by 28 percent, was to help others with material assistance including food, clothing, shelter, and even money: "give everybody money to buy things," "I would buy food for poor people and give them money," or direct aid such as "give food so they won't die" or "make clothes to give them." Nine percent expressed an interest in ecological matters such as protecting the natural environment or beautifying their communities. Five percent indicated they wished to stop fights or violent arguments, while 4 percent indicated a desire to remedy various political ills: "stop wars" or "stop Watergate." Some proposals sounded like the child's equivalent of the theologians' ultimate concerns: "give them love," "I would make everybody love each other," and "help people live right and be good." Finally, a few of the children see law as a means of helping people: "Make laws." "Tell them what to do." "Don't speed in their cars and don't go through red lights." The girls seemed more concerned about meeting what have been classified here as the humanitarian or personal needs of those suffering illness or other distress, while the boys expressed a much stronger interest than girls in ecological goals.

A third potentially useful indication of how kindergarten children perceive their society, its needs, and various options in interpersonal relations involves the kind of occupation they view as desirable. Almost 90 percent of the 149 children interviewed offered some response to the query: "What would you like to do when you grow up?" Almost half of the boys (but not one girl) responded by indicating they wanted to be either police officers or firefighters, an obvious reflection of the visibility these occupations enjoy among children. The girls preferred occupational roles normally associated with women; for example, 31 girls wanted to be nurses, and 10 girls wanted to be mothers.[19] From these data it seems clear that kindergarten children are only just beginning to develop an appreciation for the range of occupational roles they may eventually fill. Occupations involving distinctive uniforms that the children see frequently—policemen, firemen, nurses, and perhaps pilots—are clearly the most popular. Other roles that are dominant in the child's world—parent and teacher—account for most of the remaining preferences. Because a rather limited range of occupational choices is clearly visible to the kindergarten child, it is not appropriate to infer too much concerning public needs or social values. At this age they identify primarily with those occupations that are most visible and those glamorized by the media.

CONTEMPORARY ISSUES

How aware is a kindergarten child of those issues that are the subject of adult concern and discussion? We elected to ask our 1974 respondents about four contemporary public issues: Watergate, Vietnam, impeachment, and the energy crisis. Table 3.5 shows that, with the exception of the energy crisis, very few children were aware of these issues. Even though the interviews were conducted in the late spring of 1974 when Watergate and talk of impeachment dominated the news, only one child in ten claimed to have *heard* the word "impeachment," while 14 percent said they knew what Watergate was. When asked to explain what "impeachment" means, not a single child could respond. Impeachment, of course, is a complex and difficult subject for many adults to understand, so the inability of these children to respond is not surprising. When asked to explain "Watergate," the closest any child could come was to say "It's on the news." And when we followed with the question, "Does Watergate make the President happy or sad?", 71 percent of those who claimed to know something about Watergate believed that it made him happy! Vietnam did not fare much better. Fifteen percent of the children said they knew what Vietnam was, but only 3 percent (four boys) could connect it with a war and 4 percent could identify it as a country. Knowledgeable responses concerning Vietnam usually resulted from the personal involvement of a relative; for example, one boy volunteered, "It's in the Army. My uncle was in it."

The energy crisis was significantly more visible to the children, and their explanations were much more accurate. Over 62 percent of the respondents professed they had "heard the words," and nearly two-thirds of these were able to make an accurate comment about the energy crisis. Many equated the phrase with scarcity: "Gas

TABLE 3.5
Familiarity with Contemporary Issues (in percentages)

Response	Do you know what the word "impeach-ment" means?	Do you know what Watergate is?	Do you know what Vietnam is?	What is the energy crisis?
Yes	0	14	15	36
No	100	86	85	64

stations run out of gas or food runs out." Some believed it meant people should conserve: "Save carefully, don't turn on your toaster too much," or "You can't turn the Christmas lights on when it is Christmas." A few equated the energy crisis with inflation: "It means the prices are going higher and higher."

With respect to these contemporary public issues, the most critical question is whether knowledgeability is concentrated in children who have reached the cognitive developmental stage at which they can grasp this level of complexity, or do some children understand one issue while others are aware of a different issue. This latter pattern would suggest that knowledgeability in this area is heavily dependent on environmental stimuli in a particular child's learning situation. Not one of the 16 children who claimed to have heard the word "impeachment" could explain the meaning of Watergate.[20] The overlap between those who could identify Watergate and Vietnam and explain the meaning of the energy crisis is only 20 percent. Nevertheless, it is also the case that in the three cross-tabulations (energy crisis, Vietnam, and Watergate), the children who are able to respond to one issue are slightly more likely to respond to the others. Does this composite issue-related pattern suggest a social learning process (a specific response to environmental stimuli) or cognitive development (a general maturational process)? The pattern of our data leads us to believe that knowledge about contemporary public issues is more likely to result from social learning than from cognitive development.

These data, then, support the proposition that matters close to the center of everyday activity are the most prominent for five- and six-year-olds. The energy crisis apparently was discussed in many homes and Vietnam was real for those with relatives involved, but Watergate and impeachment were "out there" somewhere and not likely to be salient to the kindergarten child. Perhaps this is because the latter two issues are indeed more difficult to translate into terms meaningful for a five- or six-year-old and because parents are inclined to shelter their children from the "seamy side" of politics. If this is true, then Watergate may have a limited negative impact on future attitudes of these young children toward politics when compared with the potential influence of war, shortages, and want. Indeed, there may be an age threshold beyond which Watergate becomes a salient factor for shaping future attitudes toward the political regime and public authorities. Therefore, a cohort demarcation may exist in the future between the members of our panel who "missed" Vietnam and Watergate and children a few years their senior who were able to experience more directly these national traumas. This situation may potentially represent what Jennings and Niemi label a generational effect.* Such a demarcation may affect basic political attitudes and orientations in much the same way the Depression affected those who experienced it directly in contrast with those who were too young to be conscious of its impact on their lives.[21]

DEMOGRAPHIC DIFFERENCES AND POLITICAL AWARENESS

In political socialization studies the traditional approach to explaining knowledgeability is to look for correlations between differing levels of political knowledge and particular demographic characteristics such as sex, ethnic background, and sibling order. Herbert Hyman, for example, in his summary of early political socialization studies, concluded that boys exceeded girls in both their interest and information about political matters.[22] In his *Children and Politics* Greenstein found that wherever the questionnaire responses differentiated boys and girls, the boys were "more political."[23]

In an effort to measure political knowledgeability, we constructed a 20-item cognitive map covering the full range of the governmental process, from political authorities to elements of the regime, from national symbols to contemporary public issues (see Table 3.6). Specifically, these map items consist of: three symbols of the national political community—George Washington, the national Capitol, and the Statue of Liberty; seven items referring to the regime—the respective functions of policemen, soldiers, laws, politicians, elections, taxes, and whether or not we have a king in the United States; three authorities—the incumbent chief executives at the national, state, and local levels; two public issues—Watergate and the energy crisis; three references to political geography—city,

---

*For a discussion of the differentiation of age cohorts see M. Kent Jennings and Richard G. Niemi, *Generations and Politics* (Princeton, NJ: Princeton University Press, 1981), pp. 117–24. See also Roberta S. Sigel and Marilyn Brookes Hoskin, "Perspectives on Adult Political Socialization," in Renshon, ed., *Handbook of Political Socialization*, pp. 262, 285–87.

TABLE 3.6
Cognitive Map of Kindergarten Political Knowledgeability

Item	Percent Correct	Rank
Recognition of U.S. flag from among four national flags.[a]	99	1
What does a policeman do?	90	2
Does a judge work for the government?	76	3
Do we have a king in the United States?	63	4
Does a milkman work for the government?	58	5
Recognition of George Washington's picture.	52	6
What is a law?	46	7
What city do you live in?	42	8
What is the energy crisis?[b]	36	9
What does a soldier do?	34	10
Recognition of Nixon's picture.	29	11
What country do you live in?	21	12
What state do you live in?	17	13
Recognition of a picture of the Statue of Liberty.	16	14
Tell me about Watergate.	14	15
What is an election?	7	16
Recognition of a picture of the national Capitol.	5	17
Who is Ronald Reagan?	2	18
Who is Tom Bradley?	1	19
What do politicians do?	0	20
What are taxes?[c]	c	

[a] Because more than 99 percent of kindergartners recognized the U.S. flag, this item was omitted from subsequent interview schedules and from the cognitive map.

[b] The children were first asked if they had "heard" of the issue; those who had, were then asked to explain it.

[c] In kindergarten we only asked for a "yes or no" response to "Do you know what taxes are?" Twenty percent claimed that they did. In subsequent years we used an open-ended query, "What are taxes?", that required the children to explain the concept.

state and country; and two occupations (judge and milkman) testing a child's ability to distinguish between public- and private-sector roles. See Appendix D for a discussion of the items included in this map and the rationale for their selection.

In the kindergarten year only one of the 20 items in the cognitive map had a statistically significant correlation with the sex of the respondents, although in 16 out of those 20 items boys were more knowledgeable than girls (see Table 3.7).[24] One of the distinguishing characteristics between boys and girls was the latter's more frequent use of the "Don't know" response. On almost every item the girls had a higher percentage of "Don't knows" than boys. Renshon has succinctly discussed the problem of interpreting "don't know" responses in the *Handbook of Political Socialization* (p. 11), noting four possible translations: (1) attempts to reduce dissonance, (2) acts of evasion, (3) the equivalent of "I don't care," and (4) when used often, representing a high degree of confusion in the respondents (p. 11).

Fifty-eight percent of the children who attempted to respond to "What does the government do?" were boys, and twice as many boys as girls gave a response that involved a governmental activity. Of the 22 children who responded with "the President" when asked "Who does the most to run the country?", 64 percent were boys. At the same time a few more girls than boys believed that "God" or "Jesus" ran the country. These findings support the conclusion of earlier studies that the political environment is more salient to boys than to girls in the five- and six-year-old age group.

If sex is only marginally useful in distinguishing more politically knowledgeable from less knowledgeable children, what about ethnic background? Earlier studies have indicated that Anglo children are more politically knowledgeable than non-Anglo children.[25] Slightly less than one-fifth of our panel is non-Anglo. Although Anglo children are more accurate on 11 of the 20 items in the map, non-Anglo children are more knowledgeable on 8 items (see Table 3.7). Anglo children are significantly more knowledgeable than non-Anglos on two items: knowing what a law is (52 to 19 percent) and knowing what a policeman does (95 to 69 percent). Two explanations for these differences in knowledgeability might be advanced. Since non-Anglos are less positive toward the police than Anglos,[26] they may feel less inclined to offer a response to the query, "What does a policeman do?" and thus they may prefer not to express that

TABLE 3.7

Percentages of Correct Responses Among Three Demographic Variables Cross-tabulated with the Cognitive Map (NAs excluded)

	Sex			Race			Sibling-order				
	Male	Female	Sig.	Anglo	Non-Anglo	Sig.	Only	Oldest	Middle	Youngest	Sig.
Policeman[a]	95[b]	87		95	69	.001	92	97	89	88	
Judge	80	75		78	73		83	84	83	70	
King	63	64		59	81		58	61	72	61	
Milkman	50	66		57	69		50	58	69	57	
Washington	52	52		51	54		58	61	45	49	
Law	55	40		52	19	.01	58	64	52	35	
City	45	40		46	27		33	50	38	42	
Energy[c]	42	32		40	19		42	46	21	37	
Soldier	52	21	.001	35	31		42	33	25	37	.05

Nixon	33	26	26	42	33	36	24	27	.01
Country	23	21	22	20	50	36	18	13	
State	22	15	20	8	25	26	7	18	
Stat. of Liberty	19	15	17	12	8	18	17	16	
Watergate	19	11	15	12	25	15	17	11	
Election	8	7	9	0	0	3	10	9	
Capitol	9	2	5	8	17	9	0	4	
Reagan	2	2	2	4	17	0	0	1	.01
Bradley	3	0	1	4	0	3	0	1	
Politician	0	0	0	0	0	0	0	0	
Taxes[d]	23	18	18	31	42	27	18	15	

[a] See Table 3.6 for the exact wording of each of these map items.

[b] Underlining indicates most knowledgeable subgroup.

[c] NAs were *included* with "Tell me about the energy crisis" because the previous question, "Have you heard the words 'energy crisis?'" served as a filter that excluded nearly 40 percent of the sample.

[d] Analysis based on the children who responded affirmatively to "Do you know what taxes are?"

negativism in front of the adult interviewer. On the whole, however, we have been impressed with the forthrightness of these children. A second possible explanation is that non-Anglo parents may avoid discussing law-related matters that are unpleasant in front of their children, particularly if they feel powerless to change the situation.[27]

Is sibling order an effective predictor of political knowledge?[28] At this age oldest siblings are consistently more knowledgeable than younger and only children. On 10 of the 20 map items the oldest siblings are most knowledgeable, and in no instance are they least aware. Only children tend to be the next most knowledgeable group. They are the most knowledgeable on six items, but they are also the least knowledgeable on five items. This may result from the small number of only children (twelve) in our kindergarten panel causing greater statistical instability, or, it may stem from the fact that only children are largely dependent on their parents for reinforcement. On only three questions do sibling differences in political knowledge reach statistical significance, but in each instance only and oldest children are most knowledgeable.

Why are oldest siblings slightly, but consistently, more knowledgeable than others? We can eliminate the possibility of an unbalanced sex distribution; boys are not overrepresented in the oldest sibling category. However, because of a special cultural role, oldest boys, rather than oldest girls, might account for the sibling difference. Analysis indicates that the oldest boys' responses are 8 percent more accurate than the oldest girls to the 20 items, and this difference does partially account for the tendency of greater knowledge on the part of oldest siblings.[29]

Is there any evidence from these sibling data that would support either a Piagetian or a stimulus-response model of learning? There are a number of very large differences between sibling groups. When these occur, particularly when they involve children of the same sex, we believe that environmental variability is a more likely explanation than is a cognitive-developmental process. The pattern of only children seems to suggest that they may be highly dependent on the presence of particular stimuli from their parents, and, when these cues are absent, the void is not filled by conversations with older or younger siblings.

In summary the three traditional demographic variables—sex, ethnic background, and sibling order—are marginally helpful in distinguishing more knowledgeable from less knowledgeable children. The differences are usually in the hypothesized direction, but are not of a magnitude to be statistically significant. Consequently, the researchers sought to develop more effective indicators of political knowledge.

COGNITIVE VARIABLES AND POLITICAL KNOWLEDGE

Using the cognitive-developmental model of Jean Piaget, we hypothesized that in the realm of political awareness, as in other areas of learning, a maturing child moves through a series of cognitive stages during which increasingly complex understandings are assimilated. We focused on the knowledge children had about selected political objects that were hypothesized to be threshold understandings useful for demarcating different stages and levels of cognitive development. In particular, we examined the kindergartner's knowledge of the functions performed by the President and the government, as measured by responses to the queries "What does the President do when he goes to work?" and "What does the government do?" We also assigned children to stages of knowledgeability by analyzing their responses to "What are taxes?" and two questions comprising the "electoral process" variable: "What is an election?" and "Who picks the President?" See Appendix B for the criteria used in assigning stages of cognitive political awareness to responses given to these questions.

What basis do we have for selecting these concepts, rather than others, as likely to be thresholds leading to greater cognitive political awareness? The *President* is, without question, the central authority figure in the young child's political consciousness. Easton and Dennis argue that a notion of *government* provides the young child with "a conceptual device for grasping, however inchoately and awkwardly, the presence of some structure" of which individual authorities such as the President, the governor, and the policeman are a part. They found that by second grade nearly 75 percent of their eight-city sample had a rough working conception of government.[30] The concept of an *electoral process* is central to the notion of representative government; elections are the mechanisms by which the people give voice to their wishes. *Taxation* is the principal means by which authority figures acquire the resources to carry out public functions.

We assumed that children at higher stages on these four threshold cognitive variables would also be more knowledgeable about the 20 items in the cognitive map. If these threshold cognitive variables were successful in predicting levels of knowledgeability, it would be partial confirmation for the relevance of the cognitive-developmental theory of learning to the sphere of political awareness.

The data presented in Table 3.8 modestly support the Piagetian cognitive-developmental model. Of 75 possible comparisons of knowledgeability between unstaged and staged children, 49 are in the expected direction, with 8 being statistically significant. Ten of the 21 contrary cases, those where the unstaged children were more knowledgeable than the staged, occur with three items in the cognitive map: whether our country has a king, recognition of a picture of the national Capitol, and awareness that Tom Bradley is Mayor of Los Angeles. Failure to recognize the national Capitol is the source of four of the reversals. The national Capitol is not a unifying symbol of our national political community; rather, it is a symbol of political conflict and controversy. This is perhaps one reason why it does not receive as much attention in our educational curricula as a unifying symbol such as George Washington receives.[31]

We conclude that individually these four cognitive variables (what the President does, what government does, taxes, and the electoral process) do not distinguish knowledgeable from less knowledgeable kindergartners any more successfully than do the traditional demographic variables. However, when these four variables are combined into a single index, which we call the Political Understanding Index, we find that it predicts 14 of the 20 items on the cognitive map in the expected direction, and on seven of the items the relationship reaches statistical significance (see Table 3.9).

This new variable, the Political Understanding Index, may in turn be used to explore further the relationship between traditional demographic variables and political awareness. An examination of the demographic characteristics of the *nine* children who have the highest scores on the Political Understanding Index reveals that all are Anglo, six are boys, and five are either the only child or the oldest sibling in the family. Boys are overrepresented by 24 percent, Anglos by 17 percent, and only and oldest children by 26 percent, but these demographic differences on this index variable are not large enough to be statistically significant. In sum demographic differences only

TABLE 3.8
Staged Cognitive Variables Cross-tabulated with the Cognitive Map (in percentages correct with NAs excluded)

	President Do?[a]			Government Do?[b]			What are Taxes?			Electoral Process[c]		
	Un.[d]	S.[e]	Sig.	Un.	S.	Sig.	Un.	S.	Sig.	Un.	S.	Sig.
Policeman	91[f]	90		89	95		91	91		89	94	
Judge	77	77		74	85		77	77		77	84	
King	66	56		69	48	.05	62	68		62	49	
Milkman	62	53		64	46		59	59		61	52	
Washington	47	63		53	48		50	59		57	55	
Law	41	58		40	63	.05	41	77	.01	47	61	
City	38	50		38	54		42	46		47	41	
Energy	63	53		56	66		57	67		54	83	.05
Soldier	31	42	.05	29	50	.05	34	36		36	46	
Nixon	23	42		28	33		26	46		31	30	
Country	18	29		17	34	.05	21	24		21	37	
State	17	19		10	40	.001	17	23		17	29	

67

TABLE 3.8 (continued)

	President Do?[a]			Government Do?[b]			What are Taxes?			Electoral Process[c]		
	Un.[d]	S.[e]	Sig.	Un.	S.	Sig.	Un.	S.	Sig.	Un.	S.	Sig.
Statue of												
Liberty	17	15		15	21		15	23		17	19	
Watergate	11	21		10	25	.05	13	23		14	24	
Election	7	8		9	3		6	18		6	18	
Capitol	7	2		7	3		6	5		6	3	
Reagan	2	2		2	3		2	5		2	3	
Bradley	2	0		2	0		1	5		2	0	
Politician	0	0		0	0		0	0		0	0	
Taxes[g]	16	29		19	25		—	—		20	30	
Instances Most Knowledgeable	7	10		6	13		1	14		7	12	

[a] Based on the query "What does the President do when he goes to work?"
[b] Based on the query "What does the government do?"
[c] "Electoral Process" is based upon two queries: "What is an election?" and "Who picks the President?"
[d] "Un." is the abbreviation for Unstaged.
[e] "S." represents the children whose response could be staged.
[f] Underline indicates most knowledgeable category.
[g] Analysis based on the children who responded affirmatively to "Do you know what taxes are?"

68

partially account for variance among individuals on the Political Understanding Index.

Finally, in our quest for a satisfactory index of political knowledgeability among kindergarten children, we constructed a political awareness scale based on the total number of political

TABLE 3.9
Stage on the Political Understanding Index Cross-tabulated with the Cognitive Map (in percentages correct with NAs excluded)

| | Placement on Political Understanding Index | | | |
	Unstaged	Stage 1	Stage 2	Sig.
Policeman	89	<u>93</u>	89	
Judge	71	80	<u>85</u>	
King	<u>77</u>[a]	53	54	.01
Milkman	<u>66</u>	56	50	
Washington	48	48	<u>69</u>	
Law	32	49	<u>73</u>	.01
City	38	37	<u>65</u>	.05
Energy	50	59	<u>70</u>	
Soldier	28	31	<u>58</u>	.05
Nixon	23	26	<u>50</u>	.05
Country	15	23	<u>36</u>	
State	12	14	<u>42</u>	.01
Statue of Liberty	13	18	<u>19</u>	
Watergate	7	15	<u>31</u>	.01
Election	7	5	<u>15</u>	
National Capitol	<u>9</u>	2	4	
Reagan	3	0	<u>4</u>	
Bradley	2	2	0	
Politician	0	0	0	
Taxes[b]	9	21	<u>42</u>	.01
Instances Most Knowledgeable	3	1	14	

[a] Underline indicates most knowledgeable category.
[b] The analysis is based on affirmative responses to the self-report query, "Do you know what taxes are?"

symbols correctly identified by each child. Five of the political symbols presented to them in picture form were used to create this index: the national Capitol, the Statue of Liberty, the Liberty Bell, George Washington, and Abraham Lincoln. On our hierarchy of six stages of political awareness, an ability to recognize widely used political symbols is defined as being part of Stage 1, the lowest of the six stages. Because symbol recognition represents such a low level of political awareness, we refer to it as "prepolitical knowledge."

How well does this Symbol Recognition Index serve as a predictor of political knowledgeability among the children? Excluding the three symbols that are a part of the cognitive map (the national Capitol, the Statue of Liberty, and George Washington), only four of the remaining 17 map items show any pattern of increasing accuracy as we move from the 52 children who knew none of the symbols, to those who recognized one or two, or to the 19 children who knew three or four of the symbols (no child knew all five). The correlation, as measured by Pearson's r, between the number of symbols recognized by a child and the score of that child on the Political Understanding Index is .17. Recognition of political symbols, at least at the kindergarten level, appears to be a learning phenomenon that does not transfer to understanding other aspects of the political process.

CONSISTENCY ABOUT WHO GOVERNS

How logically or "ideologically" consistent are kindergarten children in identifying who governs and the type and scope of political power granted to governing authorities? To examine fully and precisely the logical consistency of our respondents, we would need two or more completely interchangeable sets of questions providing identical information. Our interview schedule does not contain this feature, but we can focus on two groups of children. One group thought that God or Jesus wields political power, while the other believed that the President is the central authority figure. These two groups emerge from responses to the four governance-related questions: "Who is the boss of the country?", "Who does the most to run the country?", "Who makes the laws?", and "Who picks the President?" Eighty-three percent (30 out of 36 children) who thought God or Jesus was the "boss" thought that God or Jesus also did the most to run the country. Sixty-eight percent of those who said God or Jesus made the laws also said that God or Jesus did the most to run the country. Again, 68 percent who felt that God or Jesus picked the President also felt that God or Jesus did the most to run the country.

How consistent in their views on governance are the children who thought the President was "boss of the country?" Did they perceive the President as all powerful, as carrying out many governing tasks ("task pooling")?[32] If they think the President is the "boss," then 38 percent also think he makes the laws and 46 percent think he "runs the country." In general children who take a religious view of political power are more likely to attribute greater power and scope to that religious authority than those who take a presidential view of governance, particularly when it involves "running the country." Of the six possible comparisons between these four governance queries, five are statistically significant at the .01 level or higher. Clearly, there is a high degree of consistency among kindergarten children in their perception of who governs.

Finally, we asked whether, in general, those children who believed the President is "boss of the country" were more knowledgeable than those children who believed that God or Jesus was "boss." When cross-tabulating the responses to the "boss" query with the other 55 items on the kindergarten interview schedule, we found that the children who respond with "President" are usually the most knowledgeable. "President responders" to the boss query are followed by the children giving "George Washington" or "Abraham Lincoln" or another governmental figure. The latter are slightly more knowledgeable than the God or Jesus group. The seven children who believe that a teacher or a principal is "boss of the country," and the one-third of the children who were unable to give a substantive response are by far the least knowledgeable.

AFFECTIVE ORIENTATION

In the kindergarten interviews four questions offer some indication of our panel's affective orientation toward government and politics:

"Are policemen your friends?" (91 percent said "yes".)

"Would you like to vote?" (75 percent said "yes".)

"Does the government listen to what your mommy and daddy say?" (64 percent answered affirmatively.)

"If you were playing in front of your house, and a policeman stopped to talk to you, what do you think he would say?" (52 percent of those who could visualize such a meeting thought it would be friendly.)

The governmental authority whose function is most likely to be known by our panel is the policeman. There is evidence to suggest that the child's image of the policeman may be an indicator of regime support in later life.[33] Earlier studies have shown that, although the young child does not accord the policeman the same position of esteem assigned the President, the typical reaction is very positive.[34] Thus, we were not surprised when over 90 percent of our respondents said "yes" when asked whether policemen were their friends. Previous research, however, indicates that we may expect this positive assessment to diminish as the children grow older.[35] In an attempt to clarify why young children believe law enforcement officers are friendly and to examine Goodman's conclusion that the policeman is a very "shadowy figure" to the 92 four-year-olds in her study, we asked the children to visualize an imaginary encounter with a policeman in front of their homes. Fifty-six percent could not give a substantive response; perhaps they had difficulty imagining such a meeting. This percentage is similar to Goodman's finding that 45 percent of her sample had vague perceptions of policemen.[36] About 23 percent of the sample providing a response indicated a friendly, nonthreatening meeting: "Hi," "Are you lost?" or "Let's be careful." This generally positive attitude toward the police is also reflected in the fact that the occupation of policeman is the one most favored by the boys in our sample. About 13 percent, however, provided a response to this hypothetical meeting that envisioned a threatening encounter: "Get out of the street" or "Never do that again!" Some of these responses may have been based on personal experiences or those of friends. One boy reported: "I have to go to court Thursday. I went through a stop sign on my bike. He asked my name, address, school—I signed my name and he signed his."[37]

We believe, then, that at least one child in ten visualizes a meeting with a police officer as potentially threatening; perhaps as many as three in ten would have this expectation if they were to talk with a police officer in front of their home. Who are the children who believe that they would receive a command or an accusation from the officer? The biggest factor seems to be ethnic background. Twenty-three percent of the non-Anglo children describe a threatening situation, compared to 7 percent of the Anglos. Also, 8 percent of the non-Anglos say that police officers are not their friends, whereas only 4 percent of the Anglos offer this negative response.

Although girls are slightly more likely than boys to believe the government will listen to their parents (68 to 61 percent), there are no sex-based differences on any of the other three affect queries. Indeed, there are no statistically significant demographic differences associated with positive and negative responses to any of these affect questions.

If few demographic differences correlate with either positive or negative political affect (except that non-Anglos appear to have more negative feelings toward the police), it seems necessary to ask whether there is any relationship between cognitive knowledge and affective orientation. On all four of our threshold variables, greater knowledge is correlated with a more positive orientation. The staged children, compared with the unstaged children, respond on the average 11 percent more positively when the four cognitive threshold variables are cross-tabulated with the responses to the question "Does the government listen to what your mommy and daddy say?" These more knowledgeable (staged) children are also on the average 5 percent more likely to want to vote and 5 percent more likely to describe a friendly meeting with the police. The Political Understanding Index indicates that staged children are 21 percent more likely to visualize a friendly meeting with the police than unstaged children and 12 percent more likely to believe that "government listens."

Of our cognitive variables the only measure to run counter to this correlation between greater knowledge and greater expression of positive affect is knowledge of political symbols.[38] The children who know the most political symbols are 25 percent *less* likely to believe that the government listens to their parents. A number of kindergarten-aged children are able to identify key political symbols, but this ability does not permit them to understand more complex political concepts or to express more positive feelings toward the government.

In conclusion, at this age children are quite positive about the political process, or, alternatively, they are very positive about matters generally and this spills over into the political realm. It would appear, however, that the more knowledgeable they are, the more positive they are. Demographic differences appear to have little effect other than in the case of ethnic background, and even with this factor, the differences are found only with non-Anglos being more negative in responding to our two queries relating to the police.

SUMMARY AND IMPLICATIONS

Kindergarten children often confuse religious with political authorities and are more likely to know famous Presidents of the past than they are to know the incumbent President. Five- and six-year-olds have a strong local orientation; they are most likely to identify their city of residence and least likely to know their state. Regime awareness among kindergartners is quite limited; fewer than 10 percent understand the term "election" or can recognize the names of both political parties. While almost half of the children could tell us what a law is, fewer than 20 percent gave reasonably accurate responses to the query "Who makes the laws?" Young children are clearer on the functions of policemen and soldiers than they are on the duties of the President, even though the latter is a highly visible authority figure. Very few are able to distinguish consistently between public and private occupations; fewer than half, for example, know that soldiers, teachers, and mailcarriers work for the government.

The kindergarten children's conception of fairness tends to cluster around the notions of equity versus privilege and adherence to rules. It was impressive to find more than two-thirds had a substantive response to the query "Tell me something that isn't fair." When asked to identify what they might do to help people, the largest categories of responses centered around efforts to provide humanitarian and material assistance to the indigent, disabled, or ill. Ecological concerns and efforts to curb violence were other public needs identified by the children. The only contemporary public issue on which more than 15 percent of the kindergartners had meaningful knowledge was the energy crisis; slightly more than one-third could discuss that problem.

The quest for satisfactory indicators of political knowledge-ability led us to consider not only traditional demographic variables but also a set of four cognitive variables. When the latter were combined into a Political Understanding Index, it enabled us to predict levels of knowledgeability on a 20-item cognitive map with reasonable accuracy. Use of this index will enable us to partially test the validity of the Piagetian cognitive-developmental model as it relates to political learning.

There appears to be a correlation between political knowledge and positive feelings toward political objects. Demographic differences have little influence on political feelings among this age group except in the case of non-Anglos, who are consistently more negative in responding to queries about the police and the law. The law and its enforcement arm represent the focal point where regime authority and the individual are most likely to meet and on occasion clash. Our findings may have exposed a matter of considerable sensitivity on the part of non-Anglos as well as a connection between cognitive knowledge and affective orientation. The analysis in future chapters will examine whether the differences between Anglos and non-Anglos kindergarten are sustained or modified. In turn, this will enable us to assess the extent to which non-Anglo children are being acculturated into the mainstream of society.

One aspect of children's orientation to the political arena that researchers have noted and attempted to explain is their expression of positive affect toward the regime and political authorities and, in particular, their positive feelings toward the President. Several hypotheses have been suggested. Kolson and Green have argued that this strong tendency can be largely attributed to an "agreement syndrome," an "acquiescent bias," that will "delude the researcher into believing that he or she has detected the presence of a cognitive or attitudinal dimension."[39] We believe, however, that open-ended questions combined with good interviewer-interviewee rapport minimize this positive response-set in our panel. Two other hypotheses stem from the psychodynamic model used by Greenstein, Easton, and Hess and described in Dawson, Prewitt, and Dawson.[40] The latter suggest that positive attitudes of a child toward her father are transferred to other authority figures. However, in the light of recent studies of the weakness of the family structure in the United States, the experiences of many children may not lead to positive feelings. A third explanation, the vulnerability hypothesis, suggests that when confronted with the awesome powers of the presidency the young child feels quite vulnerable. As a means of dealing with the anxieties created by this vulnerability, he or she comes to believe that the President will use that power in a helpful and protective way.[41] However appealing this hypothesis appears intuitively, Renshon bluntly declares that it has not been supported by empirical research, and our findings solidly support this rejection of the vulnerability hypothesis.[42] The children in our panel do not visualize the President as exercising the awesome powers of his office, but rather they describe him as sitting at his desk signing papers or preparing speeches.

The primacy model of socialization emphasizes the importance of the early childhood years for later political attitudes and behavior. Some scholars suggest that these early years are particularly important in the development of high levels of diffuse support for the political system. Easton and Dennis contend that a positive attitude toward the presidency may sustain citizen support for this institution despite dissatisfaction with the incumbent, or even a series of incumbents. They conclude that children may develop this positive orientation toward the presidency because of their early perception of the President as benevolent.[43]

One of the most important conclusions to be drawn from our data is the existence of a two-stage process in the development of widespread positive feelings toward the President. We believe that a positive predisposition toward the presidency originates in many children during the very earliest years of life, beginning with sensitivity to benevolent religious authorities. At least one-quarter of our panel believes that God or Jesus are general authorities, making no distinction between the religious and the secular realms. We hypothesize that when these children begin to become aware of the President as a powerful authority, they transfer their notion of a benevolent authority figure from the religious to the secular realm. Then, as the secular salience of the religious authorities recedes, the positive affect remains as a residue. This early positive orientation is consequently passed on, by this two-stage process, to the presidency as an institution. Bellah and Mead suggest that U.S. politicians have historically used religious authority as a support for the secular regime. Future research directed at even younger children ought to explore this benevolent religious authority transfer model, for it may explain the positive orientation to authority that many young children presently have, as well as the basis for their diffuse regime support. If this hypothesis is reasonably accurate, then the weakening of religious authority could contribute to regime instability.

The analysis in this chapter focused on the political world of the kindergartner. It described the extent of cognitive political knowledge and the affective political orientation possessed by five- and six-year-old children. These data are the base point for the analysis in the next chapter, which examines the patterns of growth in political knowledge and the changes in feelings about government and politics that occur during the next four years of a young child's life.

NOTES

1. Sandra Kenyon Schwartz, "Preschoolers and Politics," in *New Directions in Political Socialization*, eds. David C. Schwartz and Sandra Kenyon Schwartz (New York: The Free Press, 1975), Chapter 9.

2. The follow-up survey also tested recognition of the flag and other political objects.

3. R.W. Connell, *The Child's Construction of Politics* (Melbourne, Australia: Melbourne University Press, 1971), Chapter 1.

4. Dean Jaros, *Socialization to Politics* (New York: Praeger University Series, 1973), p. 33, and Richard E. Dawson, Kenneth Prewitt, and Karen S. Dawson, *Political Socialization* (Boston: Little, Brown, 1977), p. 50–53. However, Kenneth B. Clark questions whether the black-white distinction is known by young children unless it has been deliberately taught them. See *Prejudice and Your Child* (Boston: Beacon Press, 1955), Chapters 1 and 4. See also Judith D.R. Porter, *Black Child, White Child: The Development of Radical Attitudes* (Cambridge, MA: Harvard University Press, 1971), Chapter 2.

5. Gustave Jahoda, "The Development of Children's Ideas About Country and Nationality: Part II, National Symbols and Themes," *British Journal of Educational Psychology* 33: 143–53.

6. Robert N. Bellah, *The Broken Covenant: American Civil Religion in a Time of Trial* (New York: Seabury Press, 1975), and Sidney E. Mead, *The Nation with the Soul of a Church* (New York: Harper and Row Forum Books, 1975), particularly Chapter 7.

7. Fred I. Greenstein, *Children and Politics* (New Haven: Yale University Press, 1965), pp. 60–62, notes that "first awareness" of government is of the national and local levels, not the state, but "full understanding" of the working of a government level occurs first with the national government.

8. Gustave Jahoda, "The Development of Children's Ideas About Country and Nationality. Part I: The Conceptual Framework," *British Journal of Educational Psychology* 33: 47–60.

9. This and other responses suggest that these kindergartners were very open and honest in revealing what they did not know as well as what they did know. See Moore, *et al.*, "The Civic Awareness of Five and Six Year Olds," *The Western Political Quarterly* XXXIX (September 1976): 412.

10. The fact that Republicans vote in higher percentages than Democrats is summarized by Kevin Mulcahy and Richard Katz in *America Votes* (Englewood Cliffs, NJ: Prentice-Hall, 1976), p. 25. See also Raymond E. Wolfinger and Steven J. Rosenstone, *Who Votes?* (New Haven: Yale University Press, 1980), pp. 109–10.

11. Robert A. Dahl, *A Preface to Democratic Theory* (Chicago: University of Chicago Press, 1956), pp. 75–81.

12. Goodman, *Childhood Education*, p. 248.

13. Charles Andrain, *Children and Civic Awareness* (Columbus, OH: Charles E. Merrill, 1971), p. 19.

14. Jean Piaget, "Developmental Psychology: A Theory of Development." *International Encyclopedia of the Social Sciences* (New York: Macmillian, 1968) 4: 140–47. For a good discussion of Piaget's model see Andrain, *Children and Civic Awareness*, pp. 59–71.

15. Andrain, *Children and Civic Awareness*, p. 5.

16. David Easton and Jack Dennis, *Children in the Political System* (New York: McGraw-Hill, 1969), p. 222.

17. All of these relationships are statistically significant at .05 or higher.

18. Andrain, *Children and Civic Awareness*, p. 5.

19. One of the researchers asked each girl who gave a sex-stereotyped role, that is, nurse or teacher, whether she would like to be the counterpart role of doctor or principal. Only one of the 15 girls said she would. Sex stereotyping in occupational roles is statistically significant at the .001 level among these kindergartners. Earlier we have termed these children "transitional" because kindergarten is one of the first experiences outside the home, but it is a very limited one since the school day is abbreviated with the youngsters being exposed to a single teacher and normally isolated from older elementary school classmates. If these role attitudes were inculcated in the home, then perhaps broader social experiences might change them. In Chapter 7 we examine the changing occupational prefrences as our panel children grow older.

20. In Chapter 2 we suggested that it is significant that so many children were willing to say that they had not even "heard" the word "politician," for they could have tried to appear more knowledgeable. Yet, here, with public-policy issues, a number of children repeatedly claim to have "heard" words but are unable to explain them. Perhaps a few children exhibit an "agreement response set." Nevertheless, the greatest amount of overlap (claiming to have heard both "Vietnam" and the "energy crisis") is only 20 percent. Certainly, we could easily expect a number of children, aged five and six, to honestly claim to have heard a word and not be able to explain its meaning.

21. Arterton reports that many older children's post-Watergate attitudes toward the presidency have already begun to rebound or become more positive. See F. Christopher Arterton, "Watergate and Children's Attitudes toward Political Authority Revisited," *Political Science Quarterly* 90 (Fall 1975): 480–87.

22. Herbert Hyman, *Political Socialization* (New York: The Free Press, 1959), pp. 29–34.

23. Greenstein, *Children in Politics*, p. 115.

24. When the responses of boys and girls are compared on all 39 items in the kindergarten interview for which there was a correct response, the boys were more correct on 31 items (five were statistically significant), boys and girls were identical

on two, and boys were less accurate than girls on six. Although the differences between the sexes are often not great, where they do appear, they repeatedly indicate that boys have greater political awareness and knowledge than girls.

25. Greenstein, *Children in Politics*, p. 115.

26. Harrell R. Rodgers and George Taylor, "The Policeman as an Agent of Regime Legitimation," *Midwest Journal of Political Science* 15 (February 1971): 85–86. See also Edward S. Greenberg, "Children and Government: A Comparison Across Racial Lines," *Midwest Journal of Political Science* 14 (May 1970): 249–70.

27. F. Chris Garcia and Rudolph O. de la Garza, *The Chicano Political Experience: Three Perspectives* (North Scituate, MA: Duxbury Press, 1977), pp. 48–55, as well as their responses to authority, Chapter 9. See also F. Chris Garcia, ed., *La Causa Politica: A Chicano Politics Reader* (Notre Dame, IN: University of Notre Dame, 1974), especially "The Barrio as an Internal Colony," by Mario Barrera, *et al.*, pp. 281–301; and Lucius J. Barker and Jesse J. McCorry, Jr., *Black Americans and the Political System* (Cambride: MA: Winthrop Publishers, Inc., 1976), pp. 47–67.

28. Forer discovered that oldest children are generally more knowledgeable, moralistic, and better able to arrive at independent judgment than younger siblings. Lucille K. Forer with Henry Still, *The Birth Order Factor* (New York: David McKay Company, 1976), Chapters 4, 5, 6, and 9. There are a number of problems with the utilization of sibling order. First, it is highly unstable, for example, a youngest child can quickly become a "middle child." Second, it ignores family size. Finally, broken marriages and remarriages can affect it significantly; this occurred with several children in our panel.

29. Boys are on the average 6 percent more knowledgeable than girls in each sibling division; but this is almost entirely because girls are 5 percent more likely to respond "don't know" to our interview queries. Oldest girls are more knowledgeable than all other girls, and on two map items they are more knowledgeable than all of the boys as well. On five items the oldest girls are more correct than all of the boys except for the oldest boys.

30. Easton and Dennis, *Children in the Political System*, p. 112.

31. Frances Fitzgerald, *America Revised* (Boston: Little, Brown, 1979); see also, John J. Patrick, "Political Socialization and Political Education in Schools," in Renshon, ed., *Handbook of Political Socialization* (New York: Free Press, 1975), pp. 190–222.

32. Connell, *The Child's Construction of Politics*, Chapter 2.

33. See Easton and Dennis, *Children in the Political System*, p. 240, and Rodgers and Taylor, *Midwest Journal of Political Science*, pp. 72–86.

34. See Greenberg, "Children and Government: A Comparison Across Racial Lines," pp. 249–70.

35. Edward S. Greenberg, "Orientations of Black and White Children to Political Authority Figures," *Social Science Quarterly* 51 (December 1970): 561–71. See also, David Sears, "Political Socialization," in Fred I. Greenstein and Nelson Polsby, eds., *Handbook of Political Science*, Vol. 2 (Reading, MA.: Addison-Wesley, 1975), p. 105.

36. Goodman, *Childhood Education*, p. 248.

37. The inflection and the tone of voice must be known to interpret definitely how the child felt about this hypothetical meeting. When we were unsure whether a response depicted a friendly or unfriendly meeting, we coded it as friendly in order

to be able to determine more accurately the frequency of unfriendly encounters.

38. The researchers also constructed a scale based on the number of correct responses to the six public/private occupational roles presented the children. Since we did not hypothesize that the public/private distinction is a threshold political concept, we were not unduly surprised when neither correct knowledge of the private role nor of the five public roles predicted greater knowledge of the cognitive map items. When the two scales were combined, the resulting scale was no more effective than the individual scales. In fact, on the public-roles scale and on the combined scale, the children who knew either all five public roles or all six roles were actually less able to provide correct answers to the cognitive map items than the children with fewer correct responses.

39. Kenneth Kolson and Justin Green, "Response Set Bias and Political Socialization Research," *Social Science Quarterly* (December 1970): 527–38.

40. Dawson, Prewitt, and Dawson, *Political Socialization*, Chapters 3 and 4.

41. Ibid.

42. Stanley Allen Renshon, ed., *Handbook of Political Socialization: Theory and Research* (New York: The Free Press, 1977), pp. 35–36.

43. Easton and Dennis, *Children in the Political System*, Chapter 9.

4

Patterns of Expanding Political Knowledge

Which political phenomena become salient very early for most primary school children? Which political symbols are recognized before others? When do children begin to distinguish between the public and private sectors? between different geo-political jurisdictions? When and how do children become more familiar with the major issues of the day?

What is the pattern young children follow as they increase in political knowledge? Does the expansion follow a linear progression, or is growing civic awareness characterized by "spurts" at regular, or irregular, intervals? Is the declining level of political party identification and loyalty present in the adult population of the 1970s and 1980s reflected in a similar lack of partisan awareness and commitment among our school-age panel?

To provide answers to these and other questions, we utilized the 20-item cognitive map to measure the types of political knowledge found among primary school children.[1] We also made use of the nine regime-related threshold cognitive variables in an effort to operationalize the Piagetian cognitive-developmental hypothesis as it might apply to political learning. In addition, where appropriate, this study uses questions other than those in the cognitive map or those designated as threshold variables; for example, it gives special attention to three separate series of questions probing the child's understanding of laws, taxes, and political parties.

As shown in Table 4.1, the most dramatic gains between kindergarten and fourth grade are the increases of what an election is (87 percent), the recognition of the Statue of Liberty (77 percent), the knowledge that California is the state in which they reside (74

TABLE 4.1
Ranking of Accurate Responses to Cognitive Map Items by Grade Level (in percentages)

Item	Kindergarten		First Grade		Second Grade		Third Grade		Fourth Grade	
	Item	Percent Correct	Item	Percent Correct	Item	Percent Correct	Item	Percent Correct	Item	Percent Correct
What does a policeman do?	Policeman	91	Policeman	90	Policeman	94	Washington	94	Policeman	99
Does a judge work for govt?	Judge	76	Judge	84	Judge	89	Law	93	Law	99
Do we have a king in U.S.?	Law	63	Law	71	Washington	82	Policeman	92	Washington	98
Does a milkman work for govt?	Washington	58	Washington	68	Stat. of Lib.	80	Stat. of Lib.	91	Judge	97
Recognize Washington's pict?	King	52	King	66	King	77	Judge	90	City	97
What is a law?	Soldier	46	Soldier	49	Law	77	King	90	King	94
What city do you live in?	Milkman	42	Milkman	48	City	66	Carter	88	Carter	94
What is the energy crisis?	City	36	City	47	Ford	64	City	87	Election	94
What does a soldier do?	Ford	34	Ford	44	State	57	State	84	Stat. of Lib.	93

Recognize inc. Pres.'s pict?	29	Stat. of Lib.	39	Milkman	49	Election	75	State	91	State
What country do you live in?	21	State	38	Soldier	47	Soldier	56	Soldier	75	Soldier
What state do you live in?	17	Energy	30	Country	39	Energy	55	Country	70	Country
Pict of Statue of Liberty	16	Country	27	Election	36	Country	54	Energy	68	Energy
Tell me about Watergate.	14	Election	14	Energy	26	Milkman	36	Taxes	59	Taxes
What is an election?	7	Taxes	7	Taxes	21	Taxes	33	Brown	53	Brown
Picture of the Nat'l Capitol.	5	Capitol	6	Capitol	12	Brown	17	Milkman	31	Milkman
What are taxes?	a	Watergate	4	Brown	9	Capitol	14	Bradley	27	Bradley
Tell who Ron. Reagan is.	2	Bradley	3	Watergate	7	Bradley	12	Capitol	25	Capitol
Tell who Tom Bradley is.	1	Brown	3	Bradley	4	Watergate	6	Politician	10	Politician
What do politicians do?	0.0	Politicians	1	Politicians	4	Politicians	5	Watergate	7	Watergate

a See note C. Table 3.6, page 60. This ranking is based upon the pattern established in subsequent years.

percent), and the ability to recognize a picture of the incumbent President (65 percent). Two of these four, recognition of California as their state of residence and the ability to identify a picture of the incumbent President, grew steadily over the five years. By contrast, more than one-half the total gain in recognition of the Statue of Liberty (54 percent) occurred during the Bicentennial year, 1976. An understanding of what an election is grew by 39 percent between second and third grade. An environmental stimulus would also seem to account for this dramatic gain because in the late spring of 1976 presidential primaries were at their peak. This campaign may account for almost half of the total gain in awareness of the electoral process between kindergarten and fourth grade. In contrast with the name of their state of residence and the picture of the incumbent President, both of which are encountered almost daily on television newscasts, the picture of the Statue of Liberty and the concept of an election are more likely to be encountered on special occasions and at less frequent intervals. Thus, of the four most dramatic gains in political knowledge between kindergarten and fourth grade, two represent steady growth over the entire four-year period while two others reflect striking one-year increases resulting, quite probably, from interaction with stimuli in the child's political environment.

SYMBOL RECOGNITION

Utilizing the work of Connell who concluded that initial political awareness among Australian children centers around *symbol* recognition,[2] we hypothesized that those items in the cognitive map that are symbolic of the national political community (pictures of George Washington, the Statue of Liberty, and the national Capitol) would be identified first by our primary school panel. If we define general knowledgeability as the point at which 75 percent of the children are familiar with an item, we find, other than the U.S. flag, only two items—references to a policeman and a judge—meet this criterion in kindergarten and first grade. While both the policeman and judge represent significant dimensions of a polity (law enforcement and the judicial process), neither symbolizes the national community.

Six items meet the 75 percent test in second grade, including recognition of the pictures of George Washington and the Statue of

Liberty. Ten items in the third grade and eleven in the fourth grade meet this knowledgeability criterion. Two national symbols in the cognitive map, George Washington and the Statue of Liberty, were recognized by more than 90 percent of the fourth-grade pupils, along with three other national symbols not included in the map: the flag, Abraham Lincoln, and the Liberty Bell.

There was steady growth in symbol recognition over the years. In kindergarten 35 percent did not know any of the five symbols presented other than the flag. In first grade this dropped to 18 percent and then to five percent in second grade. In second grade two percent recognized all eight symbols (including, "What is the Star Spangled Banner?" and "What do we celebrate on July 4th?"). By fourth grade 21 percent correctly identified all eight symbols, and 46 percent recognized seven of the eight; two-thirds, then, of the panel recognized seven or all eight of the symbols.

Only two of the seven national symbols presented through pictures to the children in the fourth-grade-interview (the White House and the Capitol) fall below the 90 percent recognition level (see Table 4.2). The White House was recognized by 71 percent of the children while the Capitol was identified by only 25 percent. The latter recognition level is much lower than expected primarily

TABLE 4.2
Changes in Recognition of Pictures of Political Symbols (in percentages)

Unifying Symbols	K	1	2	3	4
American Flag[a]	99	a	a	a	a
George Washington	52	68	82	93	98
Abraham Lincoln	44	66	82	93	99
Statue of Liberty	16	39	80	91	93
Liberty Bell	1	14	66	91	93
Conflictual Symbols					
White House	NA	NA	52	61	71
National Capitol	5	6	12	14	25[b]

[a]After 99 percent could identify "our country's flag" from among four national flags in kindergarten, this question was dropped from the interview schedule.

[b]Forty-five percent of the fourth-grade children mistakenly thought that the Capitol was the White House, and another 4 percent said that the building pictured was in Washington, D.C.

because many children identified the Capitol as the White House even when, in third and fourth grades, they were shown a picture of the White House before being asked to identify the Capitol. A very high level of cognitive dissonance was evident among many of the children when they were confronted with pictures of the national Capitol and the White House one after the other. A number of them called the Capitol "the White House" and then seemed confused when immediately thereafter they were shown a picture that also seemed to fit their conception of the White House. These two symbols represent partisan decision-making institutions, and the controversies or conflicts that surround them, while the omnipresent flag, the Statue of Liberty, the Liberty Bell, and our two best known Presidents are all unifying symbols* in our national myth structure. Parents, teachers, and other socializing agents apparently are much more likely to draw attention to these five unifying national symbols than they are to emphasize more partisan objects like the Congress and the incumbent President. Fitzgerald's recent analysis of the U.S. history books used in the elementary schools supports this view; political conflict is often deemphasized or even avoided.[3]

GEO-POLITICAL AWARENESS AND POLITICAL AUTHORITIES

By the end of first grade more than one-third of our panel were able to identify their state of residence, while only one-quarter could name the country in which they live. In fact, the first-grade children's recognition of California as their state more than doubled during that one year, while their recognition of the city and country increased much more slowly (see Figure 4.1). Beginning with first grade the pattern reflects highest recognition of the city, followed by the state, and finally, at a significantly lower level, an ability to name their country. By the end of second grade knowledge of their city increased dramatically, although surprisingly it was not until fourth grade that over 90 percent of the children were able to correctly

---

*Dawson, Prewitt, and Dawson use the terms "consensus values" and "partisan values" to denote this distinction. They suggest that teachers are expected to disseminate consensus values while avoiding partisan ones. See *Political Socialization*, pp. 150–52.

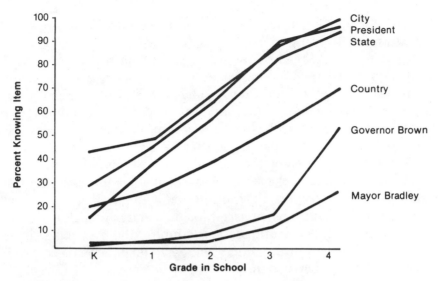

FIGURE 4.1
Growth in Knowledge of Geo-political Jurisdictions and Corresponding Chief Executives, K-4.

identify their home city. By the end of fourth grade correct recognition of the state is also over 90 percent, in marked contrast to the 70 percent who could provide the name of their country. After kindergarten this pattern of geo-political knowledge corresponds to the concentric view found by Jahoda among Scottish children.[4]

In spite of five years of ritualistic flag salutes, 30 percent of our fourth-grade children could not respond correctly when asked the name of their country.* Each day in rote fashion they "pledge allegiance to the flag of the United States of America," but this classroom routine apparently does not provide one-third of the children with an ability to articulate their country's name. Given Greenstein's findings among New Haven children that chief executives and legislatures at the national and local levels were better understood than those at the state level, we were surprised to discover that after kindergarten correct state identification ranged between 11 and 30 percent higher than recognition of the country.[5]

---

*Although there may not be much cognitive payoff from the daily pledge of allegiance, Dawson, Prewitt, and Dawson argue that "classroom ritual life" has an impact on affect in that it is a developer of basic national patriotism, loyalty, and attachment. See *Political Socialization*, pp. 146–49.

Perhaps for many children the concept of "country" is too remote, too abstract, or simply irrelevant.

Should researchers use the word "nation" instead of "country" to determine whether children associate their society with the terms "America" or the "United States"? Beginning in second grade we asked "What is a nation?" and found that prior to fourth grade fewer than 25 percent of the children recognized that synonym for country. Perhaps the 30 percent greater recognition of the state over the country was caused by the ordering of questions in the interview schedule: the name of the state was asked just before asking for the name of the country. Even if the children who mistakenly gave the name of their country when asked for their state are included with those who correctly identified their country, there would still be one-quarter of the fourth-graders who were unable to correctly tell us what country they live in.

In kindergarten only 4 percent of the children could identify correctly all three geo-political jurisdictions. Table 4.3 shows the pattern of development over the five years, grouping responses into

TABLE 4.3
Growth Pattern of Geo-political Knowledge* (in percentages)

	Grade				
Items Correct	K	1	2	3	4
All 3 Correct	4	11	26	48	67
City + State	9	14	23	30	23
City + Country	8	6	5	2	1
State + Country	1	1	2	2	1
City Only	20	16	13	6	6
State Only	3	12	7	4	—
Country Only	7	9	5	2	.04
Incorrect Responses	46	29	16	3	2
NA	1	2	3	2	—
	99	100	100	99	100.4
N =	(149)	(243)	(243)	(243)	(243)

*Based on responses to: What city do you live in? What state do you live in? What country do you live in?

all possible combinations of knowledgeability. By fourth grade two-thirds of the children were able to identify all three jurisdictions correctly, with the largest increases coming in the third and fourth grades (22 and 19 percent, respectively). In kindergarten only 22 percent of the children knew *two or more* of the geo-political levels; in first grade almost one-third were able to identify at least two. At the end of third grade more than four-fifths of the children were able to identify at least two of the three jurisdictions, and by fourth grade 92 percent knew two or more. As Table 4.3 indicates, the most frequent combination (other than knowing all three, which by second grade became the mode) is knowing both one's city and one's state. This combination more than tripled between kindergarten and third grade, reaching a peak of 30 percent at the end of third grade. The percentage of children who could not identify any of the three jurisdictions declined steadily from 46 percent in first grade to two percent in the fourth grade. The overall pattern is one of rapid and increasing knowledgeability, and it suggests the likelihood that the learning process involves at least in part the maturation of learning skills involving spatial and conceptual distinctions rather than simply interaction with environmental stimuli.

What about individual gains in knowledge of political geography? Are the children consistent in their development of this knowledge over the years, or do some of them regress? Crucial to this question is the extent to which their responses are merely guesses—albeit correct ones.* Of the six children who correctly identified all three levels of government in kindergarten, only one boy was correct in all four of the succeeding years. The responses of the other five children follow an almost random pattern in the following four years. These geo-political questions probe an area that has both spatial and conceptual dimensions. Apparently, the abstractness of the political dimension blurs spatial concreteness, and as a result many children lack consistency over the years. The aggregate pattern of rapidly increasing knowledge discussed earlier appears to fit the cognitive development model. Individual longi-

---

*Although the researchers have repeatedly reassured the panel members that our interview is not a test, many continue to refer to our interview schedule as a test—and thus may have a tendency to guess. See Kenneth Kolson and Justin Green, "Response Set Bias and Political Socialization Research," *Social Science Quarterly* 51 (December 1970): 527–38.

tudinal analysis, however, indicates that pupil knowledgeability patterns are subject to considerable variation due to guessing and possibly to differences in environmental stimuli. This suggests that a useful theory of political learning—even in a limited area such as political geography—must embrace both the cognitive-developmental and the social learning models.

With respect to awareness of political authorities, of "who governs," the pattern over the five years is one of dramatically increasing presidential salience (see Table 4.4). During kindergarten most children had difficulty distinguishing the political from the nonpolitical as evidenced by their varied conceptions of who is the "boss of the country." From a base point of approximately 15 percent in kindergarten, the percentage of children seeing the President as "boss" or doing "the most to run the country" increased to over half the panel in second grade. Each year we asked, "What does the President do when he goes to work?" The responses of one child illustrate an expanding awareness of the presidential role:

Kindergarten: "I don't know."

First Grade: "Sometimes makes speeches and works in his office."

Second grade: "Make speeches and does laws."

Third grade: "He signs bills and all that; he signs laws."

Fourth grade: "He signs bills, goes to meetings in Congress, signs laws."

By the end of the fourth grade 86 percent of the panel perceived the President as "boss of the country" and 79 percent believed that he does the most to run the country. This striking salience of the President among elementary school children is consistent with earlier studies of childhood political awareness. With the increased salience of the presidency there is a corresponding decline in the percentage of children attributing the governance function to religious authorities and former Presidents (Washington and Lincoln). There is also a decline in the percentage of children believing we have a king, from 37 percent to 6 percent over the five years.[6]

Is there a parallel between the children's growing awareness of political jurisdictions and their knowledge of the political authorities

TABLE 4.4
Children's Perception of Who Governs (in percentages)

	Grade				
Who is the boss of our country?					
	K	1	2	3	4
President	16	25	56	79	86
God or Jesus	24	14	5	1	0.4
Washington or Lincoln	16	16	12	10	2
Other	11	7	7	3	9
DK	33	29	22	7	3
Who does the most to run the country?					
	K	1	2	3	4
President	15	1	55	72	79
God or Jesus	30	a	4	1	0.4
Washington or Lincoln	7	a	4	2	0.4
Other	10	a	18	14	16
DK	37	a	19	11	4

ªNot asked in first grade

at each governmental level? The answer is no. Recognition of political authorities by our panel runs counter to their knowledge of political geography; that is, they identify the President, the governor, and the mayor in declining order of accuracy—and, for the latter two, at much lower levels (see Figure 4.1).* In part the very low recognition of mayors outside the City of Los Angeles (less than 2 percent) is because most of the towns and cities where our panel members live have nonelected, weak mayor systems (the office is rotated with the "mayor" being selected annually by the members of the city council). The mayor of Los Angeles is popularly elected with significant executive power, but about 40 percent of the panel reside

---

*Greenstein found fourth-grade New Haven children less familiar with their governor than California children were with Jerry Brown (33 to 44 percent) on the question "Who is the governor of (*state*)?", but the New Haven youngsters were much better acquainted with Mayor Richard Lee than were the Los Angeles residents with Tom Bradley (92 to 53 percent) on the question "Who is the mayor of (*city*)?"

nearly 50 miles from the civic center of Los Angeles in a different county. Consequently, it is not surprising to find that Mayor Bradley was known by only 27 percent of the entire fourth-grade panel. In a society increasingly conscious of the need for multiethnic awareness, however, it is discouraging that only slightly more than one-quarter of our Southern California panel recognized one of the leading black politicians in the United States and one who is featured regularly on local television broadcasts. A more encouraging perspective is that in fourth grade 17 percent of the children confused Mayor Bradley with Martin Luther King, Jr., perhaps a reflection of widespread public commemoration of the latter's birthday. At least some fourth-graders had become aware of the man who, more than any other, symbolizes the struggle for racial justice in the United States today.

GROWTH OF REGIME AWARENESS

By the end of fourth grade more than 90 percent of our sample understood such regime-related matters as what courts are, what judges do, what an election is, and that we do not have a king in the United States. It is noteworthy that several of these regime items are concerned with laws, their enforcement, and their application. A detailed discussion of these law-related variables is presented in Chapter 6, but it should be acknowledged here that this early recognition of law-related phenomena may provide an important insight into a child's orientation to the world of government and politics.

As noted earlier, knowledge of what an election is grew rapidly following the 1976 presidential election. By the end of fourth grade 65 percent of the youngsters described an election as a process that decides between competing candidates or issues:

"There have been a lot of elections, like for the President. Carter elected over Mr. Ford."

"It is a bunch of people who want to do something but only one can do it, so they vote on them."

"Election is like voting for somebody or like Proposition 13. You vote 'yes' or 'no.' My mom voted 'yes' on 13."

Another 29 percent said that an election simply involved "voting." When asked who can and who cannot vote in elections, nearly 70 percent noted that an age requirement must be met—and more than 26 percent correctly volunteered 18 as the minimum voting age. More than 5 percent added that a voter must also be a citizen. On the other hand, a slightly larger percentage believed that "anyone" could vote. Interestingly, a few said that the candidates themselves or the people in government could not vote in an election. This perception may result from classroom experiences where the class president is not allowed to vote (except when a tie exists) or where both the teacher and student nominees themselves are prohibited from voting. If these explanations are valid, it suggests that classroom experiences may be used by some for deciding how the world of politics functions. It is evident, then, that by the end of third or fourth grade most children understand what an election is and, in addition, some of them think that the outcome would be different if they were eligible to participate. One boy bemoaned the fact that children couldn't vote: "If children could vote, Ford would be President now."

The regime-related objects with the lowest recognition levels at the end of fourth grade include political party, senator, politician, Supreme Court, and Congress. None of these is recognized by more than 16 percent of the sample. With the exception of the Supreme Court these regime-related entities—like their counterparts among the political community symbols—are among the most partisan of the regime items. They also tend to be among the political phenomena that are most remote from the everyday life of the citizen in both geographic and psychological terms. Political parties are not very salient in the lives of young children in the late 1970s; there has been a marked decline in parental attachment to political parties and therefore a corresponding decrease in the transmission of partisan identification from parent to child is to be expected.[7]

The remaining regime measures consist of very common terms that we expected most children would recognize. At the end of fourth grade the function of an army is known by 89 percent of the sample. The vast majority said an army is to protect the country and fight enemies, but 33 fourth-graders specified that it is to protect the country *when it is attacked*. A number made references to past wars: "Defend the United States in wars like World War I and World War II." A few mentioned some causes of war, such as "to win out other armies when they get greedy." Three-quarters of the fourth-graders can also explain what a soldier does; the most frequent response referred to conflicts, for example, "fights," "kills," "shoots," or "has wars," while the second most frequent response was an explicit reference to protection of our country.

Again, three-quarters of the fourth-graders can give an example of what government does, but only 59 percent can provide a definition of "taxes." However, this represented a sizeable increase over the one-third who knew what taxes were in third grade. These percentages might be significantly higher were it not for the mistaken belief held by more than one-third of the children that the payment of utility and telephone bills is a form of taxation.* The most common referent is that associated with purchases (sales tax): "when something is 15 cents you add a penny to it" or "some extra cents." About one in five refer to general payments to government, and another 16 percent say taxes are bills that represent property taxes. Fewer than 5 percent say that they "don't know" what taxes are.

When we asked fourth-graders, "Why do people pay taxes?", 19 percent indicated that they were payments for specific government services, such as schools and aid to the poor: "it is money that goes to the government to help people—if they need jobs, food, clothes." Other children mentioned highly generalized public benefits, such as "To keep America running." Nine percent of the panel mentioned that there was a legal obligation to pay taxes—and perhaps a penalty for failure to do so: "Because the law says you have to." "They have to. If they didn't, they would have to go to jail." Finally, the largest percentage, one-quarter of the children, referred to a specific private benefit from paying taxes, such as retaining one's home and the use of various utilities. Most of those who felt that taxes were good mentioned that taxes pay for government services: "There are taxes for roads, and for the government, and for poor people. (The affective orientation of the panel toward taxes is examined in Chapter 7.) When asked "What kinds of taxes are there?", the most common response was the sales tax, followed by taxes on one's home, and then the income tax. Children also mentioned the social security tax and a number referred to the "inflation tax." Although

---

*Of course, a portion of these payments is taxation. A reference to payment of sales tax, property taxes, or other general payments to government was required in order to be coded as a knowledgeable response.

most children are familiar with the omnipresent sales tax, our probing indicates that many of them are still quite vague about the purposes for which taxes are used.

ISSUE AWARENESS

At the end of each school year, beginning in the spring of 1974, the children were asked to tell the interviewer "something" about each of three major public issues: Watergate, the energy crisis, and Vietnam. Between kindergarten and fourth grade there is a decline from 14 to 7 percent in the children who are able to comment on the Watergate episode (see Table 4.5). The panel's awareness of Watergate diminishes, we believe, because it was referred to less and less by both the media and parents following President Nixon's resignation. No doubt people in the United States desire to forget this national trauma. Nevertheless, a few fourth-graders do have some comprehension of the meaning of "Watergate," including one who said: "Illegal. In a hotel. The Democrats were talking about how to win the election, privately, and the Republicans listened and that's why Nixon was impeached." Our interview schedule also contains another question that is related to Watergate: "How did Mr. Ford become President?" Nine percent, 21 fourth-graders, are able to discuss Nixon's resignation and Mr. Ford's elevation to the presidency.

Awareness of what the energy crisis involves varies over the five years, reflecting the greater or lesser public attention this issue received, but it is consistently the best understood of the policy

TABLE 4.5
Changes in Awareness of Public Issues (percentage able to say something substantive about the issues)

	Kinder-garten	First Grade	Second Grade	Third Grade	Fourth Grade
Watergate	14	4	7	6	7
Energy Crisis	36	30	26	55	68
Vietnam	6	24	28	35	55
Unemployment				17	33
Inflation				6	15

areas. There is a steady decline in "energy awareness" following the highly visible effects of the Arab oil embargo in 1973–74, succeeded by a dramatic 29 percent increase after President Carter's energy initiatives in the spring of 1977—when he declared the battle against the overconsumption of oil to be "the moral equivalent of war." In fourth grade over half of the children who had "heard about the energy crisis" mentioned that we are running out and that we are wasting it, particularly by not turning off lights and television sets when they are not being used. Twenty percent responded with injunctions to conserve energy, to not waste it—indicating that some were being affected by adult preoccupation with this problem. There were seven children who stated that the increasing scarcity of energy was going to affect their futures and that if we did not change our wasteful behavior, there would not be any energy when they grew up—and that would not be fair. It is remarkable that at least a handful of children have begun to develop a "futures perspective"— albeit with an issue that is immediately salient in their everyday environment.

Although our interviews began near the conclusion of the Vietnam hostilities, there were progressive increases in children's awareness of this issue. This would appear to be partially attribut- able to the refugee children who became classmates of our panel members. The impact of the local sponsorship of refugee families is seen in one boy's response: "A country, and we adopted, our church, 50 people. We gave them a home because there were all those wars over there. Me and my sister collected coat hangers for them." Exactly one-half of the fourth-grade children who have "heard about Vietnam" make reference to war and fighting, while another 15 percent identify it only as a country or place. In spite of the heavy emphasis upon war and killing, 33 percent believe that Vietnam is either good or both good and bad. When asked "Why?", the children frequently mentioned that the people are "nice" and some said they were fighting for their country and freedom. In spite of their increasing knowledge about Vietnam, these children are clearly unaware of the turmoil that this divisive conflict produced in our society.

Based on these responses, it would appear that an awareness of these three political issues depends heavily on environmental stimuli. With issue areas such as inflation and unemployment— awareness of which doubled between third and fourth grade, this two-year pattern may additionally represent an increasing cognitive capacity to understand abstract political and economic phenomena.

DISTINGUISHING THE PUBLIC AND PRIVATE SECTORS

In an era such as the present when many observers believe that the scope of governmental authority has become excessive and is interfering with the private sector, it is important to determine whether children can distinguish between public and private areas of responsibility. The liberal tradition in Western political thought has stressed the importance of limiting the scope of governmental authority and has called attention to the role of the private sector as a source of stimulation and enrichment for social and economic life. The eight-city study of childhood political socialization conducted by Easton and his associates at the University of Chicago in the early 1960s sought to measure each child's awareness of the difference between the public and private spheres by asking respondents to distinguish which of six occupations "works for the government."[8] In our initial interviews with kindergarten pupils in 1974, the six occupations employed by the Easton study were used: five associated with government (policeman, soldier, judge, mailman, and teacher) and one from the private sector (milkman). Our kindergarten children were nearly as likely to think that a milkman worked for the government as they were to believe that a mailman, soldier, and teacher were governmental employees. Only in the case of the policeman and the judge did more than 50 percent of our kindergartners say "yes" they worked for the government (see Table 4.6). The inability of many five- and six-year-olds to recognize the milkman as nongovernmental prompted us to add "gas station man" as a second *uniformed* private-sector role in the first-grade interviews. When the panel members in first and second grade still had great difficulty identifying correctly the two private and five governmental occupations, we added the normally *nonuniformed* "candy store person" and the "person who gives the news on television" in a further attempt to identify possible sources of confusion between private- and public-sector occupations. With these latter roles we offered both an obvious private-sector occupation with whom most children had regular personal contact and one that would be challenging for even the most knowledgeable third- and fourth-graders. Finally, in fourth grade, we asked directly "How

TABLE 4.6
Responses to "Which Ones Work for the Government? Does a (role) Work for the Government?" (by percentage of those giving a "yes" response)

Public Roles[a]	Grade Level					Easton and Dennis[c]		
	K	1	2	3	4	2	3	4
Judge	76	84	89	90	97	86	88	89
Policeman	67	82	91	93	96	86	89	91
Soldier	49	56	68	89	87	68	79	83
Teacher[d]	46	58	52	67	71	48	55	58
Mailman	45	56	60	73	90	57	63	71
Average	57	67	72	81	88	69	75	78
Private Roles[b]								
Milkman	35	45	40	52	59	29	31	28
Gas Station Man		46	54	64	78	e	e	e
Candy Store Person				25	31	e	e	e
T.V. News Person				72	78	e	e	e

[a] Percentages represent *correct* responses.

[b] Percentages represent *incorrect* responses.

[c] These percentages are reported by David Easton and Jack Dennis, *Children in the Political System* (New York: McGraw Hill, 1969), p. 122.

[d] For purposes of this table responses of 18 parochial school pupils were categorized as correct if they believed their teachers did *not* work for the government.

[e] These pupils were not asked to identify these roles.

do you tell whether or not a person works for the government?" We expected that responses to this query would enable us to distinguish those who were merely guessing from those who in fact had a consistent criterion for deciding who works for the government and who does not.

The most striking conclusion to be drawn from this series of questions is the limited ability of the children in our panel across all five years to distinguish governmental from nongovernmental roles. Indeed, our respondents became steadily less correct in identifying the private-sector roles. Between kindergarten and fourth grade there was a 24 percent increase (from 35 to 59) among children who *incorrectly* believe that a milkman works for the government. It should be noted that because children in our panel were confronted each spring with an interview dealing largely with government, they may have been more inclined than their classmates to assume that anyone we would ask them about must work for the government. Indeed, when a comparison between our children and their nonpanel classmates was made in third grade, the only part of the interview schedule where our children had apparently been sensitized to governmental concerns was on this series of occupational questions. On the five governmental roles our third-graders were on the average 6 percent *more likely* than the third-grade respondents in the eight-city study to believe that people having those public-service occupations worked for the government. However, 114 nonsample third-grade classmates of our panel were on the average 8 percent *less likely* than the Easton-Dennis sample to believe that the five public servants did in fact work for the government. Our panel was 21 percent less accurate than the Easton-Dennis sample in saying that a milkman does work for the government (52 to 31); our nonpanel third-grade classmates were only 6 percent less correct than the third-graders in the eight-city study (37 to 31).

Even in fourth grade less than half of our panel could offer a reasonable response to the query "How do you tell whether a person works for the government or not?" Surprisingly, 5 percent asserted that "everyone works for the government." Fewer than 5 percent of those asked gave such reasonable responses as "They get paid out of taxes," "They are hired by the President (or governor)," or "They make (or enforce) the laws." Nearly 10 percent distinguished those working for the government from others by their uniforms, their vehicles, or some other visual identification. We have included in the 43 percent of the fourth-graders giving "reasonable" responses the 11 percent who said simply "Those who work for the government 'help people'" and the nearly 18 percent who suggested that they could tell who works for the government because "their job is important." The children in our panel seem more likely than those in earlier socialization studies to believe that persons in important and highly visible occupations work for the government—especially in those roles that clearly involve helping people.

The most difficult public occupation for the children to identify correctly, across all five years, was that of teacher. By fourth grade, the percentage of children identifying their teachers' employment status correctly was 71 percent, up from 46 percent in kindergarten. In contrast, the other four public-sector occupations were identified by more than 85 percent of our panel, with the judge and policeman exceeding 95 percent. It seems clear that the visibility of the policeman (on the street or in a clearly marked car) and the judge (who appears prominently in television dramas) helps youngsters to identify them as holding "important" positions in society and therefore as being part of the government. Surprisingly, the soldier and the mail carrier are less clearly identified as working for the government, even though both wear uniforms and are reasonably visible either on television or in the neighborhood.

Among the four private-sector roles used in the third- and fourth-grade interviews, the candy store person was thought to be a governmental employee by at least one-quarter of the children. In both third and fourth grades more than 70 percent of the students incorrectly identified persons giving the news on television as holding government positions. The gas station man, perhaps because he is so critical in our mobile society, was viewed as governmental by a progressively higher percentage each year beginning with 46 percent in first grade and reaching 78 percent by fourth grade. Even the milkman was thought to be a governmental employee by an increasingly higher percentage of the children. With the exception of milkman in second grade, the children each year have become progressively less correct in identifying these four private-sector roles as nongovernmental.

It is clear that primary school children—however knowledge-able they may be concerning other civic matters—do not yet grasp the distinction between the public and private sectors. Visible public figures such as policemen and judges, who are associated with the law and public order, are most easily recognized as governmental. Other public servants who are equally visible both in real life (teachers and mailmen) and in the media (soldiers) are not as easily recognized as governmental employees, with the greatest confusion arising in the case of teachers, perhaps in part because they represent such an intimate part of children's lives, whereas the rest of government seems much more remote. The greatest confusion among the private-sector roles involves, quite predictably, the television news commentator; in third and fourth grades approximately three-fourths identified this role incorrectly. Significant implications may accompany a very high percentage of elementary school children believing that television news is presented by the government. This widely held perception among these young people may deprive them of an early appreciation for the selectivity and varying interpretations presented by news gathering media in a free society. Even more critical is the possibility that they will incorrectly perceive the newscaster as being the official voice of the government. If this belief should continue through adolescence, it might cloak the television nightly news with an authoritativeness that would restrict the range of viewpoints considered by this potential electorate. Alternatively, associating television news with the government may eventually prompt some young people to reject it automatically as propaganda.

It is difficult to explain why more than half our panel—five of the nine times these questions were asked—believed that milkmen and gas station attendants are governmental employees. Some, of course, viewed these two occupations as "helping people" and therefore governmental, but unless we excuse some of those in error on the basis that they had been misled by the governmental focus of the interview—and we are inclined to view that explanation as a limited one—it would appear that primary school children in the mid-1970s viewed government as an extraordinarily pervasive phenomenon. If this perception that nongovernmental occupations are limited both in number and importance continues into adult-hood, it could portend a citizenry that fails to appreciate the important role our political tradition prescribes for individuals and institutions that are not directly associated with government. This possibility could lead us to a condition whre our people accept a kind of sociopolitical monism and excessive dependence on public authorities and sanctions that will undermine the pluralism, diversity, and voluntarism that are prerequisites for a free and open society.

POLITICIAN AND PARTIES

Fred Greenstein reported that more than 60 percent of his fourth-grade sample (1958) identified with a political party and approximately half of Easton's eight-city pupils (1961–62) made a party identification by second grade.[9] What does our mid-1970s panel know about the electoral process and political parties? When do they develop partisan preferences? Exploration of this domain was begun by asking the kindergartners whether they had *heard* the words "politician," "Republican," and "Democrat" and if they knew "Who picks the President?" as well as queries concerning elections and voting. Recognition that there is a broad electorate involved in selecting the President grew rapidly over the five years from 7 percent in kindergarten to 86 percent in fourth grade. At the latter grade level the notable misconception, held by 9 percent of the panel, was that the government or government leaders picked the President. In kindergarten 13 percent thought that God or Jesus picked the President, but by third grade not one child gave this response. In fourth grade, however, there were still two children who said that George Washington or Abraham Lincoln picked the President. Over the five years the percent responding "don't know" fell from 61 percent to only 5 percent. In fourth grade responses to "Who picks the President?" included references to the electorate choosing between alternative candidates, the age requirement for voting, and the requirement of citizenship, as well as general references to "the people," "parents," and "the voters."

In contrast to this increasing familiarity with the electoral process, however, only 10 percent of the fourth-graders could define "politician" (see Table 4.7). One of the more substantive responses to "What do politicians do?" was "They run for things, like President, mayor, treasurer. They run the government. They are always running." Another child said "If something has gone wrong, they can have a meeting and decide what to do." The few children who were modestly familiar with the term tended to associate a politician with lawmaking.

In kindergarten the children were merely asked whether they had heard of both major parties, while 26 percent claimed to have was used in an effort to avoid discouraging the children by asking party-related questions that were likely to be beyond their comprehension. We were surprised when 65 percent of our kindergartners indicated they had not hard of either party label; 9 percent said they had heard of both major parties, while 26 percent claimed to hae heard of at least one party. In each case an equal number of children, 33, claimed to have heard the words "Republican" and "Democrat."

In addition to the two self-report queries, the children in first grade were asked "What is a Republican?" and "What is a Democrat?" Only four children could give us even a vague indication of what a "Republican" is, while six could do the same for "Democrat." One child vaguely identified both party labels. All of these children responded by saying, in effect, "Democrat is the opposite of Republican" or vice versa. When we asked the first-graders whether they had heard the word "Republican," 37 percent

TABLE 4.7
Knowledge of Politician and Political Parties (by percentages)

Question	Grade				
	K	1	2	3	4
Can define "politician"	0	1	4	5	10
Claim to have "heard" Republican	22	37	62	75	86
Claim to have "heard" Democrat	22	26	46	72	79
Claim to have heard both	9	15	38	62	75
Claim to have heard neither	65	50	30	13	10
Can define Republican		0	0	0.4	2
Can define Democrat		0	0	1	3
Can define both		0	0	0.4	1
Can give a policy difference between Republican and Democrat				3	3
"Democrats are opposite of Republicans," or vice versa				3	7
Can explain what a political party is				2	7
Have heard the term "political party"				26	41
Correctly identify the "President's party"				12	16
Can give a reason for preferring a party				4	6
Have made a party identification				6	7
Democrat				3	3
Republican				3	4
N =	(149)	(238)	(236)	(240)	(243)

of the panel claimed they had, while 26 percent said they had heard the word "Democrat." The higher percentage of children claiming recognition of "Republican" may be explained by the fact that the incumbent President was a Republican. It is also possible that some children may have confused "Republican" with "Republic," which they use daily in the pledge of allegiance. By the end of first grade, 50 percent of the children still claimed *not* to have heard of either party label. Only 15 percent of the 243 said they had heard both "Republican" and "Democrat."

In second grade the number of children saying they had heard "Republican" jumped 25 percent to almost two-thirds of the panel, while "Democrat" recognition grew more slowly, rising to 46 percent. During these 1976 interviews—taken within six weeks of the California primary—some children made positive comments about President Ford, so that the 16 percent higher recognition of "Republican" may be partially attributed to a Republican incumbent in the White House. Nearly one-third of the second-graders still reported that they had not heard of either party.* The ability to say something germane about the parties grew much more slowly than the reported ability to recognize party labels: 13 children could respond to "What is a Republican?" and nine to "What is a Democrat?" Some of their responses are: "A group of people running for President." "Someone you vote." "It's different than a Republican." "Like a guy who works for the government." and "It's a donkey." None of these responses was interpreted as defining the party labels.

Because we tried not to discourage the children by asking too many "difficult" questions, we decided to wait until third grade before exploring more extensively the party domain. In that year we expanded significantly our political party questions by asking for the first time:

"Have you ever heard the words 'political party'?"

"Can you give me the name of one or two political parties?"

"Can you think of a difference between the Republican party and the Democratic party?"

"Do you like one party better than the other?"

"Which party do you like better?"

"Why do you like that party better?"

---

*These "never heard" children strongly suggest, contrary to the argument advanced by Kolson and Green, that our panel did not use these self-report opportunities to make themselves appear more politically knowledgeable than they in fact were. See Kenneth Kolson and Justin Green, "Response Set Bias and Political Socialization Research," *Social Science Quarterly* (December 1970): 530–37.

"Which political party does the President belong to?"

Table 4.7 indicates that all the new party queries requesting more than a self-report had knowledgeable responses of 7 percent or less, except for the 12 percent who knew President Carter's party affiliation. Obviously, our third-graders are not very knowledgeable about the political parties. On every substantive party query boys were more knowledgeable than girls, Anglos more knowledgeable than non-Anglos, and only and oldest children more aware than their siblings. When these 14 party items are cross-tabulated with one another, we find, as expected, that party knowledge is cumulative; children who give a knowledgeable response to one party query are much more able to answer other party questions. Even with very small Ns many of these relationships are statistically significant.

One surprising finding was that the eight children who had made an identification with the Democratic party were much more knowledgeable than the seven who preferred the Republican party. All eight "Democrats" claimed to have heard the words "political party", and five were able to suggest what a party does. In contrast, only two of the seven "Republicans" claimed to have heard this phrase, and neither could substantively tell us what a party does. Indeed, while seven of the eight who preferred the Democratic party could define for us what a "Republican" is, only two of the seven "Republicans" could tell us what a Republican is. All of the children who know what a Democrat is had also heard of "Republican," but five of the "Republicans" had not even heard "Democrat." All eight "Democrats" were able to give us a difference between the two parties, but less than half of the "Republicans" could do so. Perhaps the difference between these two groups is demographic; seven of the eight "Democrats" are boys (and four are among the dozen most knowledgeable children in the study), while four of the seven "Republicans" are girls. Consistently over the years boys tended to be more knowledgeable about politics than girls.

In fourth grade substantive party knowledge and party identification increased very slowly. The largest increase on any query was 4 percent; 16 percent could now correctly state that the President was a Democrat. While three-quarters of the children claimed to have heard of both political parties, fewer than 10 percent could tell us something about both parties (see Table 4.7). Two percent of the children could define "Republican" and 3 percent could tell us what a "Democrat" is. Party identification increased only 1 percent, to 7 percent of the sample. When asked which party they liked best, many responded that they "didn't know enough" about both parties to make a decision. Since over three-quarters could not tell us anything about either party, and because most of the remaining children could only tell us something about one of the parties, their reluctance to make an early, uninformed party identification is understandable. Those fourth-grade children who identified with the Democratic party were again consistently much more knowledgeable than their Republican counterparts.

Compared to 63 percent of Greenstein's 1958 fourth-grade sample who said they preferred one political party over another, only slightly more than 7 percent of our fourth-graders, two decades later, indicated a party preference.[10] Why this dramatic difference? A number of factors contribute to this lower party identification in our sample. First, there is the nonpartisan character of local government in California; all city and country offices are legally nonpartisan, and candidates run for office without party identification. This, combined with the heritage of cross-filing in state elections prior to 1958, has resulted in a lower salience of parties generally. There may also be a methodological explanation for this decline, both in the questions asked and the administrative procedures used to measure party identification. This study relies on open-ended questions. Earlier studies used fixed-response questionnaires with the names of the parties appearing in writing before the respondents.* These written questionnaires provide cues that are likely to trigger responses reflecting very shallow and transitory "party identification."** Perhaps the greater reliance of both children and adults on television for their political information, coupled with the very

---

*Greenstein's party identification was obtained from a question that asked: "If you were 21 now, whom would you vote for most of the time? (check one) mostly Republicans_____, mostly Democrats_____, don't know_____." Easton and Hess used "If you could vote, what would be? (Choose one) Republican_____, Democrat_____, Sometimes Democrat_____, Sometimes Republican_____, Don't know which_____, Don't know what Democrat and Republican mean_____."

**Converse has suggested that when researchers request an opinion from individuals who really have only a momentary feeling, they may be soliciting essentially nonopinions. See Philip E. Converse, "Comment: The Status of Nonattitudes," *American Political Science Review* 68 (1974): 650–60. Furthermore, if there does exist an "acquiescent bias" or "agreement syndrome" on the part of children, then it might appear with fixed-response questions.

limited reference to parties by the news media (except during presidential nominating conventions), also contributes to this decline in party recognition and identification.

But perhaps the primary explanation for the lower party identification in 1978, compared with 1958, must focus on the weakening of the party system in the United States and the dramatic lowering of party identification among adults in the late 1970s.[11] Since one-third of the children expressing a party preference specifically referred to their parents' partisan orientation, it is not surprising that many children are reflecting the lowered partisanship found in their primary role models. Parents cannot transmit something to their children that they do not themselves possess or that is not salient for them.[12]

This lessening of party identification is also accompanied by a dramatic instability in party preference among these children. We hypothesized that early party recognition (determined by the self-report queries), and particularly the ability to explain substantively the meaning of the two party labels, would be associated with early party identification. But the children in first and second grade who were able to respond to the phrase "political party" and give a vague definition of at least one party are not necessarily those who claim a party identification in third or fourth grade. Stability of party identification also fared poorly. We initially assumed that responses to open-ended questions would identify those pupils who had stable party identifications. However, there is only a partial overlap between third- and fourth-grade party identifiers. Of the seven children who said they preferred the Republicans as third graders, six stated a year later that they had no preference. When asked why he liked the Republicans best, the only consistent Republican responded "Because Abe Lincoln and Ronald Reagan are Republicans." Of the eight "Democrats" in third grade, four said they now had no party preference. Three boys, all in the top ten most knowledgeable children in the study, continued to prefer the Democratic party. One of these, however, indicated his party identification was quite tentative: "Because it is my father's party. But I might be a Republican. You never know." The eighth third-grade "Democrat" had already become a youthful party switcher— now preferring the Republican party. In short, as of fourth grade, early party recognition is only weakly associated with early party identification and early party identification appears to lack consistency.

GROWTH PATTERNS MEASURED BY
COGNITIVE THRESHOLD VARIABLES

To explore the relevance and the operationality of the cognitive-developmental theory of learning for the realm of political knowledge, we selected for each grade level from four to nine cognitive variables that were identified as organizing concepts that might, once they were understood, provide an evolving framework that could facilitate the growth of civic awareness. At each grade level the variables selected were, by design, ones that would elicit a range of responses extending from the most simplistic and superficial cognitions through more accurate though still limited generalizations, to more comprehensive and detailed descriptions of an institution, function, or political activity.* Criteria were then formulated for assigning a stage of cognitive understanding to each "stageable" response.** (See Appendix B.)

---

*After selecting the variables we hypothesized would be threshold concepts, we examined the responses to a series of other questions to determine whether they might also be predictive of general political knowledge. Six of the eight questions analyzed were potentially stageable but were not predictive of other political understanding as measured by the cognitive map. In this way we eliminated as threshold cognitive variables: "What is a court?", "What does a judge do?", "What does a policeman do?", "What does a soldier do?", "Tell me about the energy crisis.", and "How did Ford become President?" The fact that these potentially stageable variables are not predictive of other political knowledge helps to validate that the hypothesized threshold variables are in fact keys to broader political understanding. Two nonstageable questions—"What is the President's name?" and "What is the President's party?"—were very useful predictors of correctness on map items. The ability to name the incumbent President showed statistically significant correlations with the map 40 times out of a possible 100 over the five years but was particularly predictive in first and second grades, peaking in the latter year with 13 out of 20 relationships being significant. If a child does not know the incumbent President's name in first through fourth grades, this clearly places him or her in the lowest category of political knowledgeability. The President's party query was asked in third and fourth grades only and had 14 statistically significant correlations out of 40. If a child knows the President's party, this is a clear indication that he or she is in the top category of political knowledgeability.

**After the three researchers *established the criteria* enumerated in Appendix B for determining which stage was represented by a child's response to one of the threshold questions, three independent raters (a psychologist, a political scientist, and a child development specialist) were asked to stage the same responses with these criteria as their only guide. The correlation between the independent raters' staging decisions and those of the three researchers ranged from .74 to .90 for the nine threshold questions used to determine a child's stage of political awareness. The average reliability quotient was .80.

Each *level* in the hierarchy of cognitive political development implies a distinctive quality of cognitive thinking as well as a difference in the accuracy and completeness of descriptive detail. For example, the distinction between Stage 2 (Task Pooling), which is the upper stage of Level I, and Stage 3 (Critical Feature), the lower stage of Level II, focuses on the ability of the child to generalize in a meaningful way regarding the critical features of particular governmental institutions. An understanding of causation, as Merelman

TABLE 4.8
Stageable Responses for Regime Threshold Cognitive Variables (by percentages)

Threshold Variable	Kinder-garten	First Grade	Second Grade	Third Grade	Fourth Grade
What does the President do when he goes to work?[a]	32	50	50	56	77
What does the government do?[a]	26	38	47	72	79
Electoral Process:[b] What is an election? Who picks the President?	21	47	72	89	99
What are taxes?[b]	15	45	69	79	96
What is Congress?[c]			11	16	31
What is the Supreme Court?[c]			17[d]	13	23
What is a Senator?[c]				12	18
What is a political party?[c]					12
What do politicians do?[c]					10

[a] Predictor of knowledgeability for kindergarten through fourth grade.
[b] Predictor of knowledgeability for first and second grades.
[c] Predictor of knowledgeability for fourth grade.
[d] The panel was not asked "What is a court?" until third grade. Thus, second-grade responses to "What is the Supreme Court?" were inflated, but lacked a predictive capability, because many youngsters responded with a vague governmental referent, a Stage 1 response. In subsequent years the children were asked "What is a court?" immediately before they were queried about the Supreme Court. In third grade the children recognized that the latter was requesting something other than *a* court and Stage 1 responses dropped from 26 to nine. Following the lead of earlier researchers, we initiated our investigation of awareness of the court system with a query about the Supreme Court. When in third grade we finally queried the children concerning both the court system and the role of a judge, we discovered that while most are not familiar with what the Supreme Court does, they are very knowledgeable about courts in general and about the functions a judge performs.

suggests, may be a prerequisite for attaining the next level (Level III) in this hierarchy of cognitive development.[13]

In kindergarten and first grade four organizing cognitions were used as threshold variables: "What does the President do when he goes to work?", "What are taxes?", "What does the government do?" and the fourth used two queries concerning the electoral process ("What is an election?" and "Who picks the President?"). In the second-grade interviews we included a question about the legislative branch, "What is the Congress?", and the judiciary, "What is the Supreme Court?" At the end of third grade the question, "What is a Senator?" was added. By the end of fourth grade two questions asked in earlier years were recognized by the minimum 10 percent of the panel and therefore could be used as threshold variables: "What is a political party?" and "What do politicians do?" (see Table 4.8).

Congress and the *Supreme Court* were used because they represent the two coordinate branches of the national government not included in the first four threshold variables identified during the kindergarten and first grade interviews. (The bases for selecting the four threshold variables used in all five years are described in Chapter 3.) *Politician*, *senator*, and *political party* fill out more completely the figures and institutions that give substance and integrity to the processes of representative government. These nine concepts, then, appear to be central—along with such notions as law and constitution—to our governmental system. An understanding of each—at the point when cognitive skills have sufficiently developed—will, we hypothesize, promote additional understanding and insight into governmental phenomena.*

As anticipated, the percentage of children able to respond to these queries increased dramatically for those four variables staged over all five years. From a response average of 26 percent of

---

*Because the staging of the cognitive variables is a rank ordering, the interval level measurement required by factor analysis is lacking. Despite this limitation, a factor analysis involving the four original cognitive variables produces a single factor for each year except kindergarten, where, in one case, the taxes variable, we have nominal rather than ordinal measurement. This result provides confirmation that the first four cognitive variables all measure basic features of the political domain. When, beginning in second grade, additional cognitive variables are added to the Political Understanding Index, two factors emerge; one seems to be measuring the respondents' focus on the unifying and unchanging instruments of authority in the political realm, while the other factor tends to reflect a focus on more pluralistic and temporary facets of the polity.

kindergarten, the average of staged responses increased to 46 percent in first grade, to 59 percent in second, 76 percent in third, and 89 percent in fourth grade (see Table 4.9). Stage 1 responses are predominant among those children offering a substantive response

TABLE 4.9
Children at Each Stage on Four Regime Threshold Cognitive Variables, K-4 (by percentages)

	Stages	*K*	*1*	*2*	*3*	*4*
What does the	1	29	35	28	18	25
President do when	2	3	16	21	38	45
he goes to work?	3	1	0.5	1	3	10
	4	0	0	0	0	1
	Not Staged	68	49	50	41	19
What does the	1	16	17	17	14	5
government do?	2	10	20	28	50	51
	3	1	2	2	8	23
	4	0	0	0	0	2
	Not Staged	73	61	53	28	19
Electoral Process:						
What is an election?	1	19	27	17	4	1
Who picks the	2	5	17	46	61	50
President?	3	2	4	9	23	42
	4	0	0	0.5	2	6
	Not Staged	73	52	28	10	1
What are taxes?	1	14	33	42	40	21
	2	1	11	19	34	38
	3	0	2	7	7	33
	4	0	0	1	0.5	4
	Not Staged	85	54	31	19	4
Average for the	1	20	28	26	19	13
four questions[a]	2	5	16	28	46	46
	3	1	2	5	10	27
	4	—	—	0.4	0.6	3
	Not Staged	75	54	41	25	11

[a]This aggregate average for these four questions will not correspond to the summing of the average stage for each individual respondent. This is the case because the variation among individuals in the panel will not be identical to the variations in the entire group over these four variables.

in kindergarten and first grade, although in first grade there are more Stage 2 responses than Stage 1 answers to the query "What does the government do?" First grade marks the peak (28 percent) in the frequency of Stage 1 responses. During second grade the average for all four threshold variables indicates that Stage 2 responses are 2 percent more frequent than Stage 1. Third grade represents a dramatic shift of the modal response from Stage 1 to Stage 2 as the average of Stage 2 responses is more than twice the average for Stage 1. Stage 1 responses still predominate on "taxes," however. For taxes the dramatic change in stageable responses occurs at fourth grade, when Stage 2 replies outnumber Stage 1 by 38 to 21 percent. Collectively, at the end of fourth grade, Stage 2 responses represent more than three times the total responses attributed to Stage 1.

Using the four original variables over the five years a bell-shaped distribution of stage knowledgeability becomes evident (see Figure 4.2). On three of those queries, Stage 1 responses begin to decline in frequency by second grade, and the fourth, taxes, follows in third grade. Stage 2 responses can be expected to follow the same declining pattern in fifth and sixth grades. A similar pattern should prevail for Stage 3 but with a flatter and longer curve.

In order to achieve a more valid picture of the progress our panel is making up the hierarchy of stages in cognitive development, it is more appropriate to focus the analysis on the expected nine-item Political Understanding Index. The stages of our cognitive hierarchy represent a rank ordering and not an interval scale. Since Stages 1 and 2 represent the same level, we posit that it is easier to move from Stage 1 to Stage 2 than it is to move from Stage 2 to Stage 3, which is the lower stage of Level II. This seems reasonable because the latter move involves a major shift in the type of cognitive thinking required.

Stage 1, which we designate as a "prepolitical" stage, involves merely recognizing that a term is somehow associated with government. The consumer or spectator orientation that most of our citizenry have toward government and politics may be reflected in the ease with which young children recognize certain concepts as realted to government (Stage 1), but this orientation limits the children in their capacity to move toward higher stages of political understanding. The bell-shaped curve for Stage 1 is much higher and will be relatively shorter in duration than is the case with the curves for Stages 2 and 3. Based on our analysis of the original four

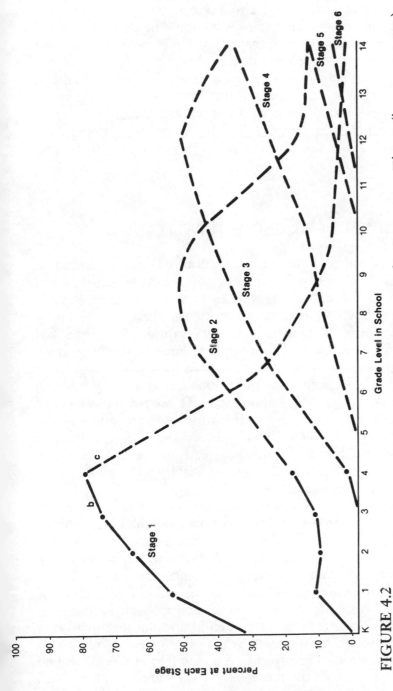

FIGURE 4.2
Actual and Projected Patterns of Cognitive Development by Stage over Time[a] (in percentages)

[a]Based on the expanded Political Understanding Index. See Table 4.9.
[b]Solid line represents present empirical data.
[c]Broken line is hypothesized pattern of political cognitive development extrapolated through first two years of college.

113

variables, it would appear to be easier to move from Stage 1 to Stage 2 than it is to move from Stage 2 to Stage 3.

Once a child has attained Stage 3, it should be easier to move to Stage 4. Since we hypothesize that Stage 4 represents the national adult mode, its pattern will not be a normal bell-shaped curve but will progress gradually until a plateau is reached, followed, perhaps, by a slight decline as an increasing number of young adults move beyond Stage 4 as a result of their college training or other politicizing experiences. Stage 3 will be longer in duration than Stages 1 and 2, and a number of citizens will never progress beyond it.

LONGITUDINAL PUPIL GROWTH PATTERNS

The threshold cognitive variables, all of which are basic to an understanding of our political system, constitute the Political Understanding Index (PUI). This index is created by averaging the stages achieved by each child on all of the threshold variables used in any given year. In kindergarten, for example, four threshold variables were staged with a maximum score achieved by a single pupil being six (an average of 1.5). The overwhelming majority of responses by kindergartners to these four questions could not be staged even as Symbol Recognition (Stage 1). Sixty-seven percent of the kindergarten children fell in the unstaged category, and the average stage for all 149 children was .30 (see Table 4.10). The percentage of children in the unstaged category falls progressively each year, even though new threshold variables were added to the PUI beginning in second grade.

Thirty-two percent of the kindergarten children achieved an average of Stage 1, and when the additional variables are included for grades 2, 3 and 4, that percentage rises progressively each year to a high of 76 percent in fourth grade. While only 1 percent of the kindergartners achieved an average of Stage 2, that percentage moved irregularly upward to a high of 17 percent in fourth grade. (If the analysis of aggregate growth is made using only the four original threshold variables, the percentage of children achieving an average of Stage 2 increases steadily each year until 63 percent reach that level in fourth grade.) The percentage of children at Stage 2 will no doubt increase through the remaining elementary and junior high school years until it is surpassed by a Stage 3 ascendancy during high school.

TABLE 4.10

Aggregate Growth Measured by the Political Understanding Index (expressed in percentages)

	Using Four Threshold Variables Across All Five Years Grade				
	K	1	2	3	4
Stage on PUI					
Unstaged[a]	67	36	20	3	0
Stage 1	32	52	49	44	14
Stage 2	1	11	29	49	63
Stage 3	0	0.4	1	5	23
Average Stage	.30	.65	.98	1.42	1.96
	Using Additional Variables in Grades 2, 3, and 4				
Unstaged	67	36	28	18	6
Stage 1	32	52	64	72	76
Stage 2	1	11	9	10	17
Stage 3	0	0.4	0	0	2
Average Stage	.30	.65	.73	1.01	1.06
No. of Variables	4	4	6	7	9

[a] Unstaged extends from .00 to .49; Stage 1 from .50 to 1.49; Stage 2 from 1.50 to 2.49; Stage 3 from 2.50 to 3.49.

If all threshold variables are considered, an average of Stage 3 does not appear for more than one child until fourth grade. If only the original four threshold variables are considered, 1 percent achieve a Stage 3 average in second grade, and 23 percent reach that stage by fourth grade.

Perhaps even more meaningful than the percentage of responses for each stage is the average stage achieved by the children at each grade level. When all nine staged variables are considered, there is a gradual but somewhat uneven progression in the average stage achieved over the five years. As they reached the end of fourth grade, the panel was only slightly above Stage 1 when using the composite PUI, which includes an increasingly complex and abstract set of variables, but at 1.96 were an average of Stage 2 on the four original threshold variables used all five years. This means, of course, that the retention of the basic four variables through all five years causes the PUI to move in an upward direction despite the fact that more difficult variables are added during the latter three years.

These additional variables help to maintain the PUI at a realistic level during the middle elementary school years. In this way the PUI retains its quality as an accurate mirror of the child's emerging political awareness.

The difference between the average stage using the original four variables and using the others that were added beginning with second grade underlines the importance of identifying new threshold variables as the children move through the elementary and secondary school years.* It seems much more realistic to say that the children were on the average slightly above Stage 1 at the end of fourth grade (when using nine threshold variables) rather than suggesting that they were at Stage 2 (as when using only the original four). Given the likelihood that the adult mean is somewhere between Stages 3 and 4, it seems unrealistic to expect the average nine- or ten-year-old child to be much above Stage 1 on this six-stage scale.

Figure 4.3 compares the individual pupil's total stage score at the end of fourth grade with his or her score after the first interview conducted either in kindergarten or in first grade. Using the original four threshold variables as the basis for computing these stage scores, 4 percent of the children failed to gain at least one stage over the period of the study. A majority of the children, 51 percent, gained two stages; the second largest category of gain was the 37 percent who advanced one stage. Seven percent showed a gain of three stages over this four- or five-year period. Using the nine threshold variables that comprise the PUI in fourth grade, 54 percent of the panel gained one stage from their initial interview, 38 percent failed to gain at least one stage, 4 percent showed a gain of two stages, and 1 percent a three-stage gain. Three percent showed a loss of one stage between the first interview and fourth grade when the nine-question PUI is used in this longitudinal analysis. As Figure 4.3 shows, the four-variable and nine-variable analyses produce very similar longitudinal patterns of pupil growth—the distinction being that the former peaks at Stage 2 while the latter reaches its zenith at Stage 1. These parallel patterns confirm that the variables added

---

*Among the threshold cognitive variables that might be added following the elementary school years are the concepts of freedom, representation, the rule of law, ideological orientation, individual rights of assembly, speech, press, and religion, as well as the role of interest groups.

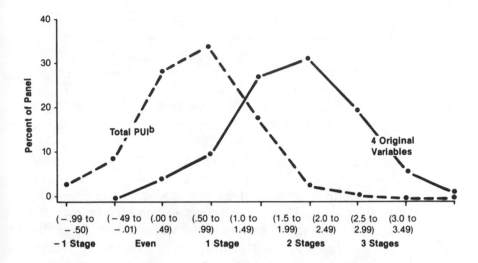

FIGURE 4.3
Contrasting Individual Pupil Gains Over Five Years on the Four Original Variables with the Expanded Political Understanding Index

[a]This is a comparison of the individual student's stage score at the end of fourth grade with that pupil's score using his or her first interview in kindergarten (149 children) or first grade (94 children).

[b]Second grade, 6 variables; third grade, 7 variables; fourth grade, 9 variables.

beginning in the second grade are in fact measuring patterns of political understanding in the same way as the original four variables.

The cognitive-developmental theory of learning has tended to emphasize patterns of sequential learning without regression. When we analyze the 878 possible growth comparisons of our pupils over the five years using the PUI, 15 percent of these comparisons showed regression.* By virtue of having added new and more difficult threshold variables to the PUI each of the last three years, a bias toward regression was introduced. When the analysis is based

---

*An error factor of .25 was used to compensate for differences that might be attributable to our inability to control all extraneous factors associated with each of the annual interviews. For this reason a regression is defined as a loss of knowledge greater than one-quarter of a stage. On the expanded PUI 35 children were at a lower stage in fourth grade than they had earlier achieved.

on the four original variables alone, 8 percent of the 878 comparisons still showed regression. Thirteen pupils, 5 percent of the panel,
were at a lower stage in fourth grade using the four original variables
than they had been using the same index during at least one of the
preceding years. Some of these regressions would appear to be
explained on the basis of traumatic events in the child's social
environment. At least four of these 13 were involved with separation
or divorce, and the family of another moved to a new community.
These longitudinal comparisons made during the early elementary
school years suggest that, although the overwhelming percentage of
pupils showed cognitive growth, there can indeed be regressions in
political understanding. These regressions in some cases may be
attributable to unusual social or emotional circumstances that the
children were coping with at the time of the interview. Under
"normal" circumstances Piagetian theory would not expect to find
such regressions in cognitive understanding, but increasingly for a
significant number of children, their social and parental circumstances are neither consistent nor comfortable.

When the number of children making their greatest gain on the
four original variables are compared from year-to-year, approximately one-fifth had their greatest increase in political knowledge in
second grade. Approximately 30 percent of the panel had their
greatest gain in third grade and an identical percentage in fourth
grade. This longitudinal analysis of when children had their greatest
gain in political knowledge suggests that during the early elementary
school grades, some children are open to significant increases in
political understanding each year. Educators should not therefore
assume that any one year provides a better opportunity than any
other for increasing a child's civic awareness.

SUMMARY AND CONCLUSIONS

Using two instruments, a 20-item cognitive map and an index
based on nine threshold cognitive variables, this study measures the
extent and the rate of growth in political awareness among school
children between kindergarten and fourth grade. Significant growth
occurred in the recognition of political symbols. Unifying symbols
such as the national flag, George Washington, and the Statue of
Liberty showed the most rapid early growth, while symbols
representing partisan institutions, the White House, and the

national Capitol, lagged substantially behind. Gains in the recognition of certain symbols such as the Statue of Liberty and the incumbent President seem attributable to environmental stimuli, for example, the Bicentennial and the presidential primaries, while gains in other areas, such as awareness of what an election is and what state the pupil lives in, were more uniform over the years and therefore more likely to be attributable to the child's developing cognitive capabilities.

In the aggregate, primary school children demonstrate steady growth in their ability to identify geo-political units such as their city, state, and nation, even though some children do not evidence consistency from year-to-year. This aggregate pattern of growth in geo-political awareness would appear to provide some support for a learning theory that emphasizes development in stages, while the individual variations suggest that environmental stimuli contribute to a child's awareness. Recognition of the chief executives heading various levels of government follows a pattern that is the reverse of the recognition of the governmental units themselves that is, children identify the President, governor, and mayor in declining order of accuracy, while the children are able to identify their city, state, and country with descending accuracy. The latter pattern corresponds to Jahoda's findings that geo-political awareness expands outward from the local area, to the region, to the nation.

In the area of regime-related phenomena, the children were best acquainted with items concerning the law, such as judges and courts, and least familiar with partisan and legislative objects, such as political parties, politicians, senators, and Congress. Some regime-related objects such as armies, elections, and taxes are presented in either the child's immediate or media-produced environment in such a way as to enable many of the youngsters to grasp their essential meaning before reaching the fourth grade.

Awareness of major public issues such as Watergate, Vietnam, and the energy crisis appears to be more a product of interaction with environmental stimuli than it is the result of increased cognitive capacity. In all three cases the level of awareness changed over time, fluctuating with variations in the attention given to those issues by the media and by parents. In the case of issues less visible to young children, such as unemployment and inflation, significant increases in recognition levels between third and fourth grades may simply represent increasing cognitive capacity to understand abstract concepts.

Primary school children, however knowledgeable in other areas, are not yet ready to grasp the distinction between the public and private sectors insofar as this understanding can be measured by their awareness of which occupations are normally associated with government. Indeed, in responding to the question of whether such private-sector occupations as a milkman, gas station man, candy store clerk, or television news person work for the government, the children became progressively less accurate as they grew older; by fourth grade a majority of the children identified three of these four private-sector occupations with government. The vitality of the private sector may be endangered by the widespread belief that positions of importance must be governmental.

Children in our mid-to-late 1970s California panel seem much less aware of politicians and political parties than those in earlier studies. Even as late as fourth grade fewer than 10 percent of our panel could cite a difference between the Republican and Democratic parties and only 6 to 7 percent claimed to prefer one party over the other. This contrasts dramatically with the 63 percent among Greenstein's 1958 fourth-grade sample from New Haven. During the past two decades there has been a substantial decline in party identification over the entire nation. In addition, the essentially nonpartisan character of local government in California, perhaps along with the heritage of cross-filing in state elections prior to 1958, gives parties a lower salience in the state. The fact that this study relies on open-ended oral interviews rather than on giving the children printed questionnaires with the party names indicated may also partially account for the substantially lower evidence of party preference among the children in our panel. Even considering these explanations for differences in party awareness and identification between Greenstein's sample and our own, there is still a major difference between the two generations, which may portend greater transciency in party loyalties and greater receptivity to media influences among those reaching voting age in the 1980s than those of earlier decades.

Using the Political Understanding Index, a pattern of steady aggregate growth among the panel members can be measured beginning with a stageable response average of 33 percent in kindergarten and culminating with 94 percent in fourth grade. Among children providing substantive responses to the four original threshold cognitive questions, Symbol Recognition (Stage 1 responses) peaked in first grade and Task Pooling answers (Stage 2 responses) reached a high of 63 percent of the panel in fourth grade. This will almost certainly be the peak year for Stage 2 responses. Between second and third grades the preponderance of our panel on these four variables shifted from symbol recognition to a task pooling conception of government. We anticipate that the third cognitive stage, Critical Feature Identifications, will reach its zenith in seventh or eighth grade. However, the expanded PUI gives a more accurate picture of actual and probable future growth patterns. Using this index, Stage 1 responses peak during fourth grade, and Stage 2 will probably continue increasing until eighth grade. Sometime during the later high school years, Stage 3 responses should surpass Stage 2 (see Figure 4.2). If this occurs, it would lend support to the Piagetian hypothesis that formal operational thinking, in this case the ability to identify critical features of political institutions and processes, emerges between ages 12 and 16.[14]

An analysis of individual growth patterns based on the expanded PUI shows that 127 of the 243 children had no regressions in knowledgeability from one year to the next. Considering the entire panel, 6 percent showed growth every year, 57 percent showed growth in at least two of the annual intervals,* 31 percent showed growth in one year, and 8 percent showed no political cognitive growth any year. All of the latter had only three years in which to show growth.

Considering only the four variables used all five years, the pattern of growth is more impressive: 16 percent showed growth every year, two-thirds showed growth in at least two years, 16 percent showed growth in only one year (over two-thirds had only three years in which to show growth), and only 1 percent showed no growth. This pattern of fairly regular growth with a limited number of regressions suggests that the cognitive-developmental theory of learning is helpful for understanding political socialization. If the first five years of formal schooling are taken as a whole, substantial percentages of children in our panel experienced significant growth during two or more years of early elementary schooling. In the next chapter we will seek to isolate the principal explanations for these patterns of growing political awareness.

---

*One hundred forty-nine children had four years in which to exhibit growth, while 94 pupils only had three years of possible growth.

NOTES

1. For a complete discussion of the rationale used to justify each of these cognitive map items, see Appendix D.

2. R. W. Connell, *The Child's Construction of Politics* (Melbourne, Australia: Melbourne University Press, 1971), Chapter 2.

3. Frances Fitzgerald, *America Revised* (Boston: Little, Brown, 1979). Earlier analyses of American history books have reached similar conclusions. For a discussion of earlier studies, as well as the possibilities for innovative teaching materials, see John J. Patrick, "Political Socialization and Political Education in Schools," in Stanley Allen Renshon, ed., *Handbook of Political Socialization* (New York: The Free Press, 1977), p. 203f.

4. Gustave Jahoda, "The Development of Children's Ideas About Country and Nationality. Part 1: The Conceptual Framework," *British Journal of Educational Psychology* 33: 47–60.

5. Fred I. Greenstein, *Children and Politics* (New Haven: Yale University Press, 1965), pp. 60–62.

6. David Easton and Jack Dennis, *Children in the Political System* (New York: McGraw-Hill, 1969), Chapter 8, "The President as a Focal Point of Political Socialization," as well as R. Sigel, "Images of the American Presidency," *Midwest Journal of Political Science* 10(1966): 123–37.

7. P. E. Converse and G. Dupeaux found that party identification among French children is acquired primarily when their parents claim such an affiliation; children with parents who do not make such a claim rarely express a party preference. See "Politicization of the Electorate in France and the United States," *Public Opinion Quarterly* 26 (1962): 1–23.

8. Easton and Dennis, *Children in the Political System*, pp. 121–23.

9. Greenstein, *Children and Politics*, p. 73; David Easton and Robert D. Hess, "The Child's Political World," *Midwest Journal of Political Science* VI (1962): 45.

10. Greenstein, *Children and Politics*, p. 73.

11. Kevin Mulcahy and Richard Katz, *America Votes* (Englewood Cliffs, NJ: Prentice-Hall, 1976); Nelson W. Polsby and Aaron Wildavsky, *Presidential Elections*, 4th ed. (New York: Scribner's, 1976), and David B. Hill and Norman R. Luttbeg, *Trends in American Electoral Behavior* (Itasca, IL: F. E. Peacock Publishers, Inc., 1980), Chapter 2.

12. Much has been written on the parental transmission of political attitudes, both methodologically and substantively. For a discussion of the methodological problems involved, see Robert Weissberg and Richard Joslyn, "Methodological Appropriateness in Political Socialization Research," in Renshon, ed., *Handbook*, pp. 46–72, as well as Paul Allen Beck, "The Role of Agents in Political Socialization," in Renshon, pp. 122–27.

13. Richard M. Merelman, "The Development of Political Ideology: A Framework for the Analysis of Political Socialization," *American Political Science Review* LXIII (September 1969): 753–58.

14. Herbert Ginsburg and Sylvia Opper, *Piaget's Theory of Intellectual Development: An Introduction* (Englewood Cliffs, NJ: Prentice-Hall, 1969), p. 181f.

5

How and Why Children Learn About Politics

Describing patterns of expanding political knowledge during the first five years of formal schooling is relatively easy when compared with the challenge of identifying the factors that might explain how and why children learn about government and politics. Clear causal connections in the learning process remain beyond the grasp of modern social science,[1] but correlations between levels of political knowledge and demographic as well as cognitive variables may help us determine those characteristics that are most closely associated with children having greater or lesser political knowledge.

In our search for correlates of political knowledge, we began with the demographic variables that earlier studies of political awareness have used, including sex, ethnic background, sibling pattern, estimated academic rank, and exposure to media, especially television. We found the expected patterns: boys were more knowledgeable than girls, Anglos slightly more aware than non-Anglos, oldest and only children more sophisticated than the others, academic high achievers significantly more knowledgeable than lower-ranking children, and television news watchers had somewhat more savvy than nonviewers. *But* the differences were not as significant as some earlier studies suggest.[2] The limited power of the demographic variables for predicting differing levels of political knowledge prompted us to seek another type of independent variable, one that we call the threshold cognitive variable—a key understanding relating to politics—which appears to open new areas of political awareness for the young child. During the first five years of this study, we were able to identify a total of nine such cognitive variables: four were used in kindergarten and first grade, two were

123

added in second grade, one more in third grade, and two in fourth. The weakest of the six cognitive independent varibles used in second grade—the ability to identify at least one governmental activity—distinguished the more knowledgeable children from the less knowledgeable as effectively as sex, which, except for academic rank, was the most powerful predictor of political knowledge among the traditional demographic variables.

After a brief discussion of the uses and limits of the five demographic variables as predictors of political knowledge, this chapter focuses on the benefits of using selected cognitive variables

TABLE 5.1
Correlations Between Five Demographic Variables and Twe **Cognitive Map Items**

	Kindergarten		First Grade		Second Grade	
Sex	Male	Female	Male	Female	Male	Female
No. of 20 map items on which most knowledge-able[a]	15	2	16	4	19	1
Average percentage of those knowing map items	37	31	44	37	55	46
Ethnic Background	Anglo	Non-Anglo	Anglo	Non-Anglo	Anglo	Non-Ang
No. of 20 map items on which most knowledge-able	12	7	11	9	12	7
Average percentage of those knowing map items	35	31	41	39	51	48
Sibling Pattern	Only Old Mid Ygst		Only Old Mid Ygst		Only Old Mid	
No. of 20 map items on which most knowledge-able	5 9 4 2		13 4 1 0		11 4 0	

in making a detailed analysis of how and why young children increase their understanding of government and politics.

DEMOGRAPHIC EXPLANATIONS FOR POLITICAL KNOWLEDGE

Sex

There is overwhelming evidence over all five years that primary school boys are more knowledgeable than girls (see Table 5.1). Of

Third Grade				Fourth Grade				Total All Years			
Male	Female			Male	Female			Male	Female		
17	1			16	4			83	12 (5 even)[a]		
61	55			66	61			53	46		
Anglo	Non-Anglo			Anglo	Non-Anglo			Anglo	Non-Anglo		
12	6			11	7			58	36 (6 even)		
59	56			64	61			50	47		
Only	Old	Mid	Ygst	Only	Old	Mid	Ygst	Only	Old	Mid	Ygst
7	4	5	1	9	7	5	0	45	28 (12 even)	11	4

(continued on next page)

TABLE 5.1 (continued)

	Kindergarten				First Grade				Second Grade			
Sibling (cont.)	Only	Old	Mid	Ygst	Only	Old	Mid	Ygst	Only	Old	Mid	Y
Average percentage of those knowing map items	36	40	34	32	49	42	39	40	58	51	49	
TV News-watching									Oft	Some	Rare	N
No. of 20 map items on which most knowledgeable									7	7	3	
Average percentage of those knowing map items									50	53	50	
Est. Academic Rank												
No. of 20 map items on which most knowledgeable												
Average percent of those knowing map items												

[a]Ties are excluded.

the 100 possible relationships over the five years, boys were more knowledgeable in 83, and girls were more knowledgeable in 12. In the remaining five cases the sexes were equally knowledgeable. The superiority of boys reached statistical significance in only 15 of the 83 instances in which they knew more than girls—less frequently than anticipated—but the overall difference is clearly evident.*

---

*In using the chi square measure of independence for the cognitive map items there is a problem of certain questions having either too few or too many children responding correctly. In kindergarten and first grade, six map items have less than 10 percent correct responses and in fourth grade one-half of the 20 items are above the 90 percent correct response level. Under these circumstances of limited variability, it is unlikely that statistically significant differences will appear.

	Third Grade				Fourth Grade				Total All Years		
62	60	57	57	67	66	62	62	54	52	48	48
Oft	Some	Rare	Nev	Oft	Some	Rare	Nev	Oft	Some	Rare	Nev
8	4	3	3	10	0	3	4	25	11	9	9
60	59	53	56	68	62	63	56	59	58	55	53
Top¼	Mid½	Low¼		Top¼	Mid½	Low¼		Top¼	Mid½	Low¼	
16	3	0		16	1	0		32	4	0	
67	59	52		70	61	57		69	60	55	

While on ten items boys were more knowledgeable than girls in each of the five years, on no single question were girls consistently more knowledgeable. In only one instance—their knowledge of what soldiers do—was the boys' knowledge sufficiently greater than girls' to be significant in all five years (see Table 5.2). Boys' perception of soldiers is also consistently different from that of girls; the former visualize soldiers as fighting while many girls describe their role as one of marching or guarding.[3] Recognition of the picture of the Statue of Liberty was the only other map item for which boys' superior knowledge reached significance in more than one year; in that case boys were significantly more knowledgeable in first, second, and third grades. On the four map questions relating to the

TABLE 5.2
Statistically Significant Correlations Between Demographic Variables and Twenty Cognitive Map Items

	Sex					Ethnic Background				
	K	1	2	3	4	K	1	2	3	4
Country										
Washington										
Statue of Liberty		*	*	*						
Nat'l Capitol				*						
King			*							
Law		*					*	*	*	
Election		*								
Politicians				*						
Taxes				*						
Policeman								*		
Soldier	*	*	*	*	*					
Pres's Picture										
Governor										*
Bradley										
State										
City			*							
Energy Crisis										
Watergate										
Judge										
Milkman										
Totals	1	4	4	5	1	2	1	1	1	0
		Sex = 15				Ethnic Background = 5				

[a]EAR stands for Estimated Academic Rank.

national community (name of country and recognition of pictures of George Washington, the Statue of Liberty, and the national Capitol), boys were more knowledgeable in each of the five years. In sum, among the children in our panel, boys are consistently more knowledgeable on a wide range of governmental matters.

Sibling Pattern					Newswatching			Est Acad Rk		Total
K	1	2	3	4	2	3	4	3	4	
								*	*	2
*								*		2
								*	*	5
		*							*	3
										1
									*	5
								*		2
									*	2
						*	*	*	*	5
*			*							3
*										6
	*									1
							*	*	*	4
		*					*	*		3
	*				*		*	*	*	5
					*			*		3
										0
										0
								*		1
										0
3	2	1	1	1	2	1	4	10	8	——

Sibling Pattern = 8   Newswatching = 7   EAR[a] = 18   53/400

In a period such as the present, when women are becoming more visible in elective and appointive offices, it is important to ask why elementary school girls systematically lag behind boys in political awareness. It would appear that it takes a very concerted effort on the part of key socializing agents—parents, schools, and mass media—to overcome the societal bias that has prompted most institutions to focus public attention on male political heroes. The children learn in school about Washington, Jefferson, and Lincoln, but they rarely hear anything about Susan B. Anthony and Jane Addams. The schools, as well as parents, perpetuate, perhaps unknowingly, the notion that political activity and public service is the province of men by continuing the long-standing emphasis on the traditional political heroes—virtually all of them male.

In some districts and even in some states, there have been concerted efforts made in recent years to eliminate sexism from the elementary school program: games are co-educational, and some teachers no longer segregate boys and girls into separate lines when entering or leaving the classroom; but even more must be done to give young children exposure to compelling role models of women who exercise power in business and government. Correcting a societal bias that spans centuries and even millenia requires an extraordinary effort that has only recently begun and has yet to equalize the aggregate levels of political awareness among elementary school girls and boys.

Ethnic Background

Approximately 19 percent of our panel are non-Anglo children, most of these Hispanic. On the 20 cognitive map items over the five years, the Anglo children were more knowledgeable 58 percent of the time. The two groups were equally knowledgeable in six instances out of the possible 100 comparisons over the five years. (See Table 5.1.) However, greater Anglo awareness reached statistical significance only five times, and on only one query did this occur in more than one year. During kindergarten, first, and second grades Anglos were significantly more knowledgeable in answering "What is a law?" Among the 36 instances in which the non-Anglo children were more knowledgeable than the Anglos, there were two map items on which the non-Anglo superiority appeared four out of five years: recognition of the incumbent President's picture and knowing that a judge works for the government. But none of these differences was statistically significant. These data suggest that there are relatively modest differences in political knowledgeability between middle-class Anglos and middle-class non-Anglos, although the pattern suggests that Anglos are slightly more knowledgeable.

Among the five demographic variables used in this study, ethnic background is clearly the *least* predictive of political awareness.

While our data suggest that there are only modest differences between Anglos and non-Anglos in their political knowledgeability, the absence of significant differences based on ethnicity may, in large measure, be attributable to the predominately middle-class character of the minority children in our panel. If a majority of the non-Anglo children in our panel had come from very low income families, it is probable that they would have differing perceptions of governmental phenomena. Even among our relatively Anglicized minority children, there were statistically significant differences in the earliest years when identifying what a law is and what a police officer does compared with those of Anglo children. But the slight Anglo superiority in certain areas of political knowledge declines modestly the longer the children are in school. It would appear that as non-Anglo children are assimilated into the mainstream Anglo culture, differences in political awareness gradually disappear.

Sibling Pattern

Is sibling order more predictive of political knowledge than sex or ethnicity? In this study we compared knowledgeability among children in four sibling configurations: "only" children, the oldest child, the youngest child, and a "middle" child having both older and younger siblings. The difference in knowledgeability among these four categories reached the .05 level of significance or higher in only eight of the 100 comparisons (see Table 5.2). Only in the responses to "What does a policeman do?" did the significant differences among siblings appear in more than one year. Nevertheless, the analysis correlating sibling position with cognitive map knowledge across five years shows that only children are ranked most knowledgeable 60 percent more often than oldest children, more than four times as often as middle children, and more than ten times as often as youngest children.* These differences are even

---

*"Only" children represent just 14 pupils in our panel of 243 and in several interesting ways they appear to be atypical of the children studied, particularly in occupational role preferences and in being represented disproportionately in the top quartile of estimated academic rank—a finding congruent with previous research. See Lucille Forer, *The Birth Order Factor* (New York: Pocket Books, 1977), Chapter 17.

more dramatic if the kindergarten year is excluded (see Table 5.1). The differences of knowledgeability among the sibling pattern is consistent every year except for kindergarten; it is conceivable that only children were less knowledgeable than oldest children that year because the former had not yet learned to "compete" in acquiring information. Our more general hypothesis is that this variation in knowledgeability on the basis of sibling placement reflects the amount and the type of interaction a child is likely to have with parents and other adults in the home and neighborhood. Zajonc and Markus have found that family size represents one form of environmental deprivation; a child's IQ declines as family size increases. IQ also declines with birth order; that is, first-born children tend to have higher IQ's than later children, with a decline for each successive sibling.[4] Potentially, only children have by far the greatest amount of interaction with adults, oldest children (having initially been only children as well as holding a special position in the family) the next greatest amount, middle children the next, and youngest children in multichild families the least adult contact. This is not to suggest that little or no political knowledge is transmitted among siblings or other children, but it does imply that in contrast with the fruitfulness of parental and other adult contacts, interaction with siblings and peers at this age is likely to be less useful in promoting greater political knowledge.

Media Exposure

Beginning in second grade the children were asked whether they watched the evening news on television. If their answer was affirmative, they were asked to estimate whether they watched it more than three times a week ("Often"), two or three times a week ("Sometimes"), or once a week or less ("Rarely"). In comparing these self-reports on the frequency of television news watching with the answers to cognitive map items, we found a very limited correlation between political knowledgeability and frequency of news watching. Only seven instances out of a possible 60 reached statistical significance, and not all of them were in the direction predicted (see Table 5.2).

There were, however, seven cognitive map items for which there is some evidence that frequent television news watching may increase knowledgeability. These are, in most instances, quite predictable: knowledge concerning elections, politicians, taxes, and Watergate. Although the percentage differences in knowledgeability were modest, those reporting the highest frequency of television news viewing (more than three times a week) were more than twice as likely to be the most knowledgeable on any given map item than those who watched only two or three times a week and nearly three times as likely to be most knowledgeable as those who watched television news once a week or less.

It has been found that a person learns from exposure to the media in proportion to the level of knowledge possessed prior to the media exposure.[5] Because very young children lack the necessary background connectives, we did not ask our panel about the frequency of their television news watching until they were in the second grade.* When comparing the three years they were questioned about viewing patterns, we found that differences in knowledgeability between regular news watchers and those who never watch the news were greatest in fourth grade. These data indicate that television news watching adds little to most children's knowledge regarding the processes and functions of government until they reach the age of nine or ten. At that time children may possess enough background to enable them to supplement prior knowledge by viewing the news on television. Clearly, it would seem by this age regular exposure to television news can make a difference in a child's political awareness, especially if messages received on television are reinforced through conversations with politically interested and knowledgeable adults. It seems clear that the two-step theory of opinion formation applies with particular relevance to young children, who may be exposed to television news but are unlikely to learn much from it unless their attention is guided by adults who point out the significance of the messages transmitted.[6]

---

*Survey results indicate that few children younger than second grade view television newscasts. A major study by Atkin also revealed that children tend to give high estimates of the amount of news they watch. For our purposes, because our interest is in comparative exposure to news viewing, overreporting does not present a problem. For a recent review of studies focusing on the media and political socialization, see Charles K. Atkin, "Communication and Political Socialization," in Dan Nimmo and Keith Sanders, eds., *Handbook of Political Communication* (Beverly Hills: Sage Publications, 1981), pp. 299–328.

Academic Rank

At the end of third grade the classroom teachers were asked to estimate whether each child in the panel would rank in the top quarter, the middle half, or the bottom quarter of all the children he or she had taught at that grade level. Comparing this estimate of academic rank with the knowledgeability of the children on the 20 cognitive map items, we found that there is a predictably high correlation between estimated academic rank and accuracy on map items; correlations reached at least the .05 level of statistical significance in almost half of the 40 cross-tabulations for third and fourth grade (see Table 5.2). Those in the top quarter academically were the most knowledgeable of the three groups in 32 of the 40 cases.* In 27 of the 40 comparisons the expected relationship between knowledgeability and estimated academic rank occurred, that is, higher-ranking children are more knowledgeable than those in lower categories. In no case was the expected pattern reversed, and in only four instances were the children in the middle half more knowledgeable than those in the top quarter, and two of those four concerned whether a milkman works for the government—one of the questions many children had great difficulty answering correctly.** There were nine instances in which children in the lowest quartile were more knowledgeable than those in the middle half. It is clear that there is an impressive correlation between general performance in elementary school and knowledgeability across a wide spectrum of political topics.

AGENTS OF POLITICAL SOCIALIZATION

Our methodology does not permit us to compare directly the relative influence of the home, school, mass media, and peer group[7] in determining the level of political awareness of elementary school

---

*Stanley Renshon mentions some of the previous findings in connection with high IQ. See *Handbook*, pp. 20, 25. See also Hess and Torney, *The Development of Political Attitudes in Children* (Garden City, NY: Doubleday, 1967), pp. 151–61.

**The more politically aware a child is, the more likely he or she is to see the scope of government as pervasive.

children. Parents and teachers were not interviewed in a systematic fashion because of the possibility that they might subsequently coach panel members. Our information about the role played by the media and peers is also indirect. Nevertheless, we do infer from regular contact with our panel that the family and especially the parents in their comments concerning candidates, issues, and governmental processes have the greatest influence over political interest and information during the first five years of elementary school. Panelists frequently referred to their parents having voted, to having strong positive or negative feelings concerning candidates as a result of parental suggestion, and to their parents' comments about problems such as inflation or the energy and water crises. The impact of the media, primarily television, is in some measure a function of parental interest and the likelihood that television news will be watched and discussed in the home.

Beginning in third and fourth grades there were frequent references to having studied an institution or process in the classroom. The role of the school during the first five years seems to have its greatest impact in familiarizing the child with the most prominent unifying political symbols: the flag, the traditional heroes—Washington and Lincoln—and several physical or architectural monuments: the Liberty Bell, the Statue of Liberty, the White House, and the national Capitol. When the political symbols used in the annual interviews are combined to create a Symbol Recognition Index, this index correlates with the map items at the .05 level or higher 40 times out of 100 possible comparisons (see Table 5.3). In fourth grade the panel members were found to be slightly above Stage 1 (see Table 4.9), which is designated at the Symbol Recognition Stage—the first of two stages at the *prepolitical level* of understanding. Therefore, it is not surprising that the substantive political content associated with these symbols remains extremely limited; children are more likely to relate tales about Washington's honesty in confessing that he cut down a cherry tree, his prowess in tossing a coin a great distance, and his wooden teeth than they are to mention his role in the American Revolution or in establishing the pattern of presidential leadership. Lincoln's assassination by an actor in the Ford Theatre is much more widely known among elementary school children than is his role in preserving the union or emancipating the slaves. In short, the school is successful in conveying those kinds of facts about political leaders and other

TABLE 5.3

Statistically Significant Relationships Between Symbol Recognition Index and Cognitive Map Items

Map Item	Grade Level					Number of Years Sig.
	K	1	2	3	4	
Country				.05	.001	2
Washington[a]		.001	.001	.001	.001	4
Statue of Liberty[a]	.001	.001	.001	.001	.001	5
National Capitol[a]	.001	.001	.001	.001	.001	5
King		.01	.05			2
Taxes			.05			1
Law		.01		.001		2
Election		.001		.001		2
Politician				.05		1
Police						0
Soldier				.01		1
Incumbent President	.001	.01				2
Incumbent Governor			.05	.05	.01	3
Mayor of Los Angeles	.01	.05	.001		.01	4
City		.001	.05			2
State		.001	.001	.05		3
Energy Crisis		.05				1
Watergate						0
Judge						0
Milkman						0
# of Symbols in Index	4 (5)	11 (6)	9 (8)	9 (8)	7 (8)	40/100

[a]Each of these map items is also a part of the Symbols Index. Annually, they represent a decreasing part of the index. If they are eliminated from consideration, still 26 of the remaining 85 comparisons are significant.

symbols that the children can identify with most easily, for example, simple virtues, physical prowess, and even violence.*

The salience of politics and government in the lives of young elementary school children remains quite low. In all five years many children made references to having "heard" of something "on the news," particularly when they were unable to offer a more substantive comment. Without threshold understandings or a cognitive structure by which to interpret and make meaningful passing media references to political phenomena, children appear to gain only an "extensive acquaintance" with what Connell calls "the phenomenal surface of politics."[8] It takes skill and persistence on the part of parents and teachers to increase substantive awareness before a child has matured to the point where abstract understandings such as the various levels of government and the distinction between public and private functions are possible.

NONDEMOGRAPHIC EXPLANATIONS FOR POLITICAL KNOWLEDGE

If the demographic and agent-related explanations for political knowledge are less satisfying than anticipated, do critical cognitive understandings provide a better explanation for how and why general political awareness increases? More specifically, do certain cognitive variables correlate better than others with the 20 map items? Do some correlate better in particular grade levels than others, and, if so, why? Are these variables precursors of clusters of new political understandings, the culmination of a widened political awareness, or simply more consistent correlates with broadened knowledge of political processes? Wide variations in the correlation between certain cognitive variables and map items would suggest that those cognitions with the highest correlations at particular grade levels may be thresholds leading to increased understanding of the political domain.

In order to achieve a meaningful understanding in any domain of human knowledge, the individual must first grasp a certain number of organizing concepts that provide a framework within which to place additional information. We believe that the political

---

*When the question, "Tell me something about Abraham Lincoln," was asked for the first time at the end of the third grade, the most common single response referred to his "being shot."

concepts we have posited as threshold variables constitute such an organizing framework for the young child's understanding of politics. The existence of such an evolving cognitive framework would appear to support the applicability of the Piagetian developmental hypothesis to the realm of government and politics. Furthermore, the systematic introduction of these key understandings by educators at appropriate grade levels may stimulate and thereby accelerate a child's civic awareness. Early presentation of critical notions about politics may in the long run help our democratic society to overcome the widespread apathy concerning public affairs that has been noted by many observers.

Our analysis hypothesized and confirmed that four threshold cognitive variables have explanatory power during kindergarten and first grades: knowing something government does, something the President does, something about taxes, and something about the electoral process (see Table 5.4). Electoral process correlates substantially better than the others with the cognitive map (see Table 5.5). Indeed, among these four threshold variables, as well as the three added in second and third grades—understanding the role of Congress, the Supreme Court, and senator, this variable has the highest proportion of statistically significant correlations with the map items across all five years. The taxes variable has the second best pattern. In fact, all the threshold items considered here have significant correlations with the cognitive map in at least one-quarter of the possible comparisons except for the President and Supreme Court variables, and even these two have proportionately almost twice as many significant correlations as did sex, the second most useful of the traditional demographic variables. In at least 60 percent of the total possible comparisons, all seven variables consistently follow the expected pattern in their relationship with the cognitive map items, that is, increasing knowledgeability on cognitive map items coresponds with progressively higher stage attainment on threshold varibles (see Table 5.4). This means that each threshold variable correlates more consistently with the cognitive map than any demographic variable used in this study except estimated academic rank.*

---

*When the nine threshold variables are combined to produce the Political Understanding Index, this index correlates at the statistically significant level over 20 percent more frequently than the estimated academic rank variable with the 84 questionnaire items for which a correct-incorrect response can be obtained.

TABLE 5.4
Knowledgeability on Twenty Cognitive Map Items by Levels with Seven Threshold Variables

	Kindergarten		First Grade		Second Grade		Third Grade			Fourth Grade		
	Unst.	Staged	Unst.	Staged	Unst.	Staged	Unst.	Lev-1[b]	Lev-2	Unst.	Lev-1	Lev-2
President Do?												
No. of 20 map items on which most knowledgeable[a]	6	10	1	17	2	18	0	4	16	1	2	13
Average percentage of those knowing map items	32	35	37	44	47	55	57	62	69	65	70	77
Government Do?												
No. of 20 map items on which most knowledgeable[a]	6	13	1	18	0	18	1	1	18	1	1	17
Average percentage of those knowing map items	31	37	37	45	46	56	56	60	69	65	69	75

TABLE 5.4 (continued)

	Kindergarten		First Grade		Second Grade		Third Grade			Fourth Grade		
	Unst.	Staged	Unst.	Staged	Unst.	Staged	Unst.	Lev-1[b]	Lev-2	Unst.	Lev-1	Lev-2
Taxes												
No. of 20 map items on which most knowledgeable	1	15	1	18	0	19	1	4	14	2	1	13
Average percentage of those knowing map items	32	39	35	49	41	57	56	63	68	54	69	74
Electoral Process												
No. of 20 map items on which most knowledgeable	4	14	1	17	0	19	0	3	15	5	2	9
Average percentage of those knowing map items					42	55	51	59	64	50	67	70
Congress												
No. of 20 map items on which most knowledgeable					0	20	0	3	15	0	3	13

Average percentage of those knowing map items							
49	62	58	67	73	67	74	79
Supreme Court							
No. of 20 map items on which most knowledgeable							
1	18	1	2	17	0	3	13
Average percentage of those knowing map items							
50	56	59	67	73	67	75	85
Senator							
No. of 20 map items on which most knowledgeable							
		1	1	16	0	1	15
Average percentage of those knowing map items							
		59	69	81	68	75	84

[a]Ties are excluded.
[b]Abbreviation for Level I.

141

TABLE 5.5
Statistically Significant Correlations Between Threshold Cogniti[ve] Variables and Twenty Cognitive Map Items[a]

	President Do?					Government Do?					What are taxes?			
	K	1	2	3	4	K	1	2	3	4	K	1	2	3
Country										*		*	*	
Washington										*				
Stat. of Liberty	*									*		*	*	
Nat'l Capitol														
King						*						*		
Law		*	*			*	*				*	*	*	*
Election			*	*			*				*	*	*	*
Politician			*	*			*	*						
Taxes			*				*							
Policeman			*											
Soldier			*			*	*			*		*	*	*
President	*	*	*				*	*				*	*	
Governor			*				*	*	*	*			*	
Bradley				*			*	*				*		
State						*	*		*			*	*	
City		*										*	*	
Energy Crisis		*						*					*	
Watergate			*					*	*					
Judge		*	*											
Milkman		*					*	*						
Totals by year	1	6	8	4	3	3	8	7	4	7	2	9	11	3

[a]In third and fourth grades many items were known by more than 90 percent o[f] panel—reducing variability and the number of statistically significant relationships (see T[able] 4.1 and the footnote to Table 5.6). The Judge and Policeman items are particularly aff[ected] by this lack of variability.

	Electoral Process				Congress			Supreme Court			Senator		Totals
K	1	2	3	4	2	3	4	2	3	4	3	4	
*	*	*	*	*			*					*	11
		*		*									4
	*	*	*			*							9
	*				*				*	*	*	*	7
	*	*											4
	*	*		*									12
					*		*						11
		*		*	*	*	*	*		*	*	*	13
	*	*			*							*	6
	*												2
*	*	*				*							13
	*	*	*	*			*						12
	*	*	*	*	*	*	*				*	*	15
	*					*	*		*	*	*	*	11
	*	*											7
	*	*	*	*									7
*								*					5
								*	*				5
				*									3
								*					4
3	13	12	5	8	5	5	6	2	4	5	4	6	161

Two additional cognitive variables—knowledge about political parties and what politicians do—reached 12 and 10 percent levels of knowledgeability in fourth grade and therefore may become more useful as predictors of general political awareness in the later elementary grades. Political party already has five statistically significant correlations with the 20 map items in fourth grade; politician has three.*

In which categories of political knowledge do the nine threshold understandings appear to be the keys to broader civic awareness? The electoral process variable is particularly useful in predicting knowledge of political geography, especially knowledge of country and city, and also an awareness of who the incumbent President and governor are (see Table 5.5). We believe that the ability to respond accurately to the electoral process questions gives a child the capacity to focus on both the political authorities competing in election campaigns and the units of political geography in which these campaigns occur. In this respect these children are reflective of the larger society's preoccupation with what has been referred to as the "horse race" aspect of our electoral system promoted by the media. We found many youngsters eager to tell us which candidate they hoped would win the next election or how much better things would be if their favorite had prevailed in the last one. This pattern is also consistent with the tendency of young children to personalize politics and to focus on individual authorities whom they believe are responsible for a "pool" of public tasks.

Knowing what taxes are is appropriately most predictive of three map items: knowing what an election is, what a law is, and what a soldier does. These high correlations may in part be reflective of the long-standing public concern over high taxes and the repeated requests for voters to approve bond issues and sales tax increases. When our panel was in fourth grade, this concern surfaced with

---

*We selected the nine variables because we hypothesized that they were not only crucial elements in our political system but were also keys to broader political understanding. The latter hypothesis was confirmed when we correlated them with the cognitive map. Six other variables were assumed not to have the same threshold quality, and by cross-tabulating them with the map items, they were found to be much less predictive of other political knowledge: "Who is the boss of the country?", "What do policemen do?", "What do soldiers do?", "Tell me about the energy crisis", What does a judge do?", and "What is a court?"

special prominence in the form of Proposition 13, a measure designed to reduce property taxes. The 1978 June primary in California was dominated by arguments over this initiative. The campaign entered the classroom in very direct ways; some youngsters mentioned the possibility that their teachers might lose their jobs and that the quality of education would decline if the proposition passed. Furthermore, many children seemed extraordinarily conscious of their parents' obligation to pay taxes because it is the law to do so and because their schools and teachers as well as the country's security depend on taxes.

Knowledge of Congress tends to be predictive of knowledge about such closely related phenomena as elections and politicians as well as who Governor Brown and Mayor Bradley are. These correlations again demonstrate the linkage between elective offices and the political authorities who hold them. It stands to reason that a child who knows about Congress, an institution composed of elected politicians, would also be aware of elections, politicians, and the two leading chief executives in the state of California.

By examining the individually staged threshold variables, we can determine that different political cognitions are of greater utility in predicting a child's level of political knowledge at different times during his or her development. Since the percentages of correct responses to the map items by kindergarten children are so low, the probability that any of the four threshold variables would be statistically predictive of general political knowledge that year is greatly reduced. Therefore, it is not surprising that none of the threshold variables is predictive of knowledge concerning more than three map items at a statistically significant level, although the overall pattern of relationships is positive. In first and second grades knowledge of the electoral process is the best predictor of cognitive map items, followed by the taxes variable (see Table 5.5). None of the seven threshold variables used at the end of third grade is a dependable predictor of general political knowledge. This is the case primarily because the variability of the responses to the map items is depressed, without an accompanying increase in the distribution of children between Level I and Level II on the Political Understanding Index (PUI). The number of map questions with 84 percent or higher correct responses increased from two to nine between second and third grade. (See the note a to Table 5.6.) At the end of fourth grade three variables—the electoral process, taxes, and government—partially reestablish their predictive capacity. This

TABLE 5.6
Statistically Significant Relationships Between the Political Understanding Index and the Cognitive Map Items[a]

| | Grade Levels | | | | | No. Years |
	K	1	2	3	4	Significant
National Community						
George Washington						0
Statue of Liberty		.001	.001		.001	3
National Capitol				.05		1
Governmental Regime						
King of the U.S.?		.05	.001			2
What is a law?	.01	.001	.001		.05	4
What is election?		.001	.001	.001	.05	4
Politician?			.001	.001	.001	3
Taxes?	.01	.001	.001	.001	.01	5
Policemen do?		.001				1
Soldier do?	.05	.001	.01	.05	.01	5
Authorities						
Incumbent President		.05	.001	.001		3
Incumbent Governor			.01	.001	.001	3
Mayor of L. A.		.001		.001	.01	3
Political Geography						
Name of country		.01	.01		.01	3
Name of state	.001	.001	.01			3
Name of city	.05	.01	.001			3
Public Issues						
Energy crisis		.05	.05		.05	3
Watergate	.01		.01	.05	.01	4
Public/Private						
Judge			.01			1
Milkman		.05				1
Totals by Grade	7	14	15	8	11	55/100

[a]The number of statistically significant correlations between the PUI and the cognitive map is severely reduced in third and fourth grades because of the number of map items having more than 84 percent correct responses. In second grade one of the two items over 84 percent is not significant, and in third and fourth grades 18 of 21 items *above* 84 percent are not significant when cross-tabulated with the PUI. In contrast, during these three years, 31 out of the 39 comparisons where knowledgeability is *below* 84 percent are statistically significant.

resurgence is in large part explained by the fact that on the average 37 percent of the panel attained Level II on these particular questions by the end of fourth grade, as compared with only 14 percent at Level II at the end of third grade (see Table 4.9). There was not a corresponding resurgence in the predictive power of the presidential duties question, because only 11 percent of the panel moved to Level II on this threshold cognitive variable.

In sum, the progression of the young child's growing political awareness appears to move from an initial grasp of several very general kinds of political phenomena, for example, what government and the President do and what taxes and elections are, to less visible but highly authoritative and very permanent institutions, the Congress and the Supreme Court. In fourth grade some children are beginning to gain an understanding of such contentious and even transitory political institutions and figures as political parties and politicians. This latter awareness may signal the beginning of the school child's appreciation for the pluralistic as opposed to the more monistic or strictly authoritative features of an open and democratic political system.*

Table 5.6 shows across all five years the extent to which knowledgeability on each of the 20 map items correlates significantly with our PUI. The two cognitive map questions having statistically significant correlations with the PUI in all five years are regime-related items: "What does a soldier do?" and "What are taxes?" The three map items with the next best patterns of correlation, significant in four out of five years, are two additional regime items: "What is an election?" and "What is a law?" and one public issue, "Tell me something about Watergate."** Beyond these five cognitive map items, there are a total of nine that have significant correlations with the PUI in three of the five years. Thus, 14 of the 20 map items are statistically correlated with this index at a significant level in at least three years. All except one of the six categories of political objects (the distinction between public and

---

*Factor analysis indicates that Congress and the Supreme Court in third and fourth grades form the foundation for one factor suggesting a unifying and unchanging authority, while political parties and politician, beginning in fourth grade, form the basis for a different factor, one that seems to focus on pluralistic and transitory values or concerns.

**Although the taxes, election, and politician map items are also contained in the Political Understanding Index, they represent a decreasing portion of that composite scale over the five years.

private sector occupations) are represented among these fourteen questions: five of the seven regime items, all three political authorities, one of the three items associated with the national community, the two public issues, and all three political geography questions. With the exception of national community symbols* and the public/private distinction, all these categories have between 60 and 70 percent of the possible comparisons statistically significant at the .05 level or higher. The distribution of correlation patterns between the PUI and the 20 items in the cognitive map suggests that in the components of this index we have identified appropriate politial phenomena to use in measuring a child's civic awareness. Indeed when the PUI is cross-tabulated with the 84 questionnaire items in the fourth-grade interview schedule for which correct or incorrect responses could be specified, nearly 70 percent involved statistically significant relationships.** The validity of the PUI is further supported by its statistically significant correlation with the Symbol Recognition Index during these years when most of the panel is still at Stage 1—Symbol Recognition.

The inability of demographic variables to explain variability in children's knowledge as measured by the PUI is confirmed by regression anlysis. Although estimated academic rank, sex, and news watching are the most accurate predictors of a child's placement on the PUI, in no instance did a single demographic variable account for more than 16 percent of the variance on the PUI. In fourth grade all five demographic variables combined account for only 25 percent of the variance. Regression analysis also indicates that over the five years the President and electoral process variables are the major determinants of placement on the PUI, followed by the government variable. In fourth grade, however, the Congress variable has the highest correlation with the PUI.

A significant question facing political socialization researchers is the extent to which the cognitive-developmental and the social learning perspectives are helpful in understanding growth in political awareness. Does one model have greater relevance than the

---

*The lack of statistical significance in this category is explained by the wide recognition of George Washington and the tendency to confuse the national Capitol and the White House.

**Many of the comparisons where statistical significance was not attained involved questionnaire items on which at least 90 percent of the responses were correct.

other in explaining variations in levels of knowledge among different types of political phenomena? As noted in Chapter 2, contemporary learning theorists usually acknowledge the influence of both external stimuli and internal maturation in varying degrees. Among the six categories of political objects in our map, regime-related items are those for which the cognitive-developmental hypothesis seems most appropriate, in large part because of their complexity and abstractness. In contrast with the regime items, identification of political authorities, public issues such as energy and Watergate, and even elements of political geography are much simpler and less abstract. These characteristics make it more likely that their understanding will be prompted to a greater extent by environmental stimuli and thus be closer to the social learning model of political education. These understandings, however, frequently involve a cognitive-developmental component.

Knowledge of public issues was found in the main to be a product of pupil exposure to parental and public discussions of these matters, particularly in the case of Vietnam and the energy crisis. With Watergate, however, the cognitive-developmental explanation has some relevance because the term involves such complex and abstract matters as partisan rivalry, allegations of corruption, and issues relating to public trust and integrity.

It would appear that a comprehensive theory of political learning must encompass both the social learning and cognitive-developmental models. Some understandings appear to be more closely related to one than the other. Frequently, however, there is a connection between the two. For example, earlier in this chapter it was noted that there had been an increase in the predictive potency of three of the four original threshold variables (elections, taxes, and government) but not the fourth (President) between third and fourth grades. Advocates of the two major learning theories take fundamentally different approaches to explaining why this partial resurgence occurred.

The social learning theorist would look to the character of the stimulus and perhaps especially to the selective exposure that children received to the Proposition 13 controversy, an election issue focusing on taxes and the high cost of certain government funtions. It did not, however, concern the President or his duties in any direct way. This theory would argue, therefore, that the variables relating to government, taxes, and the electoral process would become, to varying degrees, more salient as a result of reinforcement through stimuli in the classroom, the home, and the mass media. The relative influence of these socialization agents would, of course, vary from child to child. Therefore, these three cognitive variables would be better predictors of general political knowledge than the presidential duties question.

The cognitive-developmental hypothesis, on the other hand, would argue that only those children who had matured sufficiently in their cognitive capacities would be able to increase their political knowledge significantly during a given year. In this instance developmental advocates would note the greater variability between the percentages of children at Levels I and II in the case of three of the four original threshold cognitive variables. Because only 11 percent of the children achieved Level II on the President variable, while between 25 and 48 percent reached Level II on the other three threshold variables, the latter were understandably better at distinguishing between more and less knowledgeable children. This theory would stress that those children moving to a higher cognitive level would be better equipped to apprehend and assimilate such environmental stimuli as those produced by the Proposition 13 campaign and thereby increased their general political knowledge more effectively than those who remained at a lower cognitive level.

This latter explanation for the resurgence of three of the four threshold variables as potent predictors of political knowledge in fourth grade leads us to conclude that a composite theory of political learning is preferable to choosing between the social and developmental alternatives. Social learning, in this case exposure to the Proposition 13 stimulus, did indeed increase the political understanding of many children, but it was especially significant in increasing the general political knowledge of those who had achieved a higher level of cognitive capacity than the rest. In sum, those children who are at a more advanced stage of cognitive development assimilate more political information from their environment and thereby increase the variability among the panel members. This leads us to appreciate the fruitfulness of a composite theory of political learning that acknowledges both the role of developing cognitive capacities and systematic exposure to social and other environmental stimuli.

There is, however, one area in which neither model has yet been operative. The difference between public and private occupations is a distinction the children in our panel have failed to grasp. Indeed there is overwhelming evidence of regression. It would appear that the sociopolitical environment relating to this distinction is so complicated and confusing that cognitive maturation has not yet reached the point where the average elementary school child can distinguish consistently between those occupations normally associated with government and those that are not. Alternatively, it may well be that this distinction has not been emphasized by parents, teachers, or the public media.

From this analysis of which categories of political knowledge appear to be most closely associated with cognitive development and which are the product of social learning, it would appear that the children whose cognitive capabilities have matured earliest are, by virtue of that development, also better equipped to focus on and learn from environmental stimuli. Once children understand the meaning of election, for example, they are in a better position to begin retaining the names of candidates who are adversaries in a particular campaign. Once the principal functions of Congress are understood, then particular legislative proposals take on greater meaning for a youngster, and, if some of them involve tax matters, understanding that concept will give those measures even greater significance. In general, those political phenomena that involve a high level of abstraction, be they units of political geography or public policy issues, *are most easily grasped when a cognitive-developmental hurdle is surmounted at the same time that the child's immediate environment also contains relevant stimuli*. Countries are more easily recognized if they are engaged in well-publicized disputes or even attacking one another; energy shortages are more readily grasped when they produce domestic inconveniences such as long gas lines or parental warnings about lights being left on; a public scandal is more easily appreciated when it so preoccupies television as to disrupt regularly scheduled programming. In sum, when political phenomena involve abstract concepts, the learning process may require a significant step in cognitive development prior to the child's beginning to respond actively to social stimuli.

It is clear that students of political socialization do no yet have a unified theory of learning that will satisfactorily explain all or most of the products of this important process. What we appear to have is a better understanding of the ways in which cognitive maturation and environmental stimuli may work together in a complementary fashion to produce significant advances in political understanding. The extent to which educators generally, and curriculum planners and youth activity coordinators in particular, can begin to "orchestrate" these interactions between developmental stages and significant stimuli from the social and political environment is a question to be addressed in Chapter 8.

NOTES

1. G. David Garson, *Political Science Methods* (Boston: Holbrook Press, 1976), pp. 115–16; see also Donald T. Campbell and Julain C. Stanley, *Experimental and Quasi-Experimental Designs for Research* (Chicago: Rand McNally and Company, 1963), and Phillip J. Runkel and Joseph E. McGrath, *Research on Human Behavior: A Systematic Guide to Method* (New York: Holt, Rinehart and Winston, Inc., 1972), Chapters 2 and 3.

2. See notes 21–23, Chapter 2.

3. Jane S. Jaquette, *Women in Politics* (New York: John Wiley and Sons, 1974), p. xxxii.

4. R.B. Zajonc and G.B. Markus, "Birth Order and Intellectual Development," *Psychological Review* 82(1975): 74–88.

5. Charles Atkin and Walter Gantz, "Television News and Political Socialization," *Public Opinion Quarterly* (1978): 183–98.

6. Paul Lazarsfeld, et al., *The People's Choice*, 2nd ed. (New York: Columbia University Press, 1948), p. 151; Elihu Katz and Paul F. Lazarsfeld, *Personal Influence* (New York: The Free Press, 1955); see also, Everett Rogers and Floyd Shoemaker, *Communication of Innovation* (New York: The Free Press, 1971). Our finding of a very limited connection between the frequency of television news watching and political knowledgeability is consistent with previous research. For a discussion see Steven H. Chaffee, et al., "Mass Communication in Political Socialization," in Stanley Allen Renshon, ed., *Handbook of Political Socialization* (New York: The Free Press, 1977), p. 227f.

7. Previous research indicates that peers have little impact on levels of political knowledge and affect until after junior high. See Sara L. Silbiger, "Peers and Political Socialization," in Renshon, ed., *Handbook*, pp. 173, 179, 182f.

8. Quoted in Chaffee, et al., "Mass Communication in Political Socialization," p. 223.

6

Emerging
Sensitivity to
Law and Morality

The historic emphasis on the rule of law in U.S. society is symbolized by the assertion that "ours is a government of laws, not of men."[1] The elementary school classroom, in the emphasis it places on obeying rules, provides an early catalyst engendering a strong predisposition to comply with parent- and teacher-made rules as well as legislative enactments and court decisions.[2] Indeed, it is through governmentally developed laws that a society encourages and regulates. Law has the potential to inculcate those values preferred by influential decision makers.[3] The network of rules surrounding the maturing child regularly reinforces socially approved behavior while discouraging undesired activities. It is important, therefore, to examine what elementary school children know and how they feel about law-related phenomena. It becomes essential for students of political socialization to better understand when and how young children become aware of the law and the functionaries and processes associated with it.

The discussion in Chapter 4 indicates that, at least in the United States, knowledge of what a *law* is and what a *policeman* does develops in early childhood.[4] Young children are also surprisingly knowledgeable about what a *judge* does and the functions a *court* performs. By third grade approximately 90 percent of the children were able to offer a general description of what happens in a court and the basic duties of a judge. About one-fifth of these children associate a court with a judge, jury, or a trial setting (see Table 6.1). Another 20 percent clearly state that the court's role is to determine guilt or innocence. About 14 percent believe that a court serves a

TABLE 6.1
Perceptions of What a Court Is and What a Judge Does (in percentages)

	Grade Level	
	3	4
What is a court?		
Punitive, bad guys go there, pay fine	24.7	16.9
Adjudicative function—determine guilt	20.2	34.2
Associated with judge, jury, or trial	20.6	9.9
Inconsistent—been bad but go to determine if guilty	7.4	16.5
Facilitative—place for divorce, adoption, or dispute settlement	13.6	19.8
Other	4.9	0.8
DK	8.6	2.1
Total	100.0	100.2
What does a judge do?		
Determine guilt or innocence, right or wrong	23.0	33.3
Vague reference to court, trial, or judging	18.1	18.7
Problem solver, crime solver, helps people	16.5	17.3
Determines punishment or jail	12.3	13.6
Truth seeker, hears both sides	6.6	9.5
Other	10.3	4.1
DK	13.1	3.7
Total	99.9	100.2

facilitative function—it is a place for settlement of disputes, for divorces, and for adoptions:

> "A place where you settle things."

> "If somebody wants to have a divorce, they go there and the judge makes sure they know what they are doing."

> "A place where if you are adopted, you get to legally be a person."

Many of these responses seem to be the result of personal and peer experiences. One third-grade girl said, "My mother and father are going to court to have a divorce." A larger group, about 25 percent, believe that courts serve a punitive function—"bad guys" go there and punishment is assigned. Only half as many view this punishment function as the primary role of a judge. A slightly larger number (about 17 percent) see a judge as a problem solver, a crime solver, or one who helps people.

About 7 percent of the panel give responses that suggest, in effect, "if you aren't guilty, you wouldn't be in court." Some said that a court is where people who break laws come to defend themselves with a lawyer:

> "You go to court if you do something bad, they decide if you have to stay in jail longer."

> "When a person broke the law, they go to court to see if they are guilty—by hearing each side of the story."

One year later, as fourth-graders, more children assign an adjudicative or a facilitative role to the courts, and fewer conceive of the court as a punitive instrument. It would appear at this grade level that there is a clear division between those youngsters who focus on the impartial function of the judiciary as an arbiter acting without prejudice and other children who assume that people who go to court or appear before a judge are for the most part "bad people," guilty of some wrongdoing. The percentage of children who appear to believe that a court's role is to determine the guilt of "bad people" rises from 7 to 17 percent between third and fourth grade. It seems clear that there is a societal phenomenon that children pick up on that anyone brought before a court has ipso facto violated the law. It is possible that this general predisposition to believe that courts deal only with people who have broken the law will persist and undermine the premise of our judicial process that an accused person is innocent until proven guilty. If this were the case, it would make it even more difficult to find impartial jurors, could lead to harsher penalties, and even increase the likelihood that innocent persons will be convicted. It is also possible that a number of children, even as late as fourth grade, have not been made fully aware of the distinction between committing an illegal act and simply being accused of having done so. This is the case even though most children have themselves been wrongly accused by some adult authority of breaking a home or school rule. What is desirable, of course, is that both parents and teachers help young children distinguish between suspecting a person of wrongdoing and proving a rule or law was broken. Our data indicate that the early elementary grades are the time when most youngsters are ready to grasp this distinction.

Television is one source providing children with information about courts. This is vividly illustrated by one youngster who said that a court decides "Guilty—you're not guilty . . . sometimes a tie, six votes guilty, six not guilty; six took spray and six took stick." This perception of jury voting is influenced by viewing a television commercial extolling the virtues of two dispensers available with a leading deodorant.

The prominence of law-related concepts in the minds of young children suggests some important questions relating to the functioning of our political system. What are the implications of young children being more familiar with law-related referents than they are with other governmental institutions such as political parties or legislatures? Does knowledge of law, courts, and police foreshadow increasing knowledge about other specific areas of government during adolescence and adulthood? Is the level of a child's "legal knowledge" related to his or her feelings about politics generally? Is the cognition of and feelings about the importance of law in society a source of diffuse support for the regime?[5] Does "legal knowledge" develop in a stage-related sequence similar to the way Kohlberg believes that a moral orientation develops?[6] If this stage-type development does occur, what are the specific stages that a child passes through? Does movement to a higher "legal" stage correlate with changes in the child's perception of his or her own society in comparison with other societies?

This chapter begins with a discussion of how the young child views law. Then, to facilitate an analysis of stage-related questions, we explain how categories of legal knowledge and development were constructed. These categories (Stages and Levels) are similar to the stages of moral development employed by Lawrence Kohlberg and associates. The responses to six law-related questions are staged and their staged scores are combined to form a Law Understanding Index score. Scores on this Law Understanding Index are then correlated with demographic and key cognitive variables. Finally, a child's level of legal development is compared with his or her feelings about key aspects of the political process.

PERCEPTIONS OF LAW

Our findings reveal that despite their limited vocabulary, 46 percent of the kindergarten-aged children could offer an acceptable definition of a law—ranging from a generalized response such as "It is a rule," to a more concrete characterization, "A law means don't drive fast, no stealing, no escaping." Over the next four years the percentage of children capable of explaining the meaning of law grew to 76 percent in first grade, 85 percent in second grade, 94 percent in third grade and, by the end of fourth grade, 99 percent were able to offer an appropriate definition. The dramatic 30 percent increase between kindergarten and first grade in the ability to define a law seems to reflect the child's exposure to a series of school rules and their enforcement. This would appear to be an early instance of the "hidden curriculum" implicit in the relations and conditions prevailing in school classrooms.[7]

As kindergartners the children in our sample overwhelmingly viewed law as something that *prohibits* certain kinds of behavior: "It's something like if there is a red parking place, you can't pass a red light twice you have to go somewhere." Some believed laws perform a *prescriptive* function: "You have to do them." "Something like a rule you have to follow." None of the kindergarten children told us that laws serve a *beneficial* or *rational* purpose (see Table 6.2). By the end of third grade the percentage of prescriptive responses had grown rapidly and at the end of fourth grade a majority of the youngsters attributed a prescriptive function to laws (54 percent). Beneficial responses such as "Something that keeps the world

TABLE 6.2
Level of Response to "What Is a Law?" by Grade Level (in percentages)

Level of Response to "What Is a Law?"		Grade level				
		K	1	2	3	4
Level I—Prohibition		83	70	67	53	38
Level II—Prescriptive		17	29	28	41	54
Level III—Beneficial-rational		0	1	5	7	9
	Totals	100	100	100	100	101
	N =	(68)	(182)	(196)	(220)	(241)

organized" grew to 9 percent of the sample. Prohibitive characterizations of law decreased to about four in ten (38 percent). If, like Kohlberg, we consider the prohibitive responses to be Preconventional (Level I), prescriptive to be Conventional (Level II), and beneficial-rational to be Postconventional (Level III), our findings represent similar percentages of children at each level when compared with those found by Tapp and Kohlberg in their mid-1960s sample.[8]

Young children have been characterized by Ginsburg and Opper as believing that laws emanate from a prestigious source.[9] If this is true, then presumably young children should also have a high regard for laws. Indeed, kindergartners are most likely to identify police and religious authorities (God or Jesus) as those who make the law. Table 6.3 shows that at the end of first grade only half as many children felt these authorities were responsible for lawmaking, but three times as many now believed "the President" performed this role. Their perception of the President as the sole lawmaker reached its zenith during the third grade when 51 percent of the children implied that the President alone makes the laws. Their belief that the President is "the boss of the country" also grew

TABLE 6.3
Perceptions of "Who Makes the Laws?" by Grade Level (in percentages)

	Grade Level				
Who Makes the Laws?					
	K	1	2	3	4
Police	24	15	13	6	3
God or Jesus	15	5	2	1	0
President	11	28	43	51	38
Government	5	21	11	13	21
President Plus Others	0	2	3	7	17
Other Government Authorities	2	6	6	7	8
People/Representation Concept	0	0	1	2	4
Congress	0	0	2	1	2
Other	9	4	3	3	3
DK	34	16	14	7	4
NA	0	2	3	2	0
Total	100	99	101	100	100

rapidly during this period. Thus, many young children apparently attribute all governmental power, including the formulation of laws, to the chief executive. R. W. Connell uses the phrase "task pooling" to characterize the aggregation of political authority in a single entity.[10] By fourth grade only 38 percent of the sample implied that the President is the sole lawmaker, while 52 percent suggested that laws are the product of a collective decision-making process. This decline in the conception that the President is dominant in lawmaking and the increasing recognition that others are also involved parallels the findings in the eight-city study by Easton and Dennis completed in 1961.[11]

Several additional features of a child's perception of law change markedly during the elementary school years. The perception of the severity of punishment for a common act of lawbreaking, such as speeding, becomes more realistic as they grow older. When asked "If your mommy or daddy were speeding in their car and a policeman stopped them, what would happen to them?", the percentage who felt their parents would get a ticket increased from 77 percent in kindergarten to 92 percent by the end of second grade and remained at that level through fourth grade. Those believing that their parents would be sent to jail or arrested for speeding decreased from 15 percent in kindergarten to less than 1 percent in third and fourth grades. Greater awareness of the appropriate relationship between the seriousness of the offense and the severity of the punishment is accompanied by a strongly increased tendency (from 13 to 33 percent) to see the police officer as a helper or protector—promoter of public safety—rather than someone whose primary function is to catch law breakers—those who steal or murder—which declined from 55 to 31 percent between kindergarten and fourth grade.

We gain an important insight into the young child's beliefs about law and privilege when the responses to the parental speeding query are compared with a parallel question: "If the President were speeding in his car and a policeman stopped him, what would happen to him?" During kindergarten, first and second grades more than 20 percent of the children responded they did not know what would happen to the President in this situation. About 40 percent believed he would get a ticket (see Table 6.4). This is approximately half the number who said their parents would get a ticket for the same offense. We also noted that during kindergarten nearly 20 percent of the children felt the President would get arrested or be sent to jail but that this drops to 10 percent during first grade and

TABLE 6.4
Perceived Penalty for Presidential Speeding Violation (in percentages)

Responses to "If the President were speeding in his car and a policeman stopped him, what would happen to him?"	Grade Level				
	K	1	2	3	4
Get a Ticket	40	32	39	49	56
Go to Jail, Arrested	22	9	9	8	9
Can't be President	4	8	10	3	5
Nothing, He's President	7	17	13	11	13
Others and N/A	5	7	8	12	14
Don't Know	22	27	21	16	4
Totals	100	100	100	99	101

remains constant through fourth grade. Overall, however, as third- and fourth-graders, these children seem more aware than they were two or three years earlier that speeding is not an offense that warrants a severe penalty; 56 percent of the fourth-grade children believed the President would get a ticket if caught speeding. This is nearly 20 percent higher than a comparable response provided by Greenstein's 1969–70 sample of ten- to fourteen-year-old children.[12]

Nevertheless, many children believe that the President is not subject to the law in the same way parents are. Fourth-graders are 10 times more likely to believe that the President would be arrested or go to jail than that their parent would be similarly treated for the same offense. One child stated the President would "get arrested because *he* made the laws." Other pupils believe he would *lose his job* if he breaks the law. These responses included:

"He'd lose the presidency."

"Wouldn't be President anymore."

"Have to see the judge—six months jail—someone else to take his place."

These children evidently assumed that the President must be a model of civil obedience, adhering to an inviolable law under threat of losing his office as the penalty for its transgression. On the other hand, a larger number of children believe that *nothing* would happen to the President if he were caught speeding; indeed, they see him as above the law. Not only did several respond "Nothing," but others elaborated:

"He wouldn't get arrested because he is the President."

"Wouldn't get a ticket because he's President; the policeman would get fired."

From interviews conducted during the Watergate hearings in June 1973, Fred Greenstein notes that children at that time were more likely to believe the President would claim to be "above the law" when stopped by a police officer for speeding than were a comparable group of children whom he interviewed in 1970.[13] This would lead us to ask whether Watergate influenced perceptions of presidential equality before the law among children in our sample. Our data provide very limited support for this hypothesis. In the spring of 1975, soon after President Ford pardoned Nixon, over 17 percent of the children said nothing would happen to the President if he were caught speeding. Three years later this percentage remained at 13 percent. Among the 16 second-grade children who knew something about Watergate, 15 percent believed the President would no longer hold office if caught speeding while only 8 percent of the remaining children who knew nothing about Watergate believed he would be removed from office. One year later these percentage differences remained constant. However, at the end of fourth grade *none* of the children who knew about Watergate believed that the President would be removed from office if caught speeding. During each of these years the children unfamiliar with Watergate were slightly more likely to believe that *nothing* would happen to the President if he were caught speeding. These data suggest that Watergate had little impact on these children's conception of the penalty for presidential speeding. Rather, it seems that their growing awareness of the common penalty for a speeding offense governed an assessment of what penalty the President would receive.

Another feature of children's perceptions of law that changes markedly during the elementary school years concerns their view of citizenship. At the end of second grade when the question "What is a good citizen?" was asked for the first time, more than half the children provided very general answers: "Someone who does good things," "A good person." Fewer than 6 percent responded that a good citizen is a person who "obeys the laws." However, by the end of fourth grade, references to obeying the law grew to 37 percent of the panel, and they were more numerous than any other response. And, when the third- and fourth-grade pupils were asked, "Which is more important—to vote in an election or to obey the laws?", 92 percent said, "Obey the laws." Responses such as these provide evidence that obedience to law is engrained in the orientation of school children at a very early age and thus is a pervasive part of the political socialization process in the United States. The important socializing role of the school seems evident; this obedience-oriented view of citizen behavior is no doubt encouraged by the good citizenship awards given to those pupils who conform to the rules of the classroom. Fourth-grade children view the obligations of citizenship in nearly the same terms as adult members of society.[14] This relatively narrow, obedience-dominated approach to good citizenship introduced primarily by classroom teachers gives an early impetus to a model of political obligation that is more passive than it is active.

Finally, it can be noted that these fourth-grade children view law as the institution that protects people from danger and harm. Many see law as the instrument for avoiding violence and disorder. In response to the query, "What would happen if there were no laws?", 57 percent mentioned the likelihood of danger to persons and damage to property:

"People would steal a lot more."

"Cars would run into each other and people would get hurt."

Seventeen percent made a vague reference to "bad things" happening, but one-fifth of the sample asserted that widespread social disorder and even chaos would result from the absence of laws. They envision that:

"There would be murder all over the place."

"Everybody would get hurt and there would be nobody left."

"We would have an awful, littered, cruel, fighting country."

Without laws this 20 percent of our panel anticipate the probability of a Hobbesian world filled with a multitude of varied threats to persons and property. Indeed, some believe that life itself would not be possible without laws.*

What are the underlying causes of this impressive sensitivity to the role of law and the potential for lawlessness among these children of the 1970s? Such an explanatory quest must begin by noting long-term factors like the urbanizing trend of the past half-century and changing family patterns, as well as less authoritarian adult-child relations generally, and such more recent tendencies as the civil and student rights uprisings of the 1960s, the explosive growth of litigation,[15] and the prominence of law-related themes on television. Particularly during the prosperous decades that followed World War II, there was a gradual shift on the part of the great U.S. middle class away from economic "pocketbook" concerns in the direction of what might be termed "sociolegal" issues, including the rights of minorities, children, and deviates from mainstream life-styles. The mutually reinforcing tendencies in the classroom, in the home, and in the mass media—especially television—focusing on the rights of individuals and the protections against arbitrary authority and even majority pressures have created an intellectual and social climate in which younger and younger children become familiar with a wide range of legal matters, including not only traffic tickets, trials for burglars and murderers, but also the legal procedures leading to divorce or adoption.

The parents, as well as many of the teachers of children growing up in the 1970s, were themselves either participants in or close observers of the civil and student rights revolts of the 1960s. Some of them are now practicing in their homes and classrooms what they struggled with intellectually and emotionally a decade earlier during

---

*Further confirmation of the elementary school child's perception of the critical role of law in society is reflected in responses to the query, "If you were the boss of the whole country, what would you do to help people?" In fourth grade 14 percent said they would "make more laws."

their college and young adult years.* It is not surprising, therefore, that the young children of the 1970s have a keener and more detailed appreciation for law, individual rights, and legal processes. The tangle of demographic, economic, sociological, and psychic forces contributing to this revolution in the consciousness of law among youth cannot be sorted out with schematic or quantitative precision, but the consequences are nonetheless clear.

STAGES OF ORIENTATION TO LAW

Jean Piaget and Lawrence Kohlberg[16] have provided the basic theoretical orientation for studying the development of moral judgment and notions about law. Piaget's groundbreaking volume, *The Moral Judgment of the Child* (1932), suggests that a child's moral point of view consists of two stages. In the first stage a child is aware of rules and moral obligations, but they are not seen as mutually beneficial (Stage 2) until the child develops greater conceptual capacity.[17] Kohlberg's refinement of Piaget's scheme identified six stages of moral development: egocentric, reciprocal, social norm, system view, social contract, and universal moral principles.[18] We have used Kohlberg's scheme as the basis for constructing a six-stage hierarchy of orientation to law that we call the Law Understanding Index.

In attempting to characterize the changing orientation of young children toward law and to classify their responses to law-related questions in terms of the Law Understanding Index (hereafter referred to as LUI), this study uses answers to six questions. Two law-related questions were asked in kindergarten: "What is a law?" and "Who makes the laws?" A third was added in first grade: "Why do you like (or not like) laws?" In second and third grades, two

---

*This sensitivity to individual rights and due process of law may, on the surface, appear to conflict with the emphasis on the obedience-to-rules view of citizenship. However, the orderly classroom promoted by positive incentives to encourage good citizenship and one that emphasizes the rights of individual pupils need not be incompatible; both are built on a concept of law or rules. Indeed, a teacher who insists on a well-ordered learning environment may convey even more respect for the rights of students than another who prefers a more free-wheeling atmosphere. The latter could, on occasion, engage in rather arbitrary interventions to restrain pupils perceived as disturbing to others.

additional questions were used: "Why do we have laws?" and "Why are all the laws fair (or not fair)?" The latter was used as a follow-up to the query "Are all laws fair?" Finally, in fourth grade, a sixth law-related question was introduced: "What would happen if there were no laws?" In categorizing and staging responses to these questions, the researchers used four different criteria—scope of impact, type of impact, character of the formulation process, and implied primary goal of the legal system—each of which can be associated with particular questions used in the interview schedule (see Table 6.5). The most relevant criteria used in staging responses to the query "What is a law?", for example, are those which focus on two significant dimensions of law: (1) the scope of its impact, and (2) the type of impact it has on the citizen. Drawing on the work of Lawrence Kohlberg, we identified three distinct perceptions of the law's *scope of impact* on citizens and their community.[19] The first is the "egocentric" perception, which focuses on the way the law affects the respondent: "The law keeps *me* from getting killed or kidnapped." "The law says *I* can't be out after ten o'clock." The second is the "reciprocal" perception, which acknowledges that others may be affected by the law while continuing to emphasize the influence it has over the respondent. Reciprocal responses included: "The laws say kids can't drink beer." "Laws keep families like mine safe from robbers and murderers." The third perception is "system-wide"; it acknowledges that the laws affect the entire community or the whole society: "The laws keep our country running right." "So the country won't go berserk." Answers to "What is the law?" with an explicit or implicit egocentric focus are classified as Stage 1 responses; replies that acknowledge the reciprocal character of the legal system are defined as Stage 2 expressions; responses that clearly designate the broader community or the nation as the impact area for laws are classified as being either Stage 3 or higher, depending on the additional information concerning the *type* of impact the answer implies.

The answers provided for such questions as "Why do we have laws?" and "Why do you like (or not like) laws?" tend to focus on the *type of impact* that the legal system may have on an individual citizen or on an entire community. Very young children frequently focus on the law as an agency of physical protection or restriction: "It keeps me safe." "It stops me from jaywalking." Responses having this emphasis are viewed as charactersitic of Stage 1. If there is the implication that laws provide a more general kind of assistance-

TABLE 6.5
Orientations Toward Law

Level	Stage	Scope of Impact	Type of Impact	Character of the Formulation Process	Implied Primary Goal of the Legal System
		What is a law?	What is a law? Why do we have laws? Why do you like or not like laws?	Who makes the laws? Why are laws fair or unfair?	Why do we have laws? What would happen if there were no laws?
I Preconventional	[1] Egocentric	Egocentric (affects respondent exclusively)	Physical protection or restriction	Single (Unitary) lawmaking agency	Physical control
(Egocentric perception of the law)	[2] Reciprocal	Reciprocal (laws help others as well as me)	General assistance beyond the physical	Plural agent for lawmaking	Promotes helpful patterns of behavior
II Conventional	[3] System View	Community (or national) system-wide impact	Promotion of an orderly community	Major role for a representative body	Prevents disorder or breakdown of society

(Individual passively subordinate to the law)	4 Social Norm	Whole society	Teaches or guides the citizenry in behavior patterns suggested by the social norms	Accurate description of the role and relationship of two or more lawmaking agents	Promotes fairness and justice in society by educating as well as punishing
III Post-conventional	5 Social Contract	Whole society	An active process by which citizens help make laws as well as learn from them	Accurate description of major elements in lawmaking, giving their relative importance	Promotes a social contract involving active participation of broad community to build just society
(Individual as active shaper and reformer of the law)	6 Universal Legal Principles	Universal	Some citizens and groups seek to gain acceptance of universal principles by the community	Emphasizes the ideological assumptions underlying the influence of all major lawmaking agencies	To incorporate the principles of a higher law into the social contract and the consciousness of citizens

167

extending beyond the purely physical—as in responses such as "They help people" or "They help us live better," the answer is considered to be at Stage 2. If there is a clear implication that the respondent considers the law to be a vehicle for the promotion of an orderly community or a just and perhaps egalitarian society, the response is categorized as Stage 3 or perhaps higher. Stage 4 responses, which develop the "type of impact" dimension for the legal system, are those that emphasize the role of the law in teaching or guiding citizens toward approved behavior: "So we know what we are supposed to do." "They help us in a special way; when we don't know what to do, they tell us." We do not expect any of these young children to provide responses that are higher than Stage 4, but if they indicate that the citizens engaged in helping to make laws as well as learning from them, this would be viewed as Stage 5. Stage 6 replies would describe a process whereby citizens or groups of people attempt to gain community acceptance for universal legal principles.

Answers to the query "Who makes the laws?" as well as "Why are the laws fair (or unfair)?" focus on the character of the law *formulation* process within the political system. Those responses that indicate a single agency of lawmaking, for example, "the police" or "the President," are characterized as Stage 1 replies. If a vaguely defined plural agent is implied, as in the terms "government" or "state," the response is classified as Stage 2. If there is a clear indication that a representative body is involved in lawmaking, as in references to "Congress" or "representatives," the response is considered to be Stage 3. If a pupil gives a reasonably accurate description of a reciprocal interaction between the legislative, executive, and/or judicial roles in lawmaking, the response is classified as Stage 4. Although no children in our sample gave answers that were higher than Stage 4, we posit as characteristic of a Stage 5 or Stage 6 response some reference to the factors that frequently influence a lawmaking body, elements such as vested interests, community norms, or conceptions of a "higher" or natural law.

A fourth, more comprehensive criterion used in staging law-related questions focuses on the *implied primary goal* of the legal system. This dimension is expressed most frequently in replies to such questions as "Why do we have laws?" and "What would happen if there were no laws?" The criteria used for distinguishing the stages of legal awareness in this category are very similar to those used in staging responses addressing the "type of impact" dimension. Here again, Stage 1 responses emphasize physical control or physical protection (stopping jaywalking or preventing crashes, catching robbers or punishing murderers). Stage 2 responses imply that the primary goal of the legal system is to promote helpful and fair relationships among individuals (without suggesting a system-wide scope for this function). Those responses that address the system-wide scope of the law's impact in preventing general disorder, societal breakdown, or helping citizens achieve fairness or justice throughout the society are classified as Stage 3 or perhaps higher. If the respondent implies that the function of law is really to promote and enforce social norms or societal definitions of proper behavior, the response is viewed as being Stage 4. By the end of fourth grade no responses were higher than Stage 4. When, in the future, responses suggest that the law exists for the purpose of implementing community norms or to benefit powerful special interests, they will be considered at Stage 5. Any answers that stress that the law, in effect, exists to promote a particular view of life or a definite set of value assumptions would be Stage 6. A Stage 6 respondent might be expressing an awareness of the differences among a Marxist, a Calvinist, a Buddhist, or a Gandhian view of humanity, society, and the legal order. A keen awareness of differing social and ethical philosophies is, in fact, rare even among sophisticated adults.

Readers familiar with Kohlberg's typology will recognize that we have reversed Kohlberg's third and fourth stages. James Rest argues convincingly that, in measuring *moral development*, a system-wide view in which laws serve as a guide to the expectations of others within a larger community (Stage 4) is more encompassing and therefore an advancement over a perspective that requires face-to-face interactions to define rules for governing personal behavior (Stage 3).[20] We have concluded, however, that *legal development* proceeds in a different sequence. An examination of our panel's interview responses revealed that these children developed an awareness of the importance of "law and order" achieved by means of system-wide laws *before* having a conception of law as a vehicle that inculcates expected patterns of behavior. The reasons we posit for interchanging Stages 3 and 4 may explain why Kohlberg and Tapp were only able to use the broader levels but not the narrower stages of categorization when studying the concept of law.[21] We find it useful to conceptualize the young child's growing understanding of law as a progression from the individual outward to a broader and broader social context. Thus, a child would move from the Egocentric Stage where law is viewed as protecting him or her individually, to a Reciprocal Stage where law is believed to also protect family and friends from danger, to an even broader recognition that law protects the entire society from the lawbreaker. The perception that laws shape one's own behavior may be seen as a more advanced conception than the System Perspective. This fourth stage leads naturally to the next level where the citizen's own values make her or him an active shaper and reformer of the law.

The staging of children's responses to law-related questions provides a basis for testing several assumptions associated with the cognitive-developmental model of learning. This theory stresses the crucial role of maturation in defining the child's capacity to make moral judgements and to understand the role of laws and regulations. Kohlberg maintains that a child's progress through a series of fixed moral stages, which for the most part transcend cultural differences, is determined by the character and frequency of his or her social interactions.[22] Kohlberg also insists that movement from an initial lower stage to more advanced stages of morality represents an irreversible pattern of development.[23] Our adaptation of Kohlberg's stage-based schema enables us to test whether these assumptions are valid when applied to the development of a child's legal understanding.

In order to permit longitudinal comparison of the stages attained by an individual child over the five years of this investigation, the numerical total of the child's staged responses to the questions used was divided by the number of queries in the Law Understanding Index that year. Similar quotients for each year were then assigned to a similar stage score on the LUI. If this quotient was less than .50, the respondent was considered as unstaged. A quotient of .50 through 1.49 was scored as Stage 1, 1.50 through 2.49 as Stage 2, and 2.50 through 3.49 as Stage 3.

The data in Table 6.6 provide support for a sequence-of-stages model that describes the young child's maturing conception of the impact and purpose of law. More than 57 percent of the kindergartners were at the Egocentric (first) Stage of our developmental model, while not a single child could offer a Stage 3, System View, response. The proportion of children who were scored as Stage 1 reached a high of 75 percent during second grade and then diminished to 64 percent in third grade. By the end of fourth grade

TABLE 6.6
Stage Placement on Law Understanding Index by Grades (in percentages).

Placement on Law Understanding Index	Grade Level				
	K	1	2	3	4
Unstaged	38	23	15	3	0.4
Stage 1	57	73	75	64	30
Stage 2	4	3	7	30	69
Stage 3	0	0	0	0	1
NA	0	1	3	3	0
Total	99	100	100	100	100
Stage Average	.52	.80	.93	1.22	1.56
No. of Questions in the LUI	(2)	(3)	(5)	(5)	(6)

only 30 percent remained at this lowest stage in their orientation toward law. Reciprocal responses (Stage 2) rose from 4 percent in kindergarten to 69 percent by the end of fourth grade, while two children (1 percent) of the fourth grade sample moved to Stage 3 or System View. At the same time the number of pupils who remained unstaged decreased from a high of 38 percent in kindergarten to a single child at the end of fourth grade. This shift from more than 95 percent of the kindergartners being either unstageable or at the Egocentric Stage to over 70 percent of the fourth-grade children being at the Reciprocal or System View Stages represents dramatic support for a developmental hypothesis concerning the elementary school child's legal understanding.

The results of the longitudinal analysis also provide support for Kohlberg's claim that movement through these stages is progressive and irreversible. While 20 percent of the 243 children remained at the same stage across four years, 63 percent advanced one stage, 16 percent advanced two stages, and only two children "regressed." The average stage gain in growth between three of the four years was very similar; it measured .28 between kindergarten and first grade, .29 between second and third grade, and .34 between third and fourth grade. The gain between first and second grade was only .13 and perhaps reflected the frequent observation that for many children second grade is a time of consolidation of material presented in first grade rather than a year of significant cognitive simulation.* Although on the average 6 percent of the children regressed from the preceding year during each of the annual interviews, this may be accounted for in large part by the limited follow-up in response to the relatively brief answers many children gave to the questions comprising the Law Understanding Index.[24]

CORRELATES OF THE LAW UNDERSTANDING INDEX

Demographic

During kindergarten a child's ethnicity serves as the best demographic predictor of legal understanding. Anglo children are 24 percent more likely to be staged than are non-Anglo youngsters. This difference between Anglos and non-Anglos diminishes each year; the distinction between these groups in fourth grade is only 7 percent. The public school experience, insofar as it provides an orientation toward law, seems to serve as an assimilator of those middle-class minority youngsters attending Anglo-dominated schools.

During kindergarten oldest and only children are much more likely to be staged than are children who are youngest or who have older and younger siblings. Only children continue to be staged higher on the LUI throughout the remaining four years. After kindergarten, however, there is essentially no difference between the oldest, middle, and youngest children. As expected, youngsters who report they "often" watch the news on television are staged higher than those who seldom watch the news in the three years—second through fourth grades—when this information has been gathered. Boys are consistently more likely to be staged *and* to be staged higher on the LUI than girls. Table 6.7 reveals, however, that after second grade, differences between the sexes decline. Estimated academic rank, after first obtained in third grade, serves as the best predictor of legal development among these demographic variables.

---

*The increase from three to five questions in the LUI between first and second grade may also be an important contributor to the relatively smaller gain in legal understanding when compared with the three other years.

TABLE 6.7
Statistically Significant Relationships Between the Law Under-standing Index and Demographic and Staged Variables by Grade

	Grade Level				
	K	1	2	3	4
Demographic Variables[a]					
Sex	.05	.001	.001	ns	ns
Ethnic background	.05	.05	.05	ns	ns
Sibling pattern	ns	ns	ns	ns	ns
Newswatching			ns	ns	ns
Estimated academic rank				.05	.001
Staged Variables					
What are taxes?	.01	.001	.01	.01	.01
What does government do?	.05	.01	.001	.01	.001
What does the President do?	ns	.001	.05	.01	.001
Electoral process	ns	.001	.001	.05	.01
What is the Supreme Court?			ns	ns	.001
What is Congress?			ns	ns	.01
What is a Senator?				ns	.001
What is a political party?					.01
What does a politician do?					ns
Political Understanding Index	.01	.001	.001	.001	.001

[ns] The relationship is not statistically significant.

[a] Blank indicates information was not obtained or the variable was not staged.

To summarize, a child's ethnic background is the best predictor during kindergarten; the child's sex is most useful during first and second grades, while estimated academic rank is most reliable during grades three and four. This interpretation based upon percentage differences is supported by the results of stepwise regression analysis. Regression analysis also confirms the conclusion that demographic variables are weak predictors of a child's position on the LUI; on the average their combined explanatory power accounts for only 15 percent of the variance during these five years. Thus, we must look for other independent variables that will consistently differentiate pupils who are staged higher on the LUI from those youngsters who receive lower scores on this index.

Staged Threshold Variables

Although there is disagreement concerning the impact that intelligence has on moral development, scholars generally concur that intelligence *is related* to moral judgment and behavior.[25] Therefore, it is not surprising to find that in most comparisons, the stage a child reaches on the threshold cognitive variables serves as a more accurate predictor of the child's position on the LUI than do the demographic variables. In each of the five years the level of knowledge about what taxes are and what government does serves as a particularly accurate predictor of the child's position on the index (see Table 6.7). From first through fourth grades, understanding what the President does and how the electoral process functions serve as indicators of legal understanding, and during fourth grade, the level of information concerning what a senator is and what the Supreme Court does become very accurate predictors of a child's ranking on the LUI. As expected, in light of the above, there is a strong correlation between a child's ranking on the Political Understanding Index and his or her ranking on the Law Understanding Index in each of the five years: the higher the placement on the PUI, the higher the placement on the LUI.

In each of the five years, stepwise regression analysis reveals that the PUI variable is a more accurate predictor of a child's position on the LUI than are any of the demographic variables. In fact, in all except the fourth grade, this variable *alone* accounts for as much variance as all of the demographic variables combined. It is clear that knowledge of law is closely related to knowledge about other key features of the political process.

The Affective Realm

The preceding analysis has attempted to discover which demographic and cognitive variables are associated with various stages in the development of legal understanding. The following discussion employs the LUI to determine whether reaching a higher stage of legal understanding is associated with the way children *feel* about the political process.

Analysis indicates that placement on the LUI is related to a child's affective orientation toward the political process. Although the differences are often not statistically significant, the higher the stage of legal understanding attained, the more likely a child is to

TABLE 6.8

Statistically Significant Relationships Between the Law Understanding Index and Affect and Efficacy/Responsiveness Variables by Grade

	Grade Level				
	K	1	2	3	4
Regime Affect[a]					
Imagined encounter with a policeman	.05	ns	ns	ns	ns
Would you like to vote?	ns	ns	ns	ns	ns
Do you like laws?		.001	.01	.01	ns
Do you like government?		ns	ns	ns	ns
Is America the best country?		.05	.05	ns	ns
AFFECT INDEX	ns	.05	ns	ns	ns
Political Efficacy/Responsiveness					
Does the government listen to parents?			ns	ns	ns	.05
Would the government want to help you if you needed help?			ns	ns	ns
Why would you like to vote?			.01	ns	ns
When things in government are wrong, can we do anything?				ns	.01
Does government care what parents think?				.01	ns
If government makes a mistake, should you write a letter?				.05	.01
Does the government care about ordinary people?				ns	ns
EFFICACY/RESPONSIVENESS INDEX				ns	.01

[ns]The relationship is not statistically significant.
[a]Blank indicates information was not obtained.

respond positively when asked, "Do you like the government?" and "Would you like to vote?" The higher-staged children are much more likely to say that they "like laws"; knowledge about laws is positively associated with a favorable attitude toward them (see Table 6.8). When responding to the question, "If a policeman stopped to talk to you in front of your house, what do you think he would say?", a dramatic change occurs during the early elementary years. During kindergarten 75 percent of the higher-staged children are inclined to believe that the police would have something friendly to say to them. By contrast, 62 percent of the children who are unstaged believe the police might say something threatening. At the end of first grade, however, a majority of the unstaged children who provided a substantive response to this question now envision a friendly encounter with the police. By third and fourth grades, more than 80 percent of the lower-staged children anticipated the meeting with the police to be friendly. At the end of fourth grade, the percentage of higher-staged children who see the police encounter as friendly remains where it was at the end of kindergarten—75 percent. Thus, after second grade, the lower-staged children are more likely than the higher-staged youngsters to believe that the police will have something friendly to say to them.

The children who are staged higher on the LUI are more likely to believe that government is responsive to their needs and that they can influence governmental policy. Thus, the higher-staged pupils are more inclined to feel that the government cares about ordinary people like them, that government cares what their parents think, that ordinary people can do something about things that government does that are wrong, and that the government would help them if they needed help. An increasing number of children in each succeeding year provided conditional responses expressing other than "Yes," "No," or "Don't Know" replies. These "qualified" answers are usually supplied by the higher-staged children. Thus, as children view law from a societal, rather than an individualistic, perspective, they also come to realize that governmental responsiveness is not automatic; it is dependent upon the presence of certain conditions. The pattern described above is clearly exemplified by responses to another query, "Does the government listen to what your mom and dad say?" During first and second grades, the higher-staged children were more likely to respond "Yes" or to qualify their responses, than were children staged lower on the LUI. During third and fourth grades, lower-staged children were more likely to unequivocally say that the government listens to their parents than were the more knowledgeable youngsters. However, among the latter children, the percentage who gave a "qualified" positive response increased each year. The higher-staged children are also much more inclined to say that if the government makes a mistake, it is best to write a letter rather than do nothing. Finally, comparison of a child's position on the LUI with his or her score on the Efficacy/Responsiveness Index (discussed in Chapter 7) shows that a higher stage on the LUI is associated with a higher ranking on

TABLE 6.9

Percentage of Children Responding "No" to the Question "Is America the Best Country in the World?" by Stage on the Law Understanding Index

Grade	Stage On The Law Understanding Index		
	Unstaged	Stage 1	Stage 2
First	26	37	a
Second	22	28	a
Third	b	36	46
Fourth	b	34	43

[a]Only six first-graders and 16 second-graders were scored as Stage 2.

[b]Only seven third-grade children and one fourth-grade child were unstaged.

the Efficacy/Responsiveness Index. At the end of fourth grade, this relationship is statistically significant at the .01 level. Thus, a growing awareness of the scope, impact, and purpose of law is related to a growing sense of political efficacy and a belief that the government is responsive to citizen needs.

Is the movement among stages of orientation toward laws also related to an assessment of national "goodness?" An examination of the responses to the question "Is America the best country in the world?" shows that, in each year from first through fourth grade, those children at a higher stage of legal understanding are more inclined than those at a lower stage to respond that America is *not* necessarily the best country in the world (see Table 6.9). Although the differences are not large (ranging from 6 to 10 percent), the pattern is consistent. It would thus appear that as children begin to consider the interests of others in explaining the purpose, scope, and impact of law, they are also inclined to see that other nations may be as "good" as their own. If movement to higher stages of legal development promotes a more positive view of other nations, then concerted efforts to promote this growth may be an effective way of decreasing parochial attitudes and of increasing individual citizen sensitivity to cross-cultural and national diversity.

IMPLICATIONS

Several conclusions that are important for the functioning of a political sytem flow from these findings. In the first place an understanding of law and its role in society seems to be a central focus for a child's developing knowledge of the political system. Children know more about laws and key functionaries in the legal system than they know about other aspects of the governmental process. This understanding, however, is related to their knowledge of other features of the political process, as well as to their positive feelings about citizenship. Moreover, the degree of understanding concerning the role of law in society is positively related to the perceived responsiveness of government and to an ability of a citizen to influence its decisions and actions. Thus, an increasing understanding of law seems to provide the foundation both for a child's basic understanding of the political process and for an increasingly positive attitude toward it. If one desires to build more positive support for political institutions among the citizenry, the promotion of a fairer and a more just legal system is perhaps the way to initiate this effort.

Earlier in this chapter we reported that a higher stage on the Law Understanding Index corresponds with a less ethnocentric perception of the United States. The discovery that Stages 3 and 4 of legal development are a reversal of Kohlberg's corresponding stages of moral development provides the potential for encouraging children to modify their world view. The children's perception that law prevents social disorder develops prior to a realization that law serves an educational function—guiding the citizenry into patterns of behavior suggested by social norms. If educators appreciate this requence in a child's understanding of the role of law in society, they may then facilitate movement at an earlier age to the third and subsequently the fourth stage of legal development. If children can be "taught" to achieve a higher stage of moral development, as several researchers contend, similar efforts in the area of legal understanding might promote an earlier and deeper appreciation for other people and their cultures.[26] This intercultural sensitivity might then persist into adulthood and help diminish expressions of national parochialism.[27]

NOTES

1. John Schmidhauser notes this phenomenon in *The Supreme Court: Its Politics, Personalities, and Procedures* (New York: Holt, Rinehart and Winston, 1960), Chapter 1.

2. The significance of the concept of support is discussed by Walter Murphy, Joseph Tanenhaus, and Daniel Kastner in *Public Evaluations of Constitutional Courts, Alternative Explanations* (Beverly Hills: Sage Publications, 1973).

3. See Robert A. Dahl, *A Preface to Democratic Theory* (Chicago: University of Chicago Press, 1956), pp. 75–81.

4. See Table 4.1.

5. This concept is defined as the fundamental type of support that undergirds a political system. See David Easton and Jack Dennis, *Children in the Political System* (New York: McGraw-Hill, 1969), Chapter 3.

6. The moral development literature is summarized by Lawrence Kohlberg in "Development of Moral Character and Moral Ideology" in M. L. Hoffman and L. W. Hoffman eds., *Review of Child Development Research*, Vol. I (New York: Russell Sage Foundation, 1964), pp. 383–432. Kohlberg discusses the philosophic under-pinnings for moral stage theory in "From Is to Ought: How to Commit the Naturalistic Fallacy and Get Away With It in the Study of Moral Development," in T. Mischel, ed., *Cognitive Development and Epistemology* (New York: Academic Press, 1971), pp. 151–235. The theory of moral developmental stages is presented by Kohlberg in "Stage and Sequence: The Cognitive-Developmental Approach to Socialization," in D. A. Goslin, ed., *Handbook of Socialization Theory and Research* (Chicago: Rand McNally, 1969), pp. 347–480 and "Moral Stages and Moralization: The Cognitive-Developmental Approach," in T. Lickona, ed., *Moral Development and Behavior* (New York: Holt, Rinehart and Winston, 1976), pp. 31–53.

7. John J. Patrick, "Political Socialization and Political Education in Schools," in Stanley A. Renshon, ed., *Handbook of Political Socialization* (New York: The Free Press, 1977), pp. 204–206.

8. Kohlberg and others have found a relationship between legal development and moral development. See June Tapp and Lawrence Kohlberg, "Developing Senses of Law and Legal Justice," *Journal of Social Issues* 27(1971): 65–91. The perceptions of law we used here are those explicated by Kohlberg in Lickona.

9. Herbert Ginsburg and Sylvia Opper, *Piaget's Theory of Intellectual Development: An Introduction* (Englewood Cliffs, NJ: Prentice-Hall, 1969), Chapter 4.

10. R. W. Connell, *A Child's Construction of Politics* (Melbourne, Australia: Melbourne University Press, 1971), Chapter 2.

11. By fifth grade a majority of their sample believed that Congress was more responsible for making the laws than were the President or the Supreme Court. See Easton and Dennis, *Children in the Political System*, p. 119.

12. Fred I. Greenstein, "The Benevolent Leader Revisited: Children's Images of Political Leaders in Three Democracies," *American Political Science Review* 69 (December 1975): 1388.

13. Greenstein, "The Benevolent Leader," pp. 1393–97.

14. Lewis Bowman and G.R. Boynton, *Political Behavior and Public Opinion* (Englewood Cliffs, NJ: Prentice-Hall, 1974), pp. 205–207.

15. The United States has traditionally been regarded as a litigious society. Heightened use of this avenue of redress for grievances in the 1970s has been accompanied by a two-fold increase among members of the legal profession during that decade. See a report of the ABA summarized in the *Los Angeles Times*, Sunday August 8, 1981 (Section A17). See also A. E. Howard, "The Law: A Litigation Society," *The Wilson Quarterly* V(Summer 1981): 98–109.

16. The sixth volume of the series by Sohan Modgil and Celia Modgil is devoted to the works of Piaget and Kohlberg concerning the Cognitive-Developmental Approach to Morality. See *Piagetian Research: Compilation and Commentary* (Windsor: NFER Publishing Company Ltd, 1976). See also James Rest's development typologies in *Development in Judging Moral Issues* (Minneapolis: University of Minnesota Press, 1979), Chapter 1.

17. Jean Piaget, *The Moral Judgment of the Child* (New York: The Free Press, 1965). This work was originally published in 1932.

18. See Rest, *Development in Judging Moral Issues*, pp. 7–12; Modgil and Modgil, *Piagetian Research*, pp. 59–61; Lickona, *Moral Development and Behavior*, Chapter 2. Ronald Duska and Mariellen Whalan provide a simplified explanation of Kohlberg's stages in *Moral Development* (New York: Paulist Press, 1975), Chapter 11.

19. See Lickona, *Moral Development*.

20. Rest, *Development in Judging Moral Issues*, pp. 27–32.

21. Tapp and Kohlberg, *Journal of Social Issues*, pp. 71–79.

22. Lickona, *Moral Development and Behavior*, Chapter 2; Rest, *Development in Judging Moral Issues*, Chapter 1.

23. See Rest, *Development*. C.B. Holstein, using 53 upper-middle-class families, found that some regression occurred at the higher stages. The possibility that measurement error might account for this finding was advanced, however. See "Irreversible, Stepwise Sequence in the Development of Moral Development: A Longitudinal Study of Males and Females," *Child Development* 47: 51–61.

24. Ibid. We must remember that pupils are being forced into a stage. Although they may exhibit qualities of a lower stage of development, they are scored at a higher stage when the balance of responses tips the scale in the direction of the higher stage. Thus, measurement error could account for a substantial portion of the "regression" among these children.

25. Lickona, *Moral Development and Behavior*, Chapters 2, 3, 4, 12, and 17.

26. Kohlberg contends that children can be "aided" in moving to a higher stage of moral development when faced with the need to resolve a hypothetical moral dilemma.

27. Richard Wilson argues that the political socialization process can foster mature moral behavior. See "Political Socialization and Moral Development," *World Politics* XXXIII (January 1981): 153–77.

PART III

CONCLUSIONS

7

Political Knowledge and Political Feelings and Values: A Two-Way Street?

Political feelings, like political knowledge, appear to be learned as a result of both maturational processes and interaction with environmental stimuli. However, psychological researchers are not in agreement regarding the connections between cognition, affective orientation, and behavior. Thoreson states that the connection between cognitive theories and behavioral change is largely unexplored, and, by implication, the connection between cognition and affect is in a similar state.[1] Albert Bandura, discussing the connection between external circumstances and individual achievement declares that the relation is reciprocal rather than unidirectional.[2] The exact nature of the reciprocal relation between cognition and affect is left unspecified, but elsewhere Bandura proposes that a person's behavior can be changed if an individual has the expectation that he or she can perform a given action.[3] Positive or negative expectations have important implications for much political behavior in a democratic polity.

Décarie in *The Development of Affect* reports that Piaget assumes a threefold relationship between mental and emotional development; they are inseparable, develop parallel to one another stage by stage, and they are interactive.[4]

For Piaget, cognition and affectivity are inseparable from one another and they are irreducible one to the other: "There are not affective behaviors and cognitive behaviors: they are always both at the same time. These two characteristics become distinct only through analysis since abstraction permits a study of their respective mechanisms

whereas in reality both aspects are present simultaneously."[5]

Décarie proceeds to declare that if cognition and affect are
inseparable, then

it is a pseudoproblem to ask which comes first or which
causes which. One aspect does not produce the other, nor
is one aspect anterior to the other; rather, they are both
complementary, since neither can functionally exist without the other.[6]

Using Piaget's emphasis on the "intricate interactions" between
affectivity and intelligence, we will accept as a working hypothesis
that there is a strong linkage between affect and cognition and will
proceed to explore the relationship between greater and lesser
political knowledge and greater or lesser positive affect and efficacy
among young children.

It is not appropriate, however, to designate certain political
feelings as being more accurate or "correct" than others. Some, of
course, like tolerance, may be especially helpful or harmful in a
particular system trying to promote certain values, such as individual liberty or group discipline. Because political feelings must be
evaluated in the light of the goals of a particular system or subgroup
within a system, it is not useful to posit any general theory of
political affect based on a single hierarchy of stages or levels. It does
seem important, however, to measure whatever correlations may
exist between a higher or lower level of political knowledge, on one
hand, and positive or negative feelings toward selected political
phenomena, on the other. The following discussion, therefore, will
not focus so much on the processes by which political feelings are
acquired as on the connections between positive, neutral, or
negative affect and knowledge of the political realm.

It is essential, moreover, that students of political socialization
acknowledge the critical importance generalized positive feelings
toward the basic institutions and processes of the regime have for
political stability in every national community, whether democratic
or authoritarian. Greenstein was one of the first political scientists to
argue that the very early years of a child's life provide the foundation
for an orientation toward political institutions in the adult years.[7]
This early orientation may be extremely important because David
Easton reminds us that, in order to remain viable, every political

system requires a minimum level of generalized positive affect or "diffuse support."[8]

In this study we have attempted to address the following questions concerning political affect: What connection is there between knowledge of public affairs and the political feelings of our panel? Are positive or negative feelings toward the political process associated with any particular demographic characteristics? Do the children in our panel have a high level of diffuse support for our political system? If so, in what ways is it expressed? Does the level of diffuse support increase or diminish during the elementary school years? Do children assume their opinions are heard, or are they inclined to believe that political authorities will ignore their preferences? If the government did something wrong, would they take action to correct the situation, or would they feel powerless? If they requested aid from the government, do they believe it would respond positively, or would their appeal for help be ignored? Is the highly visible local police officer viewed as friendly or threatening?

Beginning in second grade the children were asked: "Why would you like to vote?" Typical responses included:

"It would be fun."

"I don't like Carter—want a different President."

"I think kids should have their rights too. They should have their rights to vote."

"It tells that you took part in our country's needs."

"When not enough people vote and they get somebody I don't care for, I'd like to vote and help."

"I'd vote for the President who is the best—who I can trust."

"Because it will make the people you are voting for happier if you vote for them."

"Because it gives you a choice."

Some indicated they didn't want to vote:

"I don't know which President to pick—don't know who's best."

"I don't think it would be very fun. Too many papers to fill out."

"Have to think who to vote for. It would be a hard decision."

"Don't like it. Every time I lose."

Will the children who tell us that they want to vote actually go to the polls when they become adults? If so, the United States will experience a revolution in electoral behavior when these children reach voting age. Eighty-four percent of our fourth-graders say they want to vote, and the primary reason is because they want to have a choice in selecting the President or some other elected official. In fact, a surprising number make forceful comments against the injustice of the minimum age requirement for voting: "He's our President, too. We should have a choice." If we accept Bandura's contention concerning the efficacy of expectations, then these positive expectations on the part of these children, if maintained, have important implications for their future participation in our democratic system.

INDICES OF AFFECT AND EFFICACY/RESPONSIVENESS

In order to explore systematically the emerging attitudes of our panel toward various political objects and relationships, we asked six affect-related questions in kindergarten and gradually expanded the interview schedule so that by fourth grade it included 23 affect queries (see Appendix A). These questions were designed to measure different dimensions of the child's feelings concerning the national community, the governmental regime, his or her political efficacy (the potency of the self as a political actor), and the government's responsiveness (the government as a potentially helpful resource). Attitudes concerning the national community were determined by responses to "Is America the best country in the world?" and "What makes you most proud to be an American?" Regime affect was based on responses to "Do you like government?", "Do you like laws?", "Would you like to vote?", and "If you were playing in front of your house and a policeman stopped to talk to you, what do you think he would say?" In order to obtain a composite picture of an individual child's feelings about the national community and elements of the political regime, we devised an

Affect Index composed of the student responses to five of these six questions.* The responses of pupils were coded as *positive* (replies of "yes" except in the case of a friendly meeting with a policeman), and *negative* ("no" or an unfriendly encounter with the police). A total affect score, which could range from a positive five if all responses were positive to a negative five if all responses were negative, was obtained for each child; a qualified response was coded as a zero.** For purposes of analysis the children are grouped into four categories of positive responses (positive and extremely positive). Only one negative category is used because so few children were · scored below the neutral category. This Affect Index is available for first through fourth grades.

Because political efficacy and governmental responsiveness are complementary dimensions of the same political relationship between the citizen and the government, they have been consolidated into a single Efficacy/Responsiveness Index. This index is available for third and fourth grades and is obtained by cumulating the responses that were clearly positive (efficacious/responsive) or negative (nonefficacious/nonresponsive) for these five questions. Efficacy was determined by responses to:

1. "Do you think when things in government are wrong, people like us can do something about it?"
2. "If the government makes a mistake, should you write a letter to the government or just forget about it?"

Governmental responsiveness† was determined by:

---

*The question, "What makes you most proud to be an American?", did not yield any negative affect-related responses.

**Only two of the five questions ("Would you like to vote?" and "... what would a policeman say?") were asked in the kindergarten interview, but all were asked from first through fourth grades.

†Using the insight of George Balch, Jennings and Niemi distinguish between "internal" and "external" political efficacy. The former focuses on the respondent's feelings about his or her own ability to understand or influence the actions of government while the latter focuses on the likelihood that government will respond if the respondent does make some demand on it. We have considered it clearer to refer to the latter as "governmental responsiveness" rather than using the internal-

3. "Does the government listen to what your mom or dad say?"*
4. "Would the government want to help you if you needed help?"
5. "Do the people running the government care about ordinary people like us?"

PATTERNS OF AFFECT

Table 7.1 presents the changes in responses to the questions comprising the Affect and Efficacy/Responsiveness Indices over five years. It is immediately apparent that these children have positive feelings toward a variety of political phenomena: more than 80 percent of the fourth-graders want to vote and believe that the government "cares about ordinary people like us," three-quarters claim that they "like government" and "like laws," and nearly two-thirds think that the government would "want to help them if they needed help." In each year more than 90 percent said "yes," policemen are their friends. Among the four regime affect questions there is an average increase of 10 percent toward the positive between first and fourth grades. More than half of this gain is accounted for by the increasingly positive responses to "Would you like to vote?" These data suggest the presence among elementary school children of a high level of diffuse support for the political system—but it is not without qualification. During these years there is an average 6 percent *decrease* in positive responses to the efficacy/responsiveness queries. As they grow older, many of these youngsters begin to qualify their responses to these affect questions; for example, the percentage of qualified responses to "Does the government listen to what your mom or dad say?" increases from 6 percent in first grade to 33 percent in fourth grade. There are similar

---

external distinction suggested by Balch. See M. Kent Jennings and Richard G. Niemi, *Generations and Politics* (Princeton: Princeton University Press, 1981), pp. 409–10.

*The question "Does the government care much about what your mom and dad think?" was not used in constructing the Efficacy/Responsiveness Index because it measured essentially the same degree of responsiveness as this "does the government listen" query.

TABLE 7.1
Affect and Efficacy/Responsiveness Questions by Grade (in percentages)

				Grade			
Affect Index Questions		K	1	2	3	4	Increase/ Decrease
Is America the best country in the world?	Yes		48	49	30	30	−18
	No		33	26	39	40	+7
	Qualified		0	1	5	5	+5
	DK		17	21	26	25	+8
Do you like the government?	Yes		77	81	73	76	−1
	No		15	10	3	4	−11
	Qualified		3	3	3	1	−2
Do you like laws?	Yes		80	81	80	75	−5
	No		7	6	3	0.4	−6
	Qualified		4	6	14	23	+19
Would you like to vote?	Yes	64	74	77	77	84	+20
	No	9	13	10	7	7	−2
Imagined encounter with a neighborhood policeman.	Friendly	20	24	28	41	37	+17
	Unfriendly	12	17	17	13	24	+12
	DK	48	53	45	37	32	−16
Efficacy/Responsiveness Index Questions							
Does the government listen to what your mom and dad say?	Yes	54	50	47	53	42	−12
	No	15	27	18	15	10	−5
	Qualified		6	10	17	33	+27
Do you think when things in the government are wrong, people like us can do something about it?	Yes				64	57	−7
	No				14	14	0
	Qualified				12	19	+7·

(continued)

TABLE 7.1 (continued)

Efficacy/ Responsiveness Questions		K	1	2	3	4	Increase/ Decrease
					Grade		
If the government makes a mistake, should you write a letter to the government or forget it?	Write				43	48	+5
	Forget It				43	25	−18
	Qualified				7	22	+15
Would the government want to help you, if you needed help?	Yes			76	70	64	12
	No			7	2	4	−3
	Qualified			4	13	24	+20
Does the government care about ordinary people like us?	Yes				84	85	+1
	No				3	3	0
	Qualified				3	8	+5

though less dramatic increases in the percentage of qualified responses to the other efficacy/responsiveness questions. There is also a tendency for the children to feel increasingly positive toward government, while at the same time becoming less optimistic about its responsiveness and their ability to influence its performance.

This tendency is perhaps a reflection of the primary school child's optimistic predisposition toward public authorities and political participation, which is moderated by a progressively more realistic sense that government is *not* able to respond to the individual needs and concerns of all citizens. When asked "Would the government want to help you if you needed help?", many children responded with a query of their own: "Do you mean just me?" If told "yes," they often said something like "probably not, but if there were others, then maybe it would." Some of the children, then, recognized that matters of broad concern or widespread deprivation are more likely to elicit a response from government than isolated cases of individual need.*

Responses to the question *"Why* do you like (or not like) government?" offer additional evidence confirming the generally positive orientation the elementary school child expresses when he or she says, "Yes, I like the government." The perception that the government makes laws to help and protect people by promoting an orderly and fair society comes through clearly from the 76 percent who said they liked government. Typical responses include: "They try to help us," "They make laws," "It helps keep things fair," and "They keep things in order." A very small percentage are more specific: "I like the peace treaty they are trying to make [reference to the Camp David Accords] and what they are doing about the power shortage," and "When some country attacks, they have military services to protect us; and they don't rule us, we vote." But the norm among fourth-graders is to leave the rationale for liking government at a very high level of generality. Some simply say, "It (or he) is 'nice,' 'fair,' or 'does good things.'" A substantial portion of the children, even in fourth grade, personalize the government, either because they confuse "government" with "governor" or because they have a "task-pooling" conception of government involving a single in-dividual or a small group. It may well be that this personalizing of government contributes to the young child's feeling that it is a caring and responsive entity.

FEELINGS ABOUT THE UNITED STATES, AUTHORITIES, AND TAXES

In dramatic contrast with the generally positive tenor of responses to the regime affect queries, the question, "Is America the best country in the world?", evoked a sharply declining percentage of positive responses. There was an 18 percent drop in affirmative replies between first and fourth grades and a 7 percent increase in negative responses over this same period. In third and fourth grades

*The responses of these children appear to run counter to previous findings that seventh- and eighth-graders have unrealistic feelings of "personal clout." See Hess and Torney, *The Development of Political Attitudes in Children*, Chapter 4.

we were surprised to find that only 30 percent of our panel agreed that "America is the best country in the world." By this age, an impressive percentage of these children evidenced an awareness of the relativity of values, particularly when it comes to judging countries. When asked this evaluative question about the United States, some youngsters offered such answers as: "It depends on your point of view. There are lots of problems and crime everywhere," "It depends on where you live and what you think," and "You can't judge countries by their population or anything." It seems clear that by fourth grade a majority of the youngsters appreciated the difficulty of identifying any country or people as "the best in the world": "There are better countries than America, but no country is the best. They are all about the same," and "A country shouldn't be judged because each country has different customs, culture, and its own way of living."

This recognition that all communities have their strengths and weaknesses comes in part from the cross-cultural perspective that begins to emerge in the social studies curriculum during the elementary school years. The exposure to other cultures and peoples through television, which reinforces any firsthand experience children may have with immigrant families or through foreign travel, has a notable impact on their perceptions of other countries as well as of their own society. Television documentaries on crime,[9] delinquency, drugs, and abuse of public trust, reinforced by parental comments, no doubt contribute to such negative perceptions of the United States as:

"The streets are too dirty and it is too corrupted."

"We have rules that are not fair."

"Asia is pretty civilized. They bow down to their teachers there and we don't."

The four follow-up queries to our question, "Is America the best country in the world?", illustrate the panel's increasing ability to qualify judgments as well as developing a capacity for empathy. Five percent, for example, recognized that others may believe that their country is superior. But more importantly, our probes in this area provide evidence of what Sigel and Hoskin call "relative affect." This concept suggests an orientation to a political community that holds that, when compared with others, it is at least as deserving of affection as any other.[10] When the fourth-graders were asked "Do you like any other country better than ours?", 61 percent answered "no," while another 19 percent said they did not know. This is in contrast to the 30 percent who originally said the United States is the best country in the world. After eliminating the 7 percent of the panel who mistakenly declare that they like another state or city of the United States better than our country, there are only 12 percent who indicated a preference for another nation or continent. When asked "why," one-quarter of these youngsters indicated that their parents, relatives, or friends were from the preferred other nation. Nearly half gave an environmental response, indicating that the other country was more beautiful or had more interesting wildlife, especially when referring to Africa. When the remaining members of the panel were asked why they did not like another country better, relative affect was gain evidenced: one-third said they were unfamiliar with other countries, while another 7 percent liked it here because they are "used to" our country. Relative affect, which is in part based on the lack of familiarity with any alternative, is less supportive of a political community than positive affect, but still contributes to overall diffuse support.

Although most children are not inclined to offer either positive or negative judgments when asked by an interviewer to "tell me something about a political authority like Jimmy Carter or Gerald Ford," a very small number, approximately 10 percent, do offer some indication of their feelings about the incumbent President. These voluntary expressions of feeling are as likely to be negative as they are to be positive. Some fourth-graders offering their feelings about President Carter said:

"He helps the country."

"He is a fair President."

"He is trying his best to help the U.S."

"He ain't a very good President; he sold the Panama Canal."

"Some things he's good at and some not that good. We could have had that bomb to help us, but he said 'no.'"

"Yucky; I hate him."

Those expressing negative views are more likely than the positive students to offer specific reasons for their dislike of the President.

Their references to such issues as the neutron bomb and the Panama Canal Treaty suggest the likelihood that they have picked up their views from parents or perhaps outspoken classroom teachers. A few youngsters gave evidence of developing a pattern of distrust concerning political authorities. One fourth-grader offered the following in response to "tell me something about Jimmy Carter": "He's like Nixon, 'cause Nixon lied about Watergate. This guy Carter said he wouldn't sell the Panama Canal, but he did."

The taxing and policing powers of government affect the average citizen more than most others. Beginning in second grade we began probing the panel's affective orientation to taxes in terms of their "goodness" or "badness." Over the three years, those declaring that taxes are "bad" increased from 17 to 26 percent. Typical of the children who believe that taxes are bad is the following dialogue between a fourth-grade girl and the interviewer:

Q: What are taxes?

A: Taxes are extra money that you put on what you pay.

Q: What kinds of taxes are there?

A: Sales tax—in clothing, food; income tax.

Q: Why do people pay taxes?

A: Because they have to.

Q: Are taxes good or bad?

A: Bad.

Q: Why?

A: Because you are paying extra money.

Repeatedly, taxes were seen as "bad" because one is forced to pay "extra money"—perhaps more than he should—and usually this is associated with the sales tax, the revenue source children are most likely to encounter on a regular basis. It also seems clear that a majority of the children answering that taxes are "bad" have little or no conception of what taxes are used for. They are viewed simply and purely as an "extra payment" on top of the purchase price. When parents are mentioned in any responses to questions involving taxes, it is always that they do not like taxes; no children mentioned that their parents liked them. Representative of these responses is that of a fourth-grade girl: "I don't like giving money away. Sometimes they keep raising the taxes and my mom and dad get mad."

Fourth grade (1978) was the year in which two-thirds of the Californians who went to the polls approved the Jarvis Initiative limiting property taxes. Yet, 63 percent of our fourth-graders still maintained that taxes are either good (40 percent), or at least partially good (23 percent), because of the services they provide. One girl's responses are representative:

Q:	What are taxes?	**A:**	It's a certain amount of money you have to pay— that goes toward the government.
Q:	What kinds of taxes are there?	**A:**	Sales tax—each one dollar, six cents to government to help people. No food taxes.
Q:	Why do people pay taxes?	**A:**	Money that goes to government to help people—if they need jobs, food, clothes.
Q:	Are taxes good or bad?	**A:**	Good.
Q:	Why?	**A:**	They help people who need help.

THE KNOWLEDGE-AFFECT RELATIONSHIP

One of the primary questions to be addressed in the study of political affect is whether there is any correlation between feelings toward government, on the one hand, and the level of political knowledge an individual has on the other. Although we have cross-tabulated five political affect questions with children's scores on the Political Understanding Index (see Table 7.2), we have not been able to identify any consistent patterns between political knowledge and positive feelings toward government. On most of these five affect questions, in most of the years they were asked, the highest percentage of positive feelings (the "yes" responses) were in one of the top two categories of political understanding, but it is also true

TABLE 7.2
Political Affect Index Cross-tabulated with the Political Understanding Index (in percentages)

	Political Understanding Index Categories			
	Less Knowledge		More Knowledge	
	1	2	3	4
Is America the best country in the world? (Percentage of "Yes" responses)				
First Grade	48	52	47	48
Second Grade	51	47	55	50
Third Grade	16	34	30	50
Fourth Grade	29	30	33	22
Do you like government? (Percentage of "Yes" responses)				
First Grade	83	79	80	89
Second Grade	81	81	95	75
Third Grade	65	72	82	83
Fourth Grade	81	69	83	91
Do you like laws? (Percentage of "Yes" responses)				
First Grade	71	81	88	85
Second Grade	82	84	90	75
Third Grade	81	82	78	83
Fourth Grade	86	78	70	65
Would you like to vote? (Percentage of "Yes" responses)				
Kindergarten	71	80	81	a
First Grade	73	72	81	85
Second Grade	67	81	94	92
Third Grade	75	90	87	100
Fourth Grade	69	87	86	96

	Political Understanding Index Categories			
	Less Knowledge		More Knowledge	
	1	*2*	*3*	*4*
Imagined encounter with a neighborhood policeman. (Percentage of "friendly" encounters)				
Kindergarten	21	22	72	a
First Grade	21	29	26	23
Second Grade	20	25	39	50
Third Grade	62	28	44	51
Fourth Grade	29	55	43	44

[a] No kindergartners reached this level of knowledgeability on the PUI.

that the more knowledgeable the children were, the more likely they were to qualify these positive feelings.*

In response to our questions, "What makes you most proud to be an American?", the most politically knowledgeable pupils are also the most likely to give a substantive response with political implications. This pattern becomes more pronounced as the child moves through the elementary grades (see Table 7.3). Conversely, the least politically knowledgeable pupils have consistently been more likely to give extremely vague responses such as "It's nice," "It's pretty," or to answer, "Don't know." Substantive responses to the "What makes you most proud . . . " question tended to center predominantly around abstract concepts such as freedom or friendship, though some children specified material benefits such as cars, nice homes, new clothes, and good schools. It seems clear that

---

*The query "Do you like laws?" elicited a larger percentage of qualified responses in all years than did any of the other four affect questions. The "qualifiers" reached 23 percent in fourth grade, and their exclusion from the "yes" responses accounts for the inverse relationship between liking laws and political knowledge in that year (see Table 7.2).

TABLE 7.3
What Makes You Most Proud to be an American? (Percentage of Political Responses Cross-tabulated with Categories on the Political Understanding Index)

| | Political Understanding Index Categories | | | |
| | Less Knowledge | | More Knowledge | |
Grade Levels	1	2	3	4
First	17	22	29	33
Second	2	13	31	50
Third	2	16	40	50
Fourth	7	26	40	70

the political rhetoric about freedom (and the priority our society gives to material production and distribution) has reached at least one-third of these children by the midpoint in their elementary school careers.

Among the four questions used to measure regime affect, there is a marked difference between the pattern of responses to the police encounter question and the other three queries. This suggests to us that affect relating to the police officer may be heavily influenced by either personal or secondhand experiences.* Some children gave specific examples of situations in which they interacted with the police. There is virtually no consistent pattern between political knowledgeability and whether a child believes a chance encounter with a police officer is likely to be friendly or unfriendly (see Table 7.2). In kindergarten and second grade the more knowledgeable are more likely to envision a friendly encounter, but in first and third

---

*A content analysis of the qualities demonstrated in the portrayal of government officials in television programs and in children's literature suggests that law enforcement officials are among the most soothing, reassuring, comforting, and protecting of all public servants including teachers, hospital workers, and soldiers. See Thomas R. Marshall, "The Benevolent Bureaucrat: Political Authority in Children's Literature and Television," *The Western Political Quarterly* 34 (September 1981): 389–99. Because many of our children did not perceive a chance encounter with a police officer as likely to be friendly, we feel that this result suggests that children are perhaps more heavily influenced by first- and secondhand experiences involving the police than they are by the portrayal of police officers on television or in the books they read.

grades the pattern is unclear. The overall irregularity of the relationship between political knowledge and feelings concerning such a hypothetical meeting leads us to conclude that direct or indirect experiences are influencing respondents. Moreover, many of those who have had no contact with police officers apparently have difficulty imagining such an encounter. During kindergarten, first, and second grades approximately one-half of our panel responded that they did not know what the police officer might say.

On the other hand, a positive correlation between political knowledgeability and positive affect appears in each of the three remaining Affect Index questions. With few exceptions there is a general pattern wherein the more knowledgeable children are more likely to say "yes," they like government and "yes," they would like to vote. Likewise, in most years the less knowledgeable children are more likely to give a negative or "don't know" response. With respect to the question of whether a child likes laws, there appears to be a reversal of pattern between second and fourth grades. But this apparent reversal is in fact because the more knowledgeable a child becomes, the more likely he or she is to offer a qualified response to this query. Typical of the qualified responses are:

"Some of them aren't fair and some of them are."

"I like most laws because they keep order in the country. Some of the laws, like the Jarvis property tax limitation amendment, I don't like because of the possible loss of police and teachers."

"Most of them are helpful to us, but some are not really that good. I don't like the law about killing whales."

"I like some laws. The one I like best is against child abuse."

Responses such as these increased from 4 percent in first grade to 23 percent in fourth grade. This is further evidence supporting the conclusion that, as the young child becomes politically more knowledgeable, he or she is more likely to qualify responses to affect-related questions.[11]

When these individual affect queries were combined to form an Affect Index, this index showed very little correlation with political knowledge.* In part, this is because the members of the panel were so uniformly positive in their feelings toward government (see Table 7.4).** The individual scores on the composite Affect Index ranged from a positive five to a negative three. Each year between 18 and 32 percent of the children were extremely positive; that is, they had no negative responses to our five queries and no more than one qualified response. In all four years negative affect as measured by the index was 10 percent or less, and until fourth grade the combined neutral and negative responses together annually comprised about 15 percent of the panel. In fourth grade the percentage of children having a composite negative Affect Index score doubled to 10 percent, while an additional 13 percent were scored as neutral. Thus, in fourth grade almost one-quarter of the children are now scored as negative or neutral. However, this is perhaps not as much a growth in negativism regarding government as it is a heightened realism on the part of those children qualifying their responses to two of the affect queries (see Table 7.1). On the other hand, this tendency to qualify may be an intermediate step in the direction of adolescent and adult skepticism that has pervaded society in the United States over the last decade.

The increasing tendency of the more knowledgeable children to qualify their responses to affect questions represents a second explanation for the low correlation between the Affect Index and the Political Understanding Index. From second grade on a number of the most knowledgeable children are not in the highest affect category. This is true because qualified responses to affect questions were considered to be neutral affect (scored as a zero), and therefore some children as they become more knowledgeable have a tendency to qualify their responses and thus their Affect Index is scored less positively. These knowledgeable "qualifiers" cause the positive

---

*We considered several configurations that combined the negative and neutral children into a single category while varying the number of positive categories. Some of these categorizations result in more statistically significant relationships between affect and knowledgeability, but we believe that the four categories used in our index are most appropriate for two reasons: (1) negative affect is not the same as being neutral, and (2) the category containing all positive responses is conceptually separable from the category containing subjects giving one or more negative responses.

**The problem of the measurement of limited variability is discussed in detail by Robert Weissberg and Richard Joslyn, "Methodological Appropriateness..." in Renshon, ed., Handbook, pp. 53–58.

TABLE 7.4
Distribution of Affect Across Grade Levels (in percentages)

	Grade[b]			
Affect Variance	*1*	*2*	*3*	*4*
Negative[a]	3	5	5	10
Neutral	12	10	8	13
Positive	64	53	63	59
Extremely Positive	21	32	24	18
	99	100	100	100

[a] Because of the positive orientation of the panel all negative totals are combined into one category. All totals from +1 to +3 are in the positive category. The extremely positive category consists of those pupils who either gave all positive responses or only one neutral (qualified) response.

[b] Because only two affect queries were asked in kindergarten an Affect Index was not used in that year.

category to be on an average 4 percent more knowledgeable on the PUI than the extremely positive children.

Previous research has found that as children mature they become less positive toward the polity.[12] But the connection between variations in knowledge and this increasingly negative orientation is not clear. What we find in our study is that the generally positive attitude of the children toward the polity is found at all levels of political knowledge. This suggests the existence of widespread diffuse support among early elementary school children. If this basic orientation were to persist in later years, it would promote political system stability.

POLITICAL KNOWLEDGE AND EFFICACY/RESPONSIVENESS

Our data indicate the more politically knowledgeable a young child is, the more likely he or she is to have a strong sense of political efficacy and a greater propensity to become involved in political life. This linkage is supported by all except one of the five questions used in the Political Efficacy/Governmental Responsiveness Index (see Table 7.5). In third and fourth grades we used two efficacy queries: "If something in the government is wrong, can ordinary people like

TABLE 7.5

Political Efficacy/Governmental Responsiveness Questions Cross-tabulated with the Political Understanding Index (in percentages)

| | Political Understanding Index Categories | | | |
| | Less Knowledge | | More Knowledge | |
	1	2	3	4
Do you think, when things in the government are wrong, people like us can do something about it? (Percentage giving "Yes" or qualified responses)				
Third Grade	72	70	86	92
Fourth Grade	61	70	88	81
If the government makes a mistake, should you write a letter to the government or forget it? (Percentage responding "Should write a letter")				
Third Grade	24	52	51	74
Fourth Grade	41	74	83	82
Does the government listen to what your mom and dad say? (Percentage giving "Yes" or qualified responses)				
Kindergarten	54	70	81	a
First Grade	58	65	59	52
Second Grade	42	64	65	75
Third Grade	70	71	69	83
Fourth Grade	54	75	83	83
Would the government want to help you, if you needed help? (Percentage giving "Yes" or qualified responses)				
Second Grade	77	85	87	83
Third Grade	79	83	89	84
Fourth Grade	75	88	90	95

	Political Understanding Index Categories			
	Less Knowledge		More Knowledge	
	1	2	3	4
Do people running the government care about ordinary people like us? (Percentage giving "Yes" or qualified responses)				
Third Grade	84	85	93	100
Fourth Grade	79	95	95	96

[a]No kindergartners reached this level of knowledgeability on the PUI.

us do anything about it?" and "If the government does something wrong, should you write a letter or just forget about it?" In the responses to these questions, the pattern is for the more knowledge-able child to say "yes," we can do something about government's mistakes and to indicate that writing a letter is preferable to just forgetting about the error. A number indicated that if they did not write, the problem might become more serious. Conversely, the less knowledgeable a child is, the more likely he or she is to insist that ordinary people cannot do anything about governmental errors and that just forgetting about it is the preferable alternative.

As is usual in most such response patterns, the more know-ledgeable are also more likely to qualify their responses. Examples of qualified responses by fourth-graders are:

> "If it's real bad, write a letter, but they usually don't make big mistakes."

> "Well, if you were a person who really cared about it, you'd probably write a letter, but most people would forget about it."

> "It depends on how serious a mistake they make."

> "If it's important, like having to pay more money, then you should write a letter."

In the answers to the three questions relating to governmental responsiveness, there is a general tendency for the more knowledgeable children to believe the government is more attentive and responsive than is the case with the less knowledgeable. This is particularly well illustrated by responses to the third- and fourth-grade query about whether the people running the government care about ordinary people like us: the more knowledgeable a child is, the more likely he or she is to believe that government is a caring institution that will act responsively in meeting the needs of its citizens. This positive relationship between feelings about governmental responsiveness and political knowledge becomes stronger as the child moves through the elementary grades.

What are the most likely sources of a child's perception that government, or the agents of government, are responsive? From our questions concerning who works for the government, we find that children tend to believe that virtually anyone who helps others must be a governmental employee. It is clear that government policies and programs, especially since the institutionalization of certain welfare-state policies in the mid-1930s, have themselves helped to create the impression of governmental responsiveness. Social Security for the elderly, programs of aid for the disabled and indigent as well as those temporarily out of work, special assistance for farmers and businesses, both large and small, and a variety of local government programs for citizens of all ages in areas such as recreation, education, and cultural affairs make highly visible the benevolent and supportive posture of government vis-à-vis the individual citizen. The presentation of the "benevolent as well as competent bureaucrat" in children's literature and on nonnewscast television programs has been demonstrated by Thomas R. Marshall through a content analysis of 274 children's stories and 465 television programs.[13] Characters associated with government—police and other judicial and law enforcement officials, educators, hospital workers, astronauts, and occasionally the military—are portrayed as being at least as comforting, protective, and competent as characters in nongovernmental roles such as parents, relatives, co-workers, friends, and neighbors.*

---

*Weissberg, using data from the Easton and Dennis eight-city study, argues that U.S. children are socialized from an early age to be "conservative collectivists" supporting a wide scope for governmental activity, but not believing that it should be increased any further. See Robert Weissberg, *Political Learning, Political Choice, and Democratic Citizenship* (Englewood Cliffs, NJ: Prentice-Hall, 1974), pp. 45–47. See, in addition, Easton and Dennis, *Annals*, 1965.

Researchers in the coming decade or two should explore whether a movement of government policies away from the service-state orientation, if such a trend should develop, would result in school children perceiving government as less caring and responsive to the needs of its citizens. It seems clear that the actions of government as interpreted by parents, educators, and the media—especially stories children read and television programs they see—play a significant role in shaping the perceptions children have of government. With such efficient media for transmitting socializing messages, it would not take long for a perception of a responsive government to be transformed into a more neutral or even a skeptical view of governmental responsiveness.

DEMOGRAPHIC CORRELATES WITH AFFECT AND EFFICACY

There appear to be several trends in which affect and efficacy are linked to demographic characteristics. Each year girls are between 3 and 5 percent more positive than boys; however, the latter are consistently more knowledgeable. Non-Anglos are slightly less positive than Anglos in each of the five years. Furthermore, those who watch television news often are slightly less positive than infrequent newswatchers. Even though girls are slightly more positive than boys, the latter had a greater sense of efficacy in both third and fourth grades. Apparently, boys are more likely to feel that they can influence the political system. In fact, among the highest scores on the Efficacy/Responsiveness Index, boys were 14 percent overrepresented. Although on the Affect Index there was only a slight difference between Anglos and non-Anglos in both third and fourth grades, the difference in Efficacy/Responsiveness between the ethnic groups in third grade is significant at .01. Thirty-two percent of the non-Anglos are in the lowest category of this index, in contrast to only 8 percent of the Anglos. In fourth grade, however, the differences narrow considerably—another indication of the role the school system appears to play in narrowing differences between ethnic subgroups in society.*[14] During both years the only sibling

---

*See Chapter 5, "Demographic Explanations for Political Knowledge," and Chapter 6, "Correlates of the Law Understanding Index."

difference was that only children tended to be highest on the Efficacy Index (they are also the most knowledgeable of the sibling groups). Finally, there is a clear tendency for those who watch the news more frequently to have higher Efficacy/Responsiveness scores.

OTHER INDICES OF POLITICAL AFFECT

Theocratic Orientation

During the kindergarten interviews we discovered that many children failed to appreciate the distinction between religious and secular authorities inasmuch as they perceived religious authorities as wielding secular power (see Chapter 3). We assumed that children with a "theocratic orientation" would consider God or Jesus as "good," and because they failed to distinguish between secular and religious authorities, we hypothesized that they would have a more positive orientation toward the political realm than did "nontheocratic" children. In addition, we hypothesized that this affective orientation would persist as the children grew older. There were four interview questions that evoked God or Jesus responses: "Who is the boss of the country?", "Who makes the laws?", "Who does the most to run the country?", and "Who picks the President?" Some children gave a theocratic response to only one of the four, while 11 percent gave a God or Jesus response to at least three of the four questions. These 17 "theocrats," on a scale of 1 to 9 (with 9 representing a totally positive affect), had an Affect Index average of 6.5 in kindergarten; the average score for the rest of the panel was 6.4. Our first hypothesis was, therefore, only marginally supported. However, when the affect scores of these 17 theocrats were compared with the panel in the fourth grade, the difference was dramatic. As a group their affect average increased to 6.6; by contrast the "secular" group's score declined to 5.5. Furthermore, if the fourth-graders who gave one or two theocratic responses to the four queries in kindergarten (25 percent) are compared with the rest of the panel, they have a positive affect score of 6.1, which is midway between the theocrats and the children with a purely "secular" orientation. These data strongly support our hypothesis that those who associate God with country will exhibit more positive affect than those who do not, and that this positive orientation will persist.

It would appear that this theocratic orientation provides a substantial basis for the development of diffuse support toward the regime and the political community. This theocratic orientation is also consistent with "civil religion" theory, which argues that leaders in the United States have associated God with country in order to promote citizen support for the regime and its policies.

Governmental Fallibility

The young child's sense of governmental fallibility is a dimension of political affect that has implications for the stability of the political system. If young citizens are socialized to believe the governing authorities are infallible, the disillusionment that is likely to erupt when they recognize government does make mistakes may diminish diffuse support and perhaps lead to civil unrest and even political disruption. We sought to measure this aspect of our panel's relationship with government by analyzing responses to two questions: "How often does the government make mistakes?" and "How often does the President make mistakes?" (see Table 7.6). The former query was asked from first grade on and the latter beginning in second grade. Although an overwhelming percentage of these children have positive feelings about government, they also readily acknowledge that the government is not perfect; it does make mistakes. From first grade on, 17 percent felt the government "often" makes mistakes and in fourth grade that percentage increased to 21. Conversely, the percentage of children believing that the government never makes mistakes declined from a high of 6.2 percent in first grade to one child by the end of fourth grade. Very similar percentages appeared in the responses to "How often do you think the President makes mistakes?" The contrast with responses provided by children studied in the early 1960s is striking: Easton and Dennis found that 30 percent of their fourth-grade sample felt that the government almost never makes mistakes and another 43 percent judged that governmental mistakes rarely occur.[15] We believe that this exaggerated trust in government erupted in the form of antigovernment demonstrations in the late 1960s when these young adults confronted the fallibility of governmental decision making. Our 1970s sample has a more realistic view of governmental fallibility; it seems likely that these children may not become as disillusioned or alienated as their predecessors a decade or two earlier.

TABLE 7.6.
Assessment of Governmental Fallibility by Grade Level and Compared to 1962 (in percentages)

Response to "How often do you think the government makes mistakes?"	1	2	3	4	Easton and Dennis[a] 4
Never	6	7	2	0.4	30
Rarely	b	b	29	33	43
Sometimes	49	51	48	45	25
Often	17	17	17	21	3[c]
DK	27	23	3	0.4	b
NA	2	3	1	0	0
	101	101	100	99.8	101
Number of Respondents	(243)	(243)	(243)	(243)	(1,499)

Response to "How often do you think the President makes mistakes?"		Grade 2	3	4	Easton and Dennis[d] 4
Never		5	2	0.4	38[e]
Rarely		b	28	35	34
Sometimes		60	52	47	25
Often		14	13	16	4[c]
DK		17	—	0.8	b
NA		4	5	0	b
		100	100	99.2	101
Number of Respondents		(243)	(243)	(243)	(1,732)

[a]These responses are reported in Easton and Dennis, *Children in the Political System*, p. 133. The researchers utilized a fixed-response questionnaire.
[b]This response category was not utilized.
[c]Easton and Dennis combined "often," "usually," and "almost always."
[d]Easton and Dennis, *Children*, p. 180.
[e]Easton and Dennis' category is "almost never."

Are student perceptions of governmental fallibility and their political knowledge related? In first and second grades the more knowledgeable children were more likely to say the government makes mistakes "often" or "sometimes," and the less knowledgeable tended to say "never" or "don't know" (see Table 7.7). Generally, the more knowledgeable a child is about politics, the more likely he or she is to say the President makes mistakes "often" (although there is a deviation from the pattern in third grade). Except for second grade, those in the middle levels of political knowledge are more likely to say the President rarely or never makes mistakes than are those who are either most or least knowledgeable. Our conclusion on this governmental fallibility issue is the hopeful one that the more knowledgeable young people become, the more they will come to understand the susceptibility to error among governmental institutions and leaders and the more likely they will be to avoid the disillusionment about politics that has plagued our society in the past.

TABLE 7.7
Governmental Fallibility Cross-tabulated with the Political Understanding Index (in percentages)

		Political Understanding Index Categories				
		Less Knowledge		*More Knowledge*		
		1	*2*	*3*	*4*	*Sig*
How often does the government make mistakes?						
First Grade:	Often	15	16	15	30	
	Sometimes	31	47	61	56	
	Never	4	5	8	7	
	Don't Know	50	32	16	7	.001
Second Grade:	Often	12	21	13	33	
	Sometimes	37	54	66	58	
	Never	11	7	3	0	
	Don't Know	40	18	18	8	.01
Third Grade:	Often	17	17	18	18	
	Sometimes	62	50	44	46	
	Rarely/Never	21	33	38	36	ns
Fourth Grade:	Often	11	25	20	22	
	Sometimes	63	43	39	61	
	Rarely/Never	26	32	42	17	ns

(continued)

TABLE 7.7 (continued)

| | | Political Understanding Index Categories | | | | |
| | | Less Knowledge | | More Knowledge | | |
		1	2	3	4	Sig
How often does the President make mistakes?						
Second Grade:	Often	14	14	13	33	
	Sometimes	48	65	72	67	
	Rarely/Never	9	4	2	0	
	Other, DK	28	17	13	0	.05
Third Grade:	Often	12	14	15	9	
	Sometimes	74	49	49	73	
	Rarely/Never	14	38	36	18	ns
Fourth Grade:	Often	18	15	16	22	
	Sometimes	54	52	39	44	
	Rarely/Never	21	33	46	35	
	Don't Know	7	0	0	0	.01

Social Values and Public Policies

From the beginning of our interviewing we have tried to identify the kinds of social values and public priorities that are developing among young children. In an effort to begin exploring these embryonic attitudes and concerns, we asked the question: "If you were the boss of the whole country, what would you do to help people?" Replies were grouped in the following categories: (1) material needs such as food, clothing, and shelter, (2) a more general kind of humanitarian response involving help for the sick or elderly, (3) ecological concerns such as reducing litter or air pollution, (4) "political" responses such as making better laws or stopping wars, and (5) "nonpolitical" responses such as stopping fights or ending unfairness relating to classroom or school situations (see Table 7.8). In most years there was a tendency for the more knowledgeable to emphasize political or ecological priorities in their responses to the hypothetical question of what public needs they would seek to meet first. Among the fourth-grade replies were:

"I'd cut down on inflation, provide tax relief, and I would try to find new sources of energy."

"Try to make better laws."

"I wouldn't have people use so much energy, start using buses more."

"Help make more jobs."

There is a tendency for less knowledgeable pupils to emphasize humanitarian or vague helping instincts, such as, "do good," as well as a desire to provide material assistance (food, clothing, housing, or money). Less knowledgeable pupils clearly predominate among those who respond "don't know." The most dramatic changes in these "policy priorities" over the five years came in two categories. After second grade there was a 50 percent decline in the percentage of children emphasizing material needs (from 18 to 9 percent). At the same time, between second and third grade, there was an even

TABLE 7.8
Public Priorities by Grade Level (in percentages)

	Grade				
	K	*1*	*2*	*3*	*4*
Responses to "If you were boss of the whole country, what would you do to help people?"					
Meet material needs of people (food, clothing, shelter, money)	17	18	18	10	9
Humanitarian Concerns (help elderly, sick, distressed)	23	21	20	20	19
Ecological Priorities (conserve energy, stop pollution)	5	2	3	4	5
Political (e.g., make laws, stop wars)	3	5	3	20	35
Non-political (e.g., stop fights)	3	5	0	0	0
Other Priorities (unclassified above)	10	14	15	13	9
Don't Know	37	33	38	32	23
NA	1	2	3	1	0
Total	99	100	100	100	100

more dramatic rise in the percentage of children expressing such political concerns as making better laws and stopping wars (from 3 percent in second grade to 20 percent in third grade and 35 percent in fourth). These shifts, along with others that were much more modest, suggest not only a growing diversity in the kinds of public-policy concerns these young children have but also a growing realism on their part concerning the kinds of responsibilities our system of government is most likely to undertake.

Notions of Fairness and Unfairness

The children's responses to "tell me something that isn't fair" provide another perspective on their awareness of public issues (see Table 7.9). In the kindergarten and first-grade years, there is a clear tendency for the more knowledgeable to see unfairness in terms of such violations of norms as cheating and stealing. There was also a clear pattern in which the less knowledgeable children in first and third grades emphasized inequities or privileges as the most

TABLE 7.9
Perceptions of Unfairness by Grade Level (in percentages)

	Grade				
	K	1	2	3	4
Responses to "Tell me something that isn't fair."					
Cheating (or stealing through 2nd Grade)	23	23	22	7	10
Inequity or privilege	29	44	32	35	20
Legal or political reference	a	a	a	9	10
Discrimination (age and due process violations)	a	a	a	5	27
Violence or harm	a	a	a	11	10
Other	20	13	17	12	10
Don't Know	26	18	26	20	12
NA	3	2	3	1	1
Total	100	100	100	100	100

aThese categories were not used in kindergarten, first, and second grades because of an insufficient number of responses.

common instances of unfairness (or at least those coming to mind most quickly). It does appear that by fourth grade, however, the cheating concern is most readily identified by the least knowledgeable. The most dramatic increase between third and fourth grade involved the children becoming aware of the concept of discrimination and due process of law. More than one-quarter of the fourth-graders described unfairness in these terms:

"To give more things to one nationality or religion than to another, or to treat them better."

"Not showing evidence in a court."

"Girls can't be Senators or run for President or Vice-President."

Many provided age-related examples:

"That people over 65 can't work."

"Kids aren't allowed to vote."

"Kids can't drink beer in restaurants."

The revolution in civil rights reached a personal level for many children.

Occupational Preferences and Exemplars

The feelings children have about themselves and their relationship to society and its government can in some cases be inferred from their responses to such questions as: "What would you like to do when you grow up?" and "Tell me a famous person you would like to be like." Predictably boys very early identify the uniformed roles of police officer and firefighter as careers they would like to pursue (45 percent in kindergarten), and they also much more frequently than girls identify political figures as persons they would like to emulate (see Table 7.10). Girls, on the other hand, have a smaller range of careers, identifying nursing, teaching, and parenting as careers they would like to pursue; increasingly they specify entertainers, particularly movie and television stars, as persons they wish to be like. By the end of the fourth grade the percentage of boys

TABLE 7.10
Occupational Preferences and Exemplars Cross-tabulated with Sex (in percentages)[a]

Occupational Choices	K		1		2		3		4	
	Boys	Girls	Boys	Girls	Boys	Girls	Boys	Girls	Boys	Girls[b]
Policeman, fireman (uniformed)	45	0	35	1	28	3	16	1	15	2
Pilot, spaceman, scientist	8	1	7	0	12	5	9	1	11	2
Nurse	0	16	0	14	0	16	0	25	0	18
Doctor, dentist, vet	3	4	4	2	5	4	7	4	13	15
Teacher	3	7	3	21	0	19	2	18	1	17
Parent	0	12	0	7	0	6	0	2	0	0
Lawyer	c	c	c	c	c	c	c	c	5	0
Athlete	c	c	8	0	12	2	21	9	18	4
Other	31	31	25	18	28	19	33	29	28	32
Don't Know	9	10	13	23	9	14	13	11	10	10
sig.	.001		.001		.001		.001		.001	

Exemplars[d]

	2		3		4	
	Boys	*Girls*	*Boys*	*Girls*	*Boys*	*Girls*
Political figure[e]	43	22	22	10	20	6
Famous athlete	3	0.4	26	13	24	13
Movie or TV star	11	19	16	28	17	36
Be myself	6	4	3	6	5	6
Other	13	12	9	12	12	7
Don't Know	27	42	24	31	22	33
sig.	.01		.01		.001	

[a]Based on responses to "What would you like to do when you grow up?"

[b]The panel consists of 119 boys and 124 girls.

[c]Category not used that year. Less than 1 percent offered lawyer each year before fourth grade.

[d]Based on responses to "Tell me a famous person that you would like to be like." This request was not used in kindergarten or first grade.

[e]This category includes 4 percent in fourth grade who want to be like Washington or Lincoln (in second grade this was 18 percent). Less than 1 percent identify with a female political figure in fourth grade. In third grade five girls (2 percent) identified with a *female* political figure. Without exception the *female* figures were "Betsy Ross" or the "*wife* of the President."

215

who wanted to be police officers or firefighters is reduced by two-thirds as the diversity of their occupational choices increases significantly. By fourth grade the range of occupational preferences among girls expands even more than is true with boys, although it is still less diverse than the boys'; they begin to express a desire to be doctors, scientists, police officers, jockeys, and even Marines.[16] Simultaneously, as their occupational horizons broaden, their frequency of choosing teacher, nurse, and parent decreases. We were particularly struck by the approximately 5 percent of the children, beginning in second grade, who responded to the query about a famous person they would like to emulate by indicating quite confidently that they would prefer to be "themselves."

In order to determine whether children identified particular occupations with one sex or the other, beginning in first grade those who preferred sex-stereotyped occupations were asked whether they would like to be the counterpart role. They were also queried as to whether it was all right for the opposite sex to perform a sex-stereotyped role. Most boys and girls offering sex-stereotyped roles for themselves were quite willing to see the opposite sex occupy the same positions. More than eight out of nine of both sexes indicated that it was "OK" for boys to be nurses or stewards and for girls to be doctors and pilots.[17] From the number of fourth-grade girls wanting to be doctors, veterinarians, and especially athletes, it seems clear that sex stereotyping of both occupational choices and role models is beginning to decline. It seems likely that this decline results from the impact of the women's movement on our society as well as the wider exposure these children have to persons of both sexes employed in what were formerly sex-stereotyped occupations. The openness of both sexes to permit the other unrestricted occupational choice bodes well for the future.

Although children of both sexes appear to perceive an expanding range of career opportunities available to them (more than 50 different occupations were mentioned by fourth-graders), it is apparent that the girls have very few female political models with whom they can identify. Over the three years that the "famous person" question was asked, the only political exemplars the girls could offer were Betsy Ross and *the wife* of the President. (One girl said that she wanted "to be President, but since girls can't be President, then I want to be the wife of the President.") There was, in fact, a steady decline in references to political exemplars by children of both sexes from a high of 34 percent in second grade to a low of

13 percent in fourth grade; the latter is below the 17 percent Greenstein found in 1958.[18] The decline in political heroes is in sharp contrast to the increase in references to sports figures and entertainers from television, movies, and rock music in third and fourth grades. Indeed, when only substantive responses to this query are considered, it turns out that 64 percent of the panel mentioned either an athlete or entertainment figure as their "model" at the end of fourth grade. This aggregate trend away from political exemplars is qualified by the fact that the more political and legal understanding children had the more likely they were to name political exemplars (see Table 7.11).

The importance of visible role models in providing youngsters with exemplar suggestions is illustrated by the fact that our non-Anglo youngsters—who were primarily Hispanic or Oriental—were about half as likely as Anglos to mention athletes as persons they would like to emulate. This seems clearly attributable to the very small number of Hispanic and Oriental athletes among the professional and college teams they could have followed during the mid-1970s.

SUMMARY AND CONCLUSION

In general elementary school children are quite positive in their feelings toward the political regime and toward their country. Although very few children volunteer opinions concerning political

TABLE 7.11
The Political Understanding and the Law Understanding Indices Correlated with the Choice of Political Exemplars (in percentages)

Grade	PUI Stages				LUI Stages		
	1[a]	2	3	4	1	2	3
Second	20	33	39	58	16	31	40
Third	5	10	15	36	—	6	21
Fourth	11	10	13	26	5	10	50

[a]Stage 1 represents the least knowledgeable children, while Stages 3 and 4 include the most knowledgeable.

authorities such as the incumbent President, those who do tend to be almost evenly divided between positive and negative feelings. There is a pattern of correlation between increasing political understanding and more positive attitudes toward government, except that the most knowledgeable children are more likely than others to qualify their positive feelings. This tendency to qualify is most obvious in the children's attitudes toward laws, but it is also evident in their feelings about their own efficacy as political actors and the responsiveness of government in meeting their needs. Nonetheless, the responses of our panel lead us to conclude that elementary school children feel they can have a significant role in influencing government and that the latter will respond when there is a clear need for assistance.

While these young children have a high level of confidence in the U.S. system of government, they do not believe it to be infallible. In fact, a surprising percentage of our panel believe that both the President and the government can and do make mistakes with some regularity. Yet despite this awareness of fallibility in public institutions, these children, who were coming to their political awareness during the Watergate era, still want to vote, and they also understand why we have laws and why they must be enforced. If a tolerance for ambiguity and even paradox is a requisite for good citizenship in a democratic society, then the young child who places obedience to a fallible government above voting, and yet insists that he wants to vote, may be unconsciously developing a political orientation that is appropriate for a complex government and a conflict-ridden world.

NOTES

1. Carl E. Thoresen, ed., *The Behavior Therapist* (Monterey, CA: Brooks/Cole Publishing Company, 1980), p. 25.

2. Albert Bandura, *Social Learning Theory* (Englewood Cliffs, NJ: Prentice-Hall, 1977), p. 207.

3. Albert Bandura, "Self-efficacy: Toward a Unifying Theory of Behavioral Change," *Psychological Review* 84 (1977): 191–215.

4. Therese Gouin Décarie, "Affect Development and Cognition in a Piagetian Context," in Michael Lewis and Leonard A. Rosenblum, eds., *The Development of Affect, Genesis of Behavior: Volume 1* (New York: Plenum Press, 1978), pp. 184–88.

5. Ibid., p. 184.

6. Ibid.

7. Fred I. Greenstein, *Children and Politics* (New Haven, CN: Yale University Press, 1965), p. 79f. See also Dawson, Prewitt, and Dawson, *Political Socialization* (Boston: Little, Brown, 1977), pp. 59–61, 73–77.

8. David Easton, *A Systems Analysis of Political Life* (New York: Wiley, 1965), Chapters 17–21.

9. Among junior and senior high students frequent viewing of television shows portraying crime and violence is linked with an overestimation of the actual crime rate. One would expect the media might have an even greater impact on younger audiences. G. Gerbner, et al., "The Demonstration of Power: Violence Profile No. 10," *Journal of Communication* 29 (1979): 177–96.

10. Roberta S. Sigel and Marilyn B. Hoskin, *The Political Involvement of Adolescents* (New Brunswick, NJ: Rutgers University Press, 1981), p. 68.

11. Ibid., p. 64.

12. Ibid., Chapter 3.

13. Thomas R. Marshall, "The Benevolent Bureaucrat: Political Authority in Children's Literature and Television," *The Western Political Quarterly* 34 (September 1981): 389–99.

14. Gordon L. Berry and Claudia Mitchell-Kernan, eds., *Television and the Socialization of the Minority Child* (New York: Academic Press, 1982).

15. David Easton and Jack Dennis, *Children in the Political System* (New York: McGraw-Hill, 1969), p. 133; and Robert Hess and Judith Torney, *Development of Political Attitudes in Children* (Chicago: Aldine, 1967), pp. 52–59.

16. Despite this diversification, the girls in our panel, like those studied by Siegel, had a smaller range of occupational preferences than did boys. However, it appears as though their range of preferences is expanding considerably from the early 1970s. See C. L. F. Siegel, "Sex Differences in the Occupational Choices of Second Graders," *Journal of Vocational Behavior* 3 (1973): 15–17.

17. These findings run somewhat counter to those of Schlossberg and Goodman, who reported in 1972 that "children are much more likely to believe women should be excluded from men's jobs and vice versa." See N. K. Schlossberg and J. A. Goodman, "Children's Sex Stereotyping of Occupations," *Vocational Guidance Quarterly* 20 (1972): 266–70. Very typical of our boys' responses was one boy's answer to "Is it O.K. for a girl to be a major league baseball player?": "Sure . . . if she's good enough."

18. Fred I. Greenstein, *Children and Politics*, p. 138.

8

So What? Implications for Socialization Theory, Democratic Processes, and Civic Education

The longitudinal survey data and the concepts relating to political socialization analyzed in the preceding chapters appear near the end of a quarter of a century of research and reflection in this rapidly developing area of political science. The most notable contributions of this study lie in its five-year longitudinal base, its use of open-ended interviews beginning with children as young as five years of age, and its attempt to operationalize two very promising models for understanding growing political awareness in young children—*social learning* and *cognitive development*. Our success in this latter effort is more limited than we might wish, but important insights have emerged from this examination of patterns of political understanding among young children during the first five years of formal schooling. Efforts to account for these emerging patterns by examining alternative explanations for the youngsters' cognitive and affective orientations toward the political system provide new insights into the socialization process and its consequences.

Two primary instruments have been used to help increase our understanding of the political learning process: a 20-item cognitive map and a schema for staging threshold cognitive variables. The latter involved the development of a hierarchy of six stages of cognitive understanding that defines and distinguishes various levels of political awareness and sophistication with respect to nine structuring threshold variables.

At the outset of this study the cognitive map enabled us to demonstrate that the youngest children interviewed—five- and six-year-old kindergartners—are first able to recognize political symbols, especially *unifying symbols* representing our national political community. The nation's flag, the Statue of Liberty, and pictures of our best known Presidents—George Washington and Abraham Lincoln—as well as two representatives of the regime—the policeman and the judge—are symbols recognized by many of these young children. However, symbols and institutions representing political adversaries and conflict—the White House, national Capitol, and political parties—are not identified until later in the child's cognitive development, in part because of the abstractness of their referents as well as their conflictual character. The early focus on unifying symbols is consistent with the tendency of young children to simplify a complex political world. This tendency is further reflected in their inclination at the second stage of cognitive development to aggregate governmental functions in a way that has been described as "task pooling." There appear, however, to be environmental as well as cognitive developmental reasons for this initial recognition of unifying political symbols before beginning to identify symbols of political conflict. Textbooks, teachers, and, perhaps to a lesser extent, parents avoid discussion of the tensions and conflicts that dominate much of our political life. The legitimate interest of the school and the home in promoting order and unity may prompt them, either consciously or unconsciously, to delay introducing symbols representing divisions in policy-making responsibility and the sources of political tension or conflict. This postponing of the introduction of *conflictual symbols* is ultimately detrimental to the proper functioning of a vital, participatory democratic polity.

It appears from the kindergarten interviews as well as from those in the four subsequent years that certain key organizing or structuring concepts, which we have termed "threshold cognitive variables," constitute a framework for a young child's growing political awareness. Kindergarten children who have a concept of "what government does," for example, are more likely than those who do not to have some understanding of a wide range of political phenomena. Knowledge of what the President does, what taxes are, and the electoral process are other critical understandings that provide keys to greater political awareness among children in the early primary grades. The high correlation found between the level of understanding of the nine threshold variables and knowledge of the items on our cognitive map suggests that *growth in political awareness occurs in discrete stages characterized by qualitatively different ways of perceiving political phenomena.*

Our six stages of political awareness represent three clearly distinguishable levels of understanding: the prepolitical, the quasi-political, and the political. In the prepolitical level are found the two lowest stages of political awareness: symbol recognition and task pooling—the latter involves attributing most functions to a single entity such as the President or the police. Virtually all of the kindergartners offering "stageable" responses (26 percent of the panel) were at the prepolitical level of awarness. This means that our study begins at a point where the overwhelmingly majority (74 percent) of the youngsters have yet to reach the lowest "rung" of the politically relevant cognitive-developmental "ladder."

An awareness of *the meaning and purpose of laws* in the governmental system is another basic cognition that develops early in the life of a young child. An early familiarity with the role of laws in promoting an orderly society and preventing not only chaos, but inequities as well, appears to be the foundation for a much broader understanding of the governmental system. This may be illustrated graphically by noting that in fourth grade 69 percent of the panel are at Stage 2 on the Law Understanding Index, while only 17 percent are at Stage 2 on the Political Understanding Index. A further illustration of the central role played by an understanding of law may be found in the fact that, while the children hold a general view that the President is the dominant figure in the governing process, it is with the making of laws that they first become aware of the interdependence of the three branches of government.* As a child becomes familiar with the far-reaching implications of the legal system, he or she begins to appreciate the complexity of the process by which laws are made, the mechanisms used to enforce the laws, and the procedures involved in adjudicating disputes over the application of laws to particular situations. In our analysis of the young child's impressively rapid growth in legal understanding during the elementary school years, we begin to explain how this area of cognitive awareness provides an organizing framework for more rapid growth in other areas of political understanding.

The use of a six-stage, three-level hierarchy delineating a pattern of increasing political understanding enables us to outline the early stages of a young child's civic awareness. In particular, this schema

---

*Each year more and more of the children believe the President is both the boss of the country (86 percent in fourth grade) and the one who does the most to run the country (79 percent), in notable contast to only 38 percent of the fourth-graders who thought that *the President alone* makes the laws. Those with the latter misconception reached a peak of 51 percent in third grade, but declined in fourth grade as more and more recognized the interdependent character of law making.

permits us to contrast the mere recognition of certain objects as having some association with government with the capacity to identify critical features or functions that distinguish those objects from one another. Our six-stage hierarchy of political knowledge allows us to begin testing the relevance of alternative learning models for the political domain. Although most of the children in our sample do not get much beyond the task pooling second stage, we can, with the help of the responses of some of our brightest children, begin to see their recognition of critical features and functions emerging, particularly with such familiar phenomena as taxes and elections.

With respect to certain institutions and processes—especially those relating to executive functions—we find impressive consistency on the part of many children over the years. There are at least four questions that ask the children to identify the dominant governmental authority: "Who is the boss of our country?", "Who does the most to run the country?", "Who makes the laws?", and "Who picks the President?" Especially with reference to the first three, we found young children impressively consistent every year, tending to identify either a religious or a secular authority—usually the President—with all three tasks. There are, of course, other areas where the children are not nearly so consistent; correctly identifying units of political geography, indicating which party they prefer, and citing examples of unfairness are notable instances where inconsistencies are apparent between one year and the next. This contrasting pattern of consistency and inconsistency again reinforces the notion that young children are better able to identify the unifying mechanisms and authorities than they are to appreciate the sources of political diversity.

One of our major concerns in this study has been to examine the relevance and the possibility of interconnections between two models of the political learning process—the cognitive-developmental model, which gives primacy to internal maturational processes within the child and the social learning model, which emphasizes the role of external stimuli in the learning process. Our conclusion, which agrees with Renshon and others, is that *both models are useful, indeed complementary, for explaining growth in political understanding.* Inherited dispositions, influencing the pattern of maturational development, and social experiences, involving both the interpersonal and institutional environments, interact to shape the contours as well as the rate of political learning.[1] Innate

characteristics, inherited dispositions concerning such crucial matters as levels of physical activity and intelligence, are at least partially
modified by environmental influences, including everything from
nutrition to classroom curricula. There is, on the other hand, a sense
in which these internal predispositions "structure" the environment.
It seems clear, for example, that those children whose cognitive
capabilities mature earliest are better prepared than others to attend
to and learn from environmental stimuli. Once children understand
the meaning of "government," for example, they begin to develop a
cognitive structure that will enable them to better retain the names
of the authorities who make and implement the decisions of
government. It is also true that, as children apply their innate
intelligence to political phenomena, they begin to qualify their
perceptions and shy away from making extreme statements regarding such matters as how responsive to its citizens the government is or whether the United States is the best country in the
world. In sum, it would appear that innate characteristics such as
levels of basic intelligence and rates of cognitive maturation set the
broad parameters within which political learning takes place. As
these inner forces develop they permit more fruitful interaction with
environmental stimuli provided by parents, teachers, peers, and the
public media.

Among the categories of political phenomena used in our
interviews, the public issues, including Watergate, Vietnam, and the
energy crisis, appear to be more the product of social learning
through interaction with environmental stimuli than the result of
increased cognitive capacity. Watergate and the energy crisis, in
particular, vary in the pupil's level of awareness depending on how
much public attention they were receiving at the time of the
interviews. Awareness of Vietnam seems to depend more on having
relatives who had served in the war or the presence of refugee
children in the classroom than it does on any cognitive maturational
factor. Likewise, gains in the recognition of certain symbols such as
the Statue of Liberty or authorities such as chief executives seem
more a function of environmental stimuli—the Bicentennial cele-
bration or an election campaign—than they are attributable to any
particular increase in cognitive capacity.

The aggregate pattern of growth in geo-political awareness, on
the other hand, would appear to provide support for the cognitive-
developmental hypothesis as distinguished from social learning. In

the absence of rote memorization,* it seems clear that children must have some facility in manipulating abstractions such as city, state, and country, and particularly the concentric physical relationship among them, before they are able to identify consistently their residence in a particular city, state, and country.

The distinction between the public and private sectors, as measured by the ability to identify which occupations work for the government, is a second instance where political knowledge clearly rests on a cognitive ability to use and manipulate abstract categories in a way that fourth-graders are just beginning to master. In general, our data suggest that among the six categories of political objects contained in the cognitive map, regime-related items, because of the consistently linear pattern of growth in their understanding, are those for which the cognitive-developmental hypothesis seems most appropriate. This is primarily because of their complexity and abstractness, but the central role they play in the operation of the political system may be relevant. Law, elections, taxes, and politicians are regime-related items that seem especially important in helping us predict variations in general political knowledge among elementary school children. This predictive power we attribute to the fact that these objects represent parts of an organizing framework that helps the child put into perspective a wider range of political phenomena, especially those relating to the judicial and electoral processes. Our conclusions concerning variations among children in their patterns of political learning lead us to believe that a comprehensive theory must include both the cognitive-developmental and social learning models, with the relative importance of each depending on the category of political objects being considered.

FACTORS PROMOTING REGIME SUPPORT AND POLITICAL STABILITY

Some critics have accused political scientists of being preoccupied with system stability while neglecting the bases for social

---

*Such mechanical rituals as naming the United States of America in the daily flag salute or memorizing the city and parts of a child's complete address do not normally produce an ability to relate those three geo-political names to the labels,

change. This criticism notwithstanding, all regimes attempt to generate widespread support for their institutions and policies.[2] Without such support a nation or a particular regime is threatened with some degree of instability. Democratic regimes are able to adapt to demands for policy changes. Minor procedural and structural changes can be accommodated, but demands for systemic change are threatening to a democratic regime and to a nation's stability.

What factors help to build or to erode regime support among young children? Do the responses of these children provide clues to the origins of popular support for the basic structure and processes of the U.S. polity? Do their answers provide an explanation for the widespread perception of presidential and governmental benevolence? Are these youngsters able to distinguish between the occupant of the Oval Office and the presidency itself? During these early years, when children are at the political symbol-recognition and task-pooling stages, are they able to differentiate between a highly visible President and the rest of the government? Are children who are familiar with the trauma of Watergate inclined to be less supportive of the government than those who are not?

Before examining the evidence for early development of regime support and attachment, let us review some of the contrary evidence. First, except for the children's pervasively optimistic attitudes that have already been discussed,* it must be noted that substantive responses to several of our interview queries provide only mixed evidence of regime support. Indeed, when asked "What do you think of when you see our flag?", 30 percent of the fourth-graders say, "nothing," "don't know," or some nonspecific comment such as "it's nice" or "it's pretty." The same is even more true of the responses to "what makes you most proud to be an American?" Thirty-four percent of the children are unable to offer any response, while another 36 percent give a wide range of responses from "nothing" to "people," "friends," or "it's a nice country." Second, it is important to remember that, when the children were asked "Is America the best country in the world?", only 30 percent of the third- and fourth-graders answered affirmatively. The panel's

---

city, state and country, because the labels are not linked systematically to the particular geo-political units mentioned in those common childhood exercises.

*Rather than identifying a politically specific optimism, we may be tapping a generalized trait among young children.

pattern of substantive responses does not mean, however, that a basic national patriotism or attachment is not begin acquired by these children. It may be that something as basic as attachment to a nation, or diffuse regime support, is not amenable to survey methodology, at least not during the early elementary school years. It may also be possible that our open-ended questions do not elicit the kind of responses that provide definitive evidence of developing patriotism. In spite of these methodological problems, the children in our study do provide evidence for the thesis that a basic attachment to the nation develops during early childhood.

The children's perception of rules and laws contributes in very significant ways to regime support and governmental stability. Young children are overwhelmingly rule- and law-oriented. They frequently observe that the way to make a contribution to the welfare of our country is to "make more good laws." When children are asked whether it is better to "obey the laws or to vote in an election," the former receives virtual unanimous support. From their point of view, voting is optional. Obeying the laws, on the other hand, is a necessity—essential for the good of the entire society. They feel people need to obey the law because laws protect both the individual and his property. A good citizen is one who obeys the laws. One-fifth of the fourth-graders visualized a world without laws in stark Hobbesean terms. Laws, therefore, represent the barrier between these children and a world where everyone could do as he or she pleased—a world in which children would be particularly vulnerable. According to these children, people in a lawless world would commit all manner of evils, from running stop signs to stealing and killing. Indeed, their vision is one of a chaotic society. Their sense of the paramount importance of law and the necessity for obedience to the law forms the basis for subject-oriented, rather than participatory, attitudes that promote significant support for the regime.

A second factor contributing to diffuse regime support and stability is the widespread perception by children of presidential and governmental benevolence. Easton and Dennis hypothesized in the early 1960s that benevolence directed toward the President personally is later transferred to the office.[3] However, as Renshon has noted, empirical data are lacking for the theories that have been offered to explain why children view the President as benevolent.[4] Because 40 percent of our kindergartners believed that religious authorities—God or Jesus—wield secular authority, we hypothesized a two-step explanation for the widespread belief in presidential benevolence, with a subsequent third step leading to a perception of general governmental benevolence. Initially, children believe that benevolent religious authorities—undoubtedly because of parental- and church-inspired references to their power and goodness— govern the country.[5] Later, as they become aware of the President as a secular authority, they transfer their positive feelings to him; still later they transfer their feelings of benevolence to the office itself.

But this early theocratic orientation on the part of four out of ten kindergartners does more than provide an explanation for the genesis of presidential benevolence. This theocratic orientation is a strong contributor, along with their law and order predisposition, to diffuse regime support. Those children who exhibit strong theocratic orientations in kindergarten were significantly more positive toward the polity as fourth-graders than were other children. Furthermore, the fourth-graders who had expressed a limited theocratic response were also more positive toward government and politics than the children who had not offered any theocratic responses.

Our data support the Easton and Dennis hypothesis concerning the transfer process, wherein the developing citizen-to-be becomes able to distinguish between an occupant of the presidency and the institution. By the time these children were in third grade, they had lived under three or four Presidents. Perhaps a succession of one-term Presidents will, in itself, make it easier for children to distinguish the office from the officeholder. Thus, our data indicate that even when an occupant like Richard Nixon violates his public trust, the presidency itself still enjoys widespread support among children. The more politically aware pupils appear to be able to make this distinction as early as second grade. Approximately 8 percent of the children during the second through fourth grades can accurately describe the extraordinary events that led to Mr. Ford becoming President. These children are just as likely to be ranked in the positive or highly positive categories of our Affect Index as children who are unable to tell us about the circumstances surrounding Ford's succession to the presidency. Thus, knowledge about one of the most disheartening betrayals of public trust in our nation's history apparently did not erode support for the office of the presidency among these more knowledgeable youngsters.

A third transference of political benevolence occurs when the developing citizen is able to distinguish between the role of the presidency and the functions performed by the rest of the government. This occurs when children leave the task-pooling stage and move to Stage 3 (Critical Feature). When this transition occurs, the benevolence attributed to the presidency is transferred to the government generally. Our evidence strongly supports the conclusion that these children believe that an active and responsive government will help them if they really need help, listen to their parents, care about their parents' views, and not make mistakes capriciously. The children of the classic socialization studies of the 1950s and 1960s, as well as those used in this research, were heirs to a view of government as the active, positive promoter of the welfare state inaugurated by the New Deal. Whether or not the retrenching government of the early 1980s will dissipate the benevolence initially attributed to it by young citizens remains to be seen. In sum, our data strongly suggest that the residue of early perceptions of benevolent authorities contributes significantly to diffuse regime support.

A third factor contributing to stability and regime support is the perception among the children of the 1970s that everyone makes mistakes—from Big Bird to the President. Mistakes happen frequently, even in government, and a letter to the government might be appropriate if the mistake were sufficiently serious. This perception of the ubiquitousness of mistakes, and the elusiveness of perfection, is certain to have significant implications for our polity. These children are much more realistic about the fallibility of government than the generation of children surveyed in the 1950s and 1960s. One consequence is that they may be much less likely to become disillusioned in the future. Government inevitably makes mistakes; it is not perceived as malicious.

On the other hand, another possibility might be that this early acceptance of governmental fallibility could hasten the emergence of political cynicism. To view everyone, including the President, as prone to mistakes may, in the future, lead to a questioning of all authority. There is a further possibility. Their unquestioning acceptance of mistakes as inevitable may be in conflict with other premises shared by these children. For, although they are very realistic about the fallibility of government, they are still idealistic or, at the very least, optimistic. Each year their responses to our fairness query indicate they believe inequities and privileges are unfair, even when they themselves are the privileged. Fairness and a rough sense of equality are widely accepted values among these future citizens and could in time become standards by which governmental performance is measured. In the same vein, the children in our panel believe that the primary purpose of government is to help those in need. They assume that people who help others and whose jobs are important are, of necessity, government employees. Given this constellation of perceptions about the role of government as a helper of the needy and a promoter of justice, what might be the result if departures from these standards were not perceived as ordinary mistakes, but instead as deliberate policies? If, in the future, these children were to perceive governmental actions as patently inequitable and unfair, this developing value structure would be offended, the diffuse regime support would be undermined.

Finally, there are three related factors that may contribute to basic political stability—the lack of familiarity with alternatives, acceptance of the status quo out of habit, and the persistence of political inertia. Although few children give an affirmative answer to whether or not the United States is the best country in the world, many exhibit what Sigel and Hoskin have called "relative affect."[6] This is the only country most of the children have experienced: "I've never been to any other country." "This is my country." "I live here." "My friends live here." This country may not be perfect—but it is the only one they know.

The fact of residence over time begins to weld a bond between the developing citizen and his or her country. Long-term association, with a lack of significant exposure to alternatives, inculcates the habit of extending attachment to and support for the governing institutions in the young person's political community. The force of habit should not be underestimated as a basis for lifelong loyalty. In *Change and Habit* Arnold Toynbee stresses what a powerful influence habit can be.[7]

Although these children are eager to vote in elections, they are typically being raised in a nonpartisan milieu characterized by widespread political passivity and inertia.[8] This is substantiated in part by the significantly lower partisan awareness and party identification found among these primary school children during the mid-to-late 1970s, when compared with the levels found 15 or 20 years earlier. A mere 7 percent of our fourth-graders indicated that they preferred one party over another, and only 16 percent could tell us President Carter's party affiliation. In Greenstein's pioneering study, when children were given party names on written questionnaires, 63 percent of the fourth-graders indicated a preference for one of the two major parties.[9] This startling 56 percent difference in party identification, coupled with an almost unbelievable 71 percent lower recognition of the President's affiliation,[10] could either contribute to future stability by promoting passivity and inertia among the electorate, or it could, on the other hand, cause greater instability. If these citizens-to-be do vote in the future, and if privatistic and transitory orientations toward parties and candidates replace the more stable and easily inherited party identification of earlier generations, the new pattern may diminish stability in the system by inducing more rapid shifts from one media-packaged candidate to another at both the national and state levels.

There is some indication from the responses of our panel that there is a stronger *subject* as opposed to *participant* orientation among primary school children in the 1970s.[11] Jennings and Niemi set forth values that delineate two differing views of the good citizen—allegiant and participant. One set of virtues stresses political allegiance, obeying laws, being loyal, honoring the country, and paying taxes, while the other stresses more active, participatory components of the political repertory—being interested and paying attention to politics and taking an active role through a great variety of intensive forms of participation.[12] As fourth-graders more than a third of our children answered the query "What is a good citizen?" with a reply "One who obeys the law." Almost unanimously they assert that obeying the law is more important than voting in an election. They feel more positively toward the police officer than toward any other governmental authority figure. They see paying taxes from a legalistic perspective: when asked "Why do people pay taxes?" they typically answer "You have to. It's the law." They are increasingly less willing, as they advance through the primary grades, to tell us what they would do to help other people, if they "were the boss of our whole country." Particularly striking in this pattern of subject orientation is the significantly greater visibility of the judicial process in the eyes of young children as compared to the relative obscurity of the legislative process. The formalized, constraining, and nonpartisan character of the judicial process contrasts with the less formal and highly partisan behavior that often prevails among elected legislators and their activist supporters.

In addition, the young child's concept of *a good citizen* centers increasingly on the notion that this is a person who always obeys the law. The use of weekly or even daily "good citizen" awards in the elementary school classroom reinforces the perception that a good citizen is one who is consistently responsive to rules and regulations. At the same time, however, a number have begun to question rules such as curfews involving age discrimination, and several fourth-graders asserted that some laws discriminate on the basis of race.

On the whole the children in our panel seem to fit the passive model of citizenship. Even as fourth-graders, many explain their lack of knowledge about politics by saying, in effect, "I'm not into politics." A good citizen is a good person, who does good things, is a good sport, a good loser, a good citizen in school, and above all, one who always obeys the laws. Only 5 percent gave a response that implied a more active role in the political process. The only other attitudes that run counter to this passivity are their desire to vote and their responses to "If the government makes a mistake, should you write a letter or just forget about it?" Almost half believe that a letter would be appropriate, while another 22 percent believe that, if the problem is serious enough, a letter should be sent—so that the government will be aware of its mistake and not repeat it.

Time will tell whether these young citizens will become more participant oriented, or whether their present lack of knowledge about partisan politics will persist and support this subject orientation. The latter is more likely, in our opinion, and will contribute to the continuing domination of political campaigns by the mass media.

As we come to better understand the process by which young children learn about government and politics, and as we see that early cognitions affect the level of regime support and stability, we appreciate the opportunities for strengthening elementary school curricula to facilitate both faster learning and a more functional and realistic perception of political phenomena. It is appropriate, therefore, that we now turn our attention to the subject of the elementary school civics curriculum.

SUGGESTIONS FOR CURRICULUM DEVELOPMENT IN CIVIC EDUCATION

The lessons of this research for the primary school educator are both clear and noteworthy. It would enhance the rate and the quality of political learning among primary school children if teachers were sensitized to the threshold structuring cognitions that provide the basis for increased political awareness. If a youngster, during the kindergarten and first-grade years, were encouraged to identify the most salient political authorities (for example, the police officer, the judge, and the President) with *the government* and its functions, the concept of government would become more meaningful and subsequently the child could more readily associate other public authorities and activities with the realm of government. It would also be useful for first- and second-grade teachers to begin helping the young child sort out the components of our federal system: local, state, and national. The competency with abstractions required for understanding these jurisdictions of government—entities that are obviously beyond the child's immediate, day-to-day experience—makes understanding their interrelationships a more difficult task than mere symbol recognition. However, because highly visible national symbols are known by most children at this young age and because many of them have progressed to a "task pool" notion of government (for example, the President does "everything"), it would seem appropriate to begin helping first- and second-graders understand the division of labor that distinguishes various institutions and jurisdictions in our political system. Such an effort would perhaps counterbalance the extraordinary emphasis the young child tends to give to the President and to other chief executives.

The Western democratic tradition includes the notion of a division of political authority and the concept of checks and balances between separated powers. It would therefore seem desirable to have children from a rather young age become increasingly sensitive to the importance of legislative and judicial as well as executive authority. The children in our panel, however, persisted, even through the fourth grade, in giving predominant attention and importance to the President. Eighty-six percent of the fourth-graders perceived the President as "the boss of the country"; 79 precent believe he does the most to run our country; and 38 percent think *he alone* makes the laws. By contrast, not one child thought that Congress was "the boss of the country"; only one child (in fourth grade) believed that Congress does the most to run our country; and six children (2.5 percent) implied that Congress alone makes the laws. Just 17 percent of the fourth-grade children acknowledge a division of labor in the legislative process by suggesting that the President must cooperate with "others" in making the laws. This relatively low salience of Congress, especially when contrasted with the highly visible President, is further revealed by the fact that only 22 percent of the fourth-graders offered any response to the question "What is the Congress?" and only 16 percent were able to answer "What is a Senator?" This early and persistent concept of presidential supremacy and the absence of a notion of shared political power prevent these young children from developing an appreciation for the complex bargaining and broker-age roles both the President and Congress are called upon to play.

Nonetheless, it seems clear that by the time children reach third grade, they are normally ready to think at a sufficiently high level of abstraction to permit them to grasp not only the concept of the separation of powers within a single political jurisdiction, but also the division of labor that prevails among the different levels in our federal system. It would also seem appropriate for teachers to acknowledge both the cooperative *and* the competing (that is, partisan or institutional) relationships among the major organs of government. The value of promoting greater pupil awareness of Congress in particular is demonstrated by the fact that those children who did have an understanding of what Congress does were more knowledgeable on most of the cognitive map items than those who did not.

While children in the middle primary grades appear ready to distinguish the branches and levels of our governmental system, they do not seem to have a firm grasp of which occupations work for the government and which do not. Highly visible government agents—police officers and judges—are very early recognized as governmental by young school children, but certain other public servants with whom they do have regular contact—teachers and mail carriers—are not consistently recognized as governmental employees. On the other hand, a number of private sector workers—because they too provide services (that is, "help people")—are seen as governmental. More than 50 percent of our third- and fourth-graders identified milkmen, gas station attendants, and television news commentators as working for the government, and in the latter two cases the percentage of incorrect responses was 78 percent in fourth grade. Only the candy store person ran counter to this general misperception.

In order to help elementary school children begin to distinguish between the public and private sectors, perceive the limits of governmental authority, and understand the parameters of public service, it would seem essential that, as part of the emerging pattern of career education in the early grades, the youngsters be helped to distinguish more accurately which occupations are normally part of government service and which are not. While this may be partially a task for rote memory, the exercise will provide eight- to ten-year-old children with a means for furthering their understanding of the scope as well as the limits of government.

Two discoveries concerning the development of a child's conception of law should be of interest to curriculum planners. We have found that law is one of the first elements in the political system that children come to understand. At the end of fourth grade, children on the average were one-half of a stage higher on the Law Understanding Index than they were on the Political Understanding Index. Thus, just as the development of cognitive skills is claimed to be a necessary if not a sufficient condition for growth in moral development, so there is evidence to indicate that the development of an understanding of the role of law in society may be a necessary, if not a sufficient, condition for increased knowledge of the political world.

A second law-related finding is that the stages children pass through as they develop in their understanding of the law are not identical to the stages in moral development. Recognition of this fact by educators should enable them to facilitate earlier learning about the role of law in modern society. Specifically, the children must be helped to grasp the broader systemic impact of the law before attempts are made to teach them the particular norms of our legal system. The role of law in ordering a society should be introduced before attempting to specify the norms underlying the social order. This recommendation is based on our finding that children grasped the societal impact of law before they were very clear on the particular social norms it embodied. An acceleration of this law-related understanding may, in turn, speed up the entire political learning process.

Political socialization in a democratic as opposed to an authoritarian society involves the simultaneous promotion of the conflicting values of uniformity versus diversity, principles versus pragmatism, and even loyal support versus responsible criticism. There is an inevitable tension between these competing values—one set directed to unity, stability, consensus, and continuity while the other is oriented to pluralism, instability, conflict, and change. It is understandable, through perhaps not excusable, that public-supported school systems of the type attended by most of the children in our panel lean heavily on the side of promoting the first set of values—the enduring principles undergirding our polity, the authoritativeness of our institutions—especially the presidency and the Courts, and the importance of loyalty and commitment to our national political community. This has meant, of course, that the public school classrooms have not been very effective in introducing school children to the conflicting values that lie at the heart of a democratic political process. Andrain in his *Children and Civic Awareness* cogently described the role of the school in biasing the conception of a good citizen among young children away from a model of active, competitive participation:

> American school officials conceive that their main political responsibility involves teaching the role of a good citizen, not a partisan role. In certain respects, these two roles come into conflict. Partisan roles deal with conflict relationships; one party struggles to outmaneuver the opposition. Party norms stipulate loyalty not only to the nation but also to a sub-national group. As taught in the schools, the role of a "good citizen" stresses loyalty to a general constituency; teachers try to avoid controversies which may threaten their standing with parents, school administrators, and community leaders. Thus the school teaches children the virtues of nonpartisanship, respect for law and order, and participation in politics as individuals, not as members of organized groups, i.e., parties.[13]

It seems clear to us that the school curriculum and the teachers in particular can take a much more active role in promoting the elementary school child's appreciation for the competitive side of democratic politics and the benefits of diversity, pragmatism, and change. By giving pupils an opportunity to participate in mock elections, examine the arguments and the evidence on opposing sides of public issues, and encourage involvement with local political figures through field trips and correspondence, the teachers of third, fourth, and fifth grades can awaken earlier an interest in and perhaps even a thirst for political competition. These steps would encourage a participatory rather than a passive role in the political process.

It may be useful in the middle elementary grades (third and fourth) to begin moving from the "election" of classroom officers and monitors to experimenting with mock elections for leading public offices, when those elections are being presented in the public media and discussed by many of the children's parents at home. Under these circumstances, it is possible for a teacher to give the pupils a mock "sample ballot" and have them discuss with their parents, classmates, and interested others the arguments for and against particular issues and candidates. This involvement in the electoral processes of the adult world appeals to children and helps them develop the habit of paying attention to the names and possibly to the public positions of leading candidates. Children in one elementary school were able to recognize the name of Senator S. I. Hayakawa many months after they had "voted on him" in the school auditorium. In some cases the children were even able to offer substantive political reasons for preferring one presidential candidate, usually Carter or Ford, over the other in the 1976 presidential election.

In general, however, it was disappointing for us to find a majority of students remembering things about a candidate or officeholder that they can identify and remember easily. For example, they frequently mentioned that President Carter was a peanut farmer from Georgia with prominent teeth, an eager smile, and a brother named Billy. A few youngsters were beginning to pick up and retain some relevant information about public figures, for example, that President Nixon lied and had to give up his office. The point is that the children in the early elementary years need concrete referents from their everyday experience to relate to: an occupation they find amusing (growing peanuts), a physical feature they can remember (prominent teeth), or a kind of behavior they have experienced themselves (lying). They are just beginning to relate to public issues that have everyday referents—pollution is symbolized by the smog that makes their eyes water, energy problems are identified with long gas lines or reminders to turn off unused electricity, and a war-ravaged country like Vietnam is represented by the refugee children who appear in their classroom. Even Watergate begins to make sense to some children when it is presented in terms of a burglary to get secrets and a President lying to hide his involvement with that incident.

Identifying a public problem or issue, however, is one matter— a fairly simple one for an elementary school teacher—but helping young children form a reasonably intelligent viewpoint on such matters is quite another. It becomes easier to get youngsters in the early elementary school years to attempt to engage in meaningful political or policy analysis if they develop the capacity to grasp such complex matters as social and political causation and realize the need to evalute different sources of information, weigh competing interpretations of facts and events, and accept the legitimacy of honest disagreements over priorities and value judgments.

The elementary school classroom can contribute to the development of what John J. Patrick identifies as intellectual skills and participation skills—the foundation needed for active citizenship.[14] Where the youngsters have an interest in an issue, such as whether children should be allowed to "drink beer in restaurants" or "vote for Presidents," it may be possible to begin helping them use these public issues and decisions as vehicles for gathering and weighing evidence, analyzing processes of social and political causation, and assessing the relative weight given to different authorities. By engaging in classroom debates, taking votes on issues of general interest, writing letters to public officials, or even inviting them to appear in classrooms and school auditoriums, the process of developing the young child's participation skills can begin in the elementary school.

What is at least as important as the early introduction of these intellectual and participation experiences, however, is consistent reinforcement of these "lessons" throughout the entire educational experience. It would have limited impact on skills in either political analysis or participation if a teacher were to introduce issue or candidate debates in third or fourth grade and have children write letters or visit elected officials, but have no other teacher during the remaining eight or nine years of precollegiate education follow through with similar exercises directed to the same end. It does seem essential that clear suggestions and easy-to-implement formats for classroom discussions, debates, and communications with public decisionmakers should be a part of virtually every teacher's manual beginning with third grade.

Most young citizens in the United States are raised to believe in the myth of our infallible Founding Fathers and *The Genius of American Politics*, as Daniel Boorstin described it in his book bearing that title.[15] These myths stress that our basic political principles and institutions were, in effect, "given" almost as if by divine order and are not to be tampered with or modified in any significant way. Less is learned about the great debates, the false starts, the rampant pluralism, and the divided loyalties that characterized the early decades of our young republic. Indeed, there appears to be an overemphasis on the unifying or consensual symbols—the flag, Statue of Liberty, Liberty Bell, White House, and the most revered Presidents, Washington and Lincoln. Neglected are those symbols representing disagreement, conflict, and debate—if not outright disunity. The national Capitol, the Supreme Court, political parties, politicians, and figures such as Jefferson, Jackson, John Brown, William Jennings Bryan, the two Roosevelts, and even Woodrow Wilson may be used to dramatize the debates, the divisions, and the diversity that are so central to our continuing struggle to redefine our political values and revitalize our institutions.

It might be argued that we must build diffuse regime support on a solid foundation before we begin to expose young children to the divisions that have plagued our polity from its beginning. We would submit that a more helpful and realistic understanding of our basic pluralism and diversity, as well as our internal conflicts, if introduced at an earlier age, would prepare young children to play a more vigorous and active role in the political process in later life. In addition, they will learn two valuable lessons—recognition that their viewpoint will not prevail every time and that the polity will not always be successful in its endeavors.

We believe that school curriculum planners and those responsible for designing children's television programs should begin devising ways to convey to relatively young children the notion that our political values and institutions are not as static, unitary, or authoritative as earlier generations have been led to believe. A more realistic view of our political experience that balances the unity with the diversity, the consensus with the conflict, and the successes with the failures will enable young children to appreciate the tenuousness of our democratic experiment and the necessity for active involvement on the part of a diverse and well-informed public. If citizens are to cope with the complexity and the diversity of our political, social, and economic environment during the closing decades of the twentieth century, it is imperative that they be prepared to change as well as to preserve certain features of the existing political system.

SUGGESTIONS FOR FUTURE RESEARCH

Most studies of social and political processes conclude with suggestions for future research; this is not an exception. Some of the suggestions that follow are, in effect, a critique of the methods and instruments used in this study; others result directly from things we learned about the political awareness of primary school children.

Because we wished to map both the cognitive and affective orientations of our panel, we chose to reduce sensitization by not interviewing the parents and the teachers of our panel members. However, if we are to gain a better understanding of the role of home and school in political socialization, we must risk sensitization in order to obtain more data on the beliefs and actions of both parents and teachers. It is desirable to include systematic questioning of teachers *after* they are no longer in regular contact with panel members. Based on our experience, it would seem appropriate to begin a longitudinal study at about age three-and-one-half or four. If both the children and the parents were interviewed every two years thereafter, such a study could avoid excessive sensitization and contribute significantly to our understanding of the transmission of affect between parents and children. Well-designed, probing, open-ended questions will be needed to measure this parent-child relationship.

A better approach to measuring attachment to the national political community is necessary. Perhaps a systematic probing strategy, a la Piaget, combined with a tape recording capability might allow the researcher to explore the affective domain more thoroughly. Our need to record responses by hand was a serious limitation on our ability to ask follow-up questions without pausing to record the responses.

Although our panel included a significant percentage of non-Anglo children, it seems essential that future studies incorporate a greater diversity of ethnic and socioeconomic levels, especially children from the lower end of that scale. It is likely that the cognitions and the feelings of youngsters raised in lower income families, and especially in lower income minority homes, will have different perceptions of the U.S. political system and some of the authorities and processes that dominate it.

Our data suggest a "theocratic" explanation for the benevolence most young children see in the President and the office of the presidency. Forty percent of our kindergartners had some level of theocratic orientation to executive functions and powers. Does that percentage represent the full extent of this phenomenon among young children? Or, were other panel members also theocratic at an earlier age? Were the 40 percent those children who persisted the longest in their theocratic perspective? Is it the persistence over time of such an orientation or simply that it had been experienced that contributes to the perception of benevolence and a generally more positive affect toward the political system? Children who had a theocratic orientation in kindergarten had more positive feelings toward the political system four years later than did those children who offered no theocratic responses to our questions. Since diffuse regime support is vital to political systems, such a theocratic connection makes the study of "civil religion" important in the United States.

We are also convinced that there are many questions we used in the second, third, and fourth grades that should have been asked earlier in the study. The questions concerning the judicial process (courts and judges) as well as such law-related queries as "What would happen if there were no laws?", for example, should have been asked from the beginning, because the children evidenced a surprising familiarity with these objects the first time they were asked about them. Likewise, more affect questions should have been asked at an earlier age.

In the future it will be desirable to determine whether perceptions of benevolence persist even during periods when government social programs are being reduced. In addition, the influence that the mass media, especially television, exert on the cognitive and affective political orientations of children needs to be explored much more systematically. It is also important that future longitudinal studies test learning models other than the cognitive-developmental and social learning that we have begun testing—especially those that emphasize processes such as identification, interpersonal transfer, and simple accumulation of information over time.

Our findings also suggest an important subject for investigation among adults. We have hypothesized that the national adult mean on our six-stage hierarchy of political knowledgeability will be approximately Stage 4—although many adults may never progress beyond Stage 3. Various subgroups of U.S. society could be tested as to their stage of political knowledgeability. Groups, or perhaps even individuals, who significantly exceed or fall below the national mean could be analyzed to see if there are demographic or cognitive explanations for this divergence. This might lead to a clearer understanding of those structuring concepts that help the individual to organize the mass of sociopolitical data that frequently overwhelms even the concerned citizen.

It is impossible to formulate a perfect research design. Trade-offs must always be made. Researchers are painfully aware of the limits placed upon them by the lack of time and resources. Obviously, a national sample with hundreds of subjects would be desirable. Nevertheless, many of the research opportunities suggested above are feasible and necessary if we are to explore and delineate systematically the political socialization foundations underpinning U.S. democracy.

NOTES

1. Stanley Allen Renshon, "Assumptive Frameworks in Political Socialization Theory," in Renshon, ed., *Handbook of Political Socialization* (New York: The Free Press, 1977), pp. 16–30.

2. Dean Jaros, *Socialization to Politics* (New York: Praeger, 1973), Chapter 1; Robert Dahl, *A Preface to Democratic Theory* (Chicago: University of Chicago Press, 1956). Chapter 3 stresses the need for social training in a society's norms in order to gain consensus and stability for a society; and Robert P. Clark, Jr., *Development and Instability: Political Change in the Non-Western World* (New York: The Dryden Press, 1974), Part 2 (Chapters 5–8). Easton, however, has criticized a systems *maintenance* approach for its overemphasis on stability. He has suggested that a concern for system *persistence* would allow for greater focus on diversity, conflict, and change. See David Easton, "The Theoretical Relevance of Political Socialization," *Canadian Journal of Political Science* 1 (1968): 141.

3. David Easton and Jack Dennis, *Children in the Political System* (New York: McGraw-Hill, 1969), Chapter 9.

4. Stanley Allen Renshon, "Assumptive Frameworks in Political Socialization Theory," in Renshon, ed., *Handbook*, pp. 35–36.

5. Political scientists have in the past tended to discount the influence of religion on political attitudes because denominational affiliations were not predictive of citizen attitudes and political persuasions. However, a recent study conducted by the Search Institute of Minneapolis on the members of Congress reports that "By knowing both party affiliation and religious orientation, we can predict as much as 75 percent of the variation in voting on some scales." Peter L. Benson analyzed the members of Congress' attitudes toward religion on four continua: agentic or communal religion; vertical or horizontal religion; comforting or challenging religion; and restricting or releasing religion. See Peter L. Benson, "God is Alive in the United States Congress, But Not Always Voting Against Civil Liberties and for Military Spending," *Psychology Today* (December 1981): 47–57.

6. Roberta S. Sigel and Marilyn Brookes Hoskin, *The Political Involvement of Adolescents* (New Brunswick, NJ: Rutgers University Press, 1981), p. 68.

7. Arnold Toynbee, *Change and Habit* (London: Oxford University Press, 1966), Chapter 2.

8. For a helpful discussion on this particular type of citizen participation promoted during the early political socialization process in the United States, see

Robert Weissberg, *Political Learning, Political Choice, and Democratic Citizenship* (Englewood Cliffs, NJ: Prentice-Hall, 1974), pp. 65–67.

9. Fred I. Greenstein, *Children and Politics* (New Haven: Yale University Press, 1965), p. 73.

10. Robert Hess and Judith Torney, *Development of Political Attitudes in Children* (Chicago: Aldine Publishing Company, 1967), p. 278.

11. Gabriel Almond and Sidney Verba, *The Civic Culture* (Boston: Little, Brown, 1963), pp. 17–26.

12. M. Kent Jennings and Richard G. Niemi, *Generations and Politics* (Princeton: Princeton University Press, 1981), pp. 35–36.

13. Charles F. Andrain, *Children and Civic Awareness: A Study in Political Education* (Columbus, OH: Charles E. Merrill Publishing Company, 1971), pp. 154–55.

14. John J. Patrick, "Political Socialization and Political Education in Schools," in Renshon, ed., *Handbook*, p. 196.

15. Daniel J. Boorstin, *The Genius of American Politics* (Chicago: University of Chicago Press, 1953).

Complete List of All Questions Over the Years 1974–1978

Cognitive Questions Used at Each Grade Level for the Five Annual Interviews

	Grade Level and Year of Interview				
	K 1974	1 1975	2 1976	3 1977	4 1978
NATIONAL POLITICAL COMMUNITY					
What country do you live in?	x	x	x	x	x
Which is our flag? (Pictures of 4 flags shown)	x				
Recognition of a picture of the national Capitol.	x	x	x	x	x
Recognition of a picture of the Statue of Liberty.	x	x	x	x	x
Recognition of a picture of the Liberty Bell.	x	x	x	x	x
Recognition of a picture of the White House.			x	x	x
Recognition of a picture of George Washington.	x	x	x	x	x
Recognition of a picture of Abraham Lincoln.	x	x	x	x	x
What is the Star Spangled Banner?		x	x	x	x
What is the Bicentennial?			x		
What do we celebrate on the fourth of July?			x	x	x
What is a nation?			x	x	x
Tell me something about George Washington.				x	x
Tell me something about Abraham Lincoln.				x	x

245

	Grade Level and Year of Interview				
	K 1974	1 1975	2 1976	3 1977	4 1978
REGIME					
<u>Political Ideals</u>					
What is freedom?				x	x
<u>Government</u>					
What does the government do?	x	x	x	x	x
How does the government do that?					x
Why does the government do that?					x
What is the government?		x			
What does the word "government" mean?				x	x
<u>Executive</u>					
Who is the boss of our country?	x	x	x	x	x
Do we have a king in our country?	x	x	x	x	x
Who does the most to run our country?	x		x	x	x
What do you think the President does when he goes to work?	x	x	x	x	x
Who is the king? (If indicated that we have a king)		x	x	x	x
If Ford indicated as boss, what is his job called?		x			
<u>Legislative</u>					
Who makes the laws?	x	x	x	x	x
What is the Congress?			x	x	x
What is a Senator?				x	x
What does Congress do?					x

Grade Level and Year of Interview

	K 1974	1 1975	2 1976	3 1977	4 1978
Judicial					
What is the Supreme Court?			x	x	x
What is a court?				x	x
What does a judge do?				x	x
Electoral Process					
What is an election?	x	x	x	x	x
Who picks the President?	x	x	x	x	x
Who can vote in an election?					x
Are there any people who can't vote?					x
How did Gerald Ford become President?		x	x	x	x
How did Jimmy Carter become President?				x	x
Political Parties					
What do politicians do?	x	x	x	x	x
Tell me something about a political party.				x	x
Special Governmental Functions					
What does a policeman do?	x	x	x	x	x
What does a soldier do?	x	x	x	x	x
What are taxes?	x	x	x	x	x
Why do people pay taxes?		x	x	x	x
What is an army for?			x	x	x
What is the Board of Education (School Board)?			x	x	x

Grade Level and Year of Interview

	K 1974	1 1975	2 1976	3 1977	4 1978
Law and Law-Related					
What is a law?	x	x	x	x	x
If your mom and dad were speeding in a car and a policeman stopped them, what would happen?	x	x	x	x	x
If the President were speeding in his car and a policeman stopped him, what would happen?	x	x	x	x	x
Why do some people have to go to jail?	x	x	x	x	x
Why do we have laws?			x	x	x
AUTHORITIES					
What is the President's name?	x	x	x	x	x
Recognition of Richard Nixon's picture.	x			x	x
Can you tell me who Tom Bradley is?	x	x	x	x	x
Can you tell me who Ronald Reagan is?	x				
Can you tell me who Richard Nixon is?	x	x			
If said "President" was boss of country, what is his name?		x			
Recognition of Gerald Ford's picture.		x	x	x	x
What is a Republican?		x	x	x	x
What is a Democrat?		x	x	x	x
Can you tell me who Gerald Ford is?		x	x		

Grade Level and Year of Interview

	K 1974	1 1975	2 1976	3 1977	4 1978
AUTHORITIES (Continued)					
Can you tell me who Jerry Brown is?		x	x	x	x
Which political party does the President belong to?			x	x	x
Can you tell me who _____ (local mayor) is?			x	x	x
Recognition of Jimmy Carter's picture.				x	x
Can you tell me who Jimmy Carter is?				x	x
Tell me about Jimmy Carter.				x	x
Name of first political party mentioned.				x	x
Name of second political party mentioned.				x	x
Can you think of a difference between the Republicans and the Democrats?				x	x
Which party do you like better?				x	x
Recognition of John F. Kennedy's picture.				x	x
Can you tell me who Alan Cranston is?				x	x
Can you tell me who S. I. Hayakawa is?				x	x
Recognition of Governor Brown's picture.					x
Recognition of Mayor Bradley's picture.					x
Who is the Governor of California?					x
Who is the Mayor of Los Angeles?					x

	Grade Level and Year of Interview				
	K 1974	1 1975	2 1976	3 1977	4 1978
POLITICAL GEOGRAPHY					
Tell me, where do you live?	x	x	x		
What city do you live in?	x	x	x	x	x
What state do you live in?	x	x	x	x	x
Which other country do you like better than ours?			x	x	x
Can you tell me the name of another country (besides ours)?				x	x
Can you tell me the name of another state (besides ours)?				x	x
PRIVATE/PUBLIC SECTOR ROLES					
Does a policeman work for the government?	x	x	x	x	x
Does a soldier work for the government?	x	x	x	x	x
Does a judge work for the government?	x	x	x	x	x
Does a mailman work for the government?	x	x	x	x	x
Does your teacher work for the government?	x	x	x	x	x
Does a milkman work for the government?	x	x	x	x	x
Does a gas station man work for the government?		x	x	x	x
Does the person who gives the news on TV work for the government?				x	x
Does a candy store person work for the government?				x	x
How do you tell whether a person works for the government or not?					x

	Grade Level and Year of Interview				
	K 1974	1 1975	2 1976	3 1977	4 1978
PUBLIC POLICY ISSUES					
Tell me something about Vietnam.	x	x	x	x	x
Tell me about the energy crisis.	x	x		x	x
Tell me something about the energy problem.			x		
Tell me something about Watergate.	x	x	x	x	x
Do you know what impeachment is?	x				
Tell me about the economy.			x		
Tell me something about prices.			x		
Tell me about unemployment.				x	x
Tell me about inflation.				x	x
Tell me about crime.				x	x
TOTAL COGNITIVE QUESTIONS ASKED BY GRADE LEVEL	41	50	59	82	92

Affective Questions Used at Each Grade Level for the Five Annual Interviews

	Grade Level and Year of Interview				
	K 1974	1 1975	2 1976	3 1977	4 1978
REGIME					
Government					
Do you like the government?		x	x	x	x
Why doesn't the government make mistakes?				x	x

	Grade Level and Year of Interview				
	K 1974	1 1975	2 1976	3 1977	4 1978
REGIME (continued)					
Laws					
Do you like the laws?		x	x	x	x
Are there any laws you don't like?					x
Electoral Process					
Would you like to vote?	x	x	x	x	x
Special Governmental Functions					
Are policemen your friends?	x	x	x	x	x
If you were playing in front of your house and a policeman stopped to talk to you, what do you think he might say?	x	x	x	x	x
Are taxes good or bad?			x	x	x
Sense of Governmental Responsiveness					
Does the government listen to what your mom or dad say?	x	x	x	x	x
Would the government want to help you if you needed help?			x	x	x
Do the people running the government care about ordinary people like us?				x	x
Do people in the government care much about what your mom or dad think?				x	x

Grade Level and Year of Interview

	K 1974	1 1975	2 1976	3 1977	4 1978
<u>Sense of Political Efficacy</u>					
If the government makes a mistake, should you write a letter or just forget about it?				x	x
Do you think when things in the government are wrong that people like us can do something about it?				x	x
PUBLIC POLICY ISSUES					
Is Watergate good or bad?	x[a]	x	x	x	x
Is Vietnam good or bad?	x	x	x	x	x
Is the economy good or bad?		x			
Is the energy crisis good or bad?		x	x	x	x
Are prices good or bad?			x		
Is unemployment good or bad?				x	x
Is inflation good or bad?				x	x
Is crime good or bad?				x	x
Is it OK for a girl to be a (male stereotyped role)?				x	x
Is it OK for a boy to be a (female stereotyped role)?				x	x
AUTHORITIES					
Do you like one party better than the others?				x	x
TOTAL AFFECTIVE QUESTIONS ASKED BY GRADE LEVEL	6	10	12	22	23

[a]Does Watergate make the President happy or sad?

Evaluative Questions Used at Each Grade Level for the Five Annual Interviews

	Grade Level and Year of Interview				
	K 1974	1 1975	2 1976	3 1977	4 1978
POLITICAL IDEALS					
Tell me something that isn't fair.	x	x	x	x	x
What is a good citizen?			x	x	x
GOVERNMENT					
Why do you like government?		x	x	x	x
Why don't you like government?		x	x	x	x
GOVERNMENTAL FALLIBILITY					
How often do you think the government makes mistakes?		x	x	x	x
Why does the government make mistakes?				x	x
LAWS					
Why do you like laws?		x	x	x	x
Why don't you like laws?		x	x	x	x
Are all the laws fair?			x	x	x
Why are all the laws fair?			x	x	x
Why aren't all the laws fair?			x	x	x
Which is more important: to vote in an election or to obey the laws?				x	x
Why is it more important to obey the laws?					x
What would happen if there were no laws?					x
ELECTORAL PROCESS					
Why would you like to vote?			x	x	x

	K 1974	1 1975	2 1976	3 1977	4 1978
Grade Level and Year of Interview					

	K 1974	1 1975	2 1976	3 1977	4 1978
Why wouldn't you like to vote?			x	x	x
Why is it more important to vote?[a]					x
SPECIAL FUNCTIONS					
Why are taxes good?			x	x	x
Why are taxes bad?			x	x	x
NATIONAL POLITICAL COMMUNITY					
Is America the best country in the world?		x	x	x	x
Why is America the best country in the world?		x	x	x	x
Why is America not the best country in the world?		x	x	x	x
Do you like any other country better than ours?			x	x	x
Why do you like _____ (country) better than ours?			x	x	x
Why don't you like any other country better than ours?			x	x	x
AUTHORITIES					
Why do you like that party better?				x	x
How often do you think the President makes mistakes?			x	x	x

[a] Part of follow-up for respondents who considered voting in an election more important than obeying the laws.

	Grade Level and Year of Interview				
	K 1974	1 1975	2 1976	3 1977	4 1978
PUBLIC/PRIVATE SECTOR ROLES					
Who is more important, a judge or an athlete?				x	x
Who is more important, a police chief or a TV person?				x	x
PUBLIC POLICY ISSUES					
Why is Watergate good?		x	x	x	x
Why is Watergate bad?		x	x	x	x
Why is Vietnam good?		x	x	x	x
Why is Vietnam bad?		x	x	x	x
Why is the economy good?		x			
Why is the economy bad?		x			
Why is the energy crisis good?		x	x	x	x
Why is the energy crisis bad?		x	x	x	x
What is the worst thing that can happen to a person?		x			
If you were the boss of the whole country, what would you do to help people?	x	x	x	x	x
Why are prices good?			x		
Why are prices bad?			x		
Why is unemployment good?				x	x
Why is unemployment bad?				x	x
Why is inflation good?				x	x
Why is inflation bad?				x	x
Why is crime good?				x	x
Why is crime bad?				x	x
What is the most important problem facing America?			x	x	x

	Grade Level and Year of Interview				
	K 1974	1 1975	2 1976	3 1977	4 1978
Why is it so important? (Problem facing America)					x
TOTAL EVALUATIVE QUESTIONS ASKED BY GRADE LEVEL	2	19	31	40	44

**Self-report Questions Used at Each Grade Level for the Five Annual
Interviews**

	Grade Level and Year of Interview				
	K 1974	1 1975	2 1976	3 1977	4 1978
NATIONAL POLITICAL COMMUNITY					
What do you like best about America?		x			
What do you think of when you see our flag?		x	x	x	x
What makes you most proud to be an American?			x	x	x
REGIME					
Do you know what the word "government" means?	x				
Have you ever voted in an election?	x	x	x	x	x
Can you tell me when you voted?				x	x
Why haven't you voted?				x	x
· Have you ever heard of the words "political party"?				x	x

	Grade Level and Year of Interview				
	K 1974	1 1975	2 1976	3 1977	4 1978
AUTHORITIES					
Have you ever seen the President on TV?	x	x	x	x	x
Have you ever heard of the word "Republican"?	x	x	x	x	x
Have you ever heard of the word "Democrat"?	x	x	x	x	x
Name a famous person you want to be like.			x	x	x
PUBLIC POLICY ISSUES					
Have you heard of the word "impeachment"?	x				
Have you heard of the words "energy crisis"?	x	x	x	x	x
Have you heard of the word "Watergate"?		x	x	x	x
Have you heard of the word "Vietnam"?		x	x	x	x
What would you like to do when you grow up?	x	x	x	x	x
If offered a sex stereotyped role, would you like to be the counterpart for opposite sex?		x	x	x	x
Have you heard of the word "economy"?		x			
Have you heard anything about "prices"?			x		
Have you heard about "unemployment"?				x	x
Have you heard about "inflation"?				x	x
Have you heard about "crime"?				x	x

	Grade Level and Year of Interview				
	K 1974	1 1975	2 1976	3 1977	4 1978
TOTAL SELF-REPORT QUESTIONS ASKED BY GRADE LEVEL	8	12	13	18	18

B

Criteria for Staging Threshold Variables

Criteria for Staging Responses to "What Does the Government Do?", "How Does the Government Do That?" and "Why Does the Government Do That?"

Stage One: Symbol Recognition

Responses associate the term with property, helping people, or other very general public functions. Stage 1 responses also encompass those in which there is a confusion between government and governor.

Stage Two: Task Pooling

Responses identify the institution in a partially accurate way, but do not specify any critical feature or any distinctive function as enumerated in the Stage 3 criteria listed below. Stage 2 responses may specify helping the country or helping the President, lawmaking without any further elaboration, or extremely generalized references to actual government functions, for example, to protect people. Unless there is a clear implication of a division of governmental tasks or unless "he" refers to the governor, the use of the third person singular ("he") constitutes a Stage 2 response.

Stage Three: Critical Features

Responses specify one of the following critical features or functions:
   a) involved in law and rule making (must offer some details that imply division of labor in this process)
   b) specific reference to governing or administering a political jurisdiction (with some illustration)
   c) seeks to insure safety of either individuals or the national community (must offer some details about means or the threats, that is, go beyond phrase "protect us")

d) involved in acquisition, regulation, and allocation of economic resources, for example, taxation, protecting natural resources, and regulating or subsidizing economic activities

Stage Four: Multiple Features

Response specifies two or three of the critical features or functions enumerated in Stage 3 above.

Stage Five: Textbook Description

Response specifies with reasonable completeness all of the critical features enumerated in Stage 3 above.

Stage Six: Self-Conscious Ideological Interpretation

Response must meet the criteria for Stage 5 above but must also acknowledge the possibility of varying interpretations based on differing value or ideological assumptions.

Criteria for Staging Responses to "What Are Taxes?" and "Why Do People Pay Taxes?"

Stage One: Symbol Recognition

Responses associate the term inaccurately with a bill or payment not involving taxation, for example, a utility bill, or refer simply to "money," or identify a nongovernmental purpose to which tax revenue might be applied.

Stage Two: Task Pooling

Responses identify or imply a single specific tax, for example, property, sales (including reference to "extra money"), or income tax, or suggest a single or very generalized governmental purpose to which tax revenue might be applied.

Stage Three: Critical Features

Responses specify one of the following critical features or functions:
a) general payment to government
b) multiple sources of revenue, that is, reference to more than one of the following taxes: income, sales, property, and luxury
c) multiple government purposes to which tax revenue might be applied

d) reference to a single revenue source and a single governmental purpose to which that tax revenue might be applied

Stage Four: Multiple Features
Response specifies two or three of the critical features or functions enumerated in Stage 3 above.

Stage Five: Textbook Description
Response specifies with reasonable completeness all of the critical features enumerated in Stage 3 above.

Stage Six: Self-Conscious Ideological Interpretation
Response must meet the criteria for Stage 5 above but must also acknowledge the possibility of varying interpretations based on differing value or ideological assumptions.

Criteria for Staging Responses to "What Is an Election?" and "Who Picks the President?"

Stage One: Symbol Recognition
Responses associate the process with government but are extremely vague or inaccurate; references to meeting(s) and discussion(s) are included in this stage.

Stage Two: Task Pooling
Responses identify the notion of a broad electorate without implying any restrictions on participation, a general reference to voting with a specific implication of choice, or reference to voting for one specific office with the implication that it represents the full extent of electoral opportunity, for example, voting for the President.

Stage Three: Critical Features
Responses specify one of the following critical features or functions:
  a) notion of a broad electorate, limited by a few demographic restrictions; age, residence, citizenship
  b) choice between competing candidates or alternative positions on public issues

c) reference to such phenomena as nominating process or campaigns
d) reference to multiple offices or differing jurisdictions

Stage Four: Multiple Features
Response specifies two or three of the critical features or functions enumerated in Stage 3 above.

Stage Five: Textbook Description
Response specifies with reasonable completeness all of the critical features enumerated in Stage 3 above.

Stage Six: Self-Conscious Ideological Interpretation
Response must meet the criteria for Stage 5 above but must also acknowledge the possibility of varying interpretations based on differing value or ideological assumptions.

Criteria for Staging Responses to "What Is the Congress?"

Stage One: Symbol Recognition
Responses associate the term with government, politics, or an important public entity, but are extremely vague or inaccurate in describing the relationship, or identify it as a group of people without specifying a governmental association, or associate it with Washington, D.C., only.

Stage Two: Task Pooling
Response identifies the institution or process in a partially accurate way but does not specify or imply a critical feature of Congress enumerated in the Stage 3 criteria listed below. Stage 2 responses may include reference to two or more of the Stage 1 criteria, identification as a presidential helper or aide; mention of Senate, House of Representatives, or Congress; reference to elections or being voted for; or participating in voting but no reference to lawmaking.

Stage Three: Critical Features
Responses specify one of the following critical features or functions:
a) represent states, people, or group interests

b) law or rule making body, or refers to interaction with the President in decision making
c) responds to citizen appeals for assistance—ombudsman function
d) oversees the administration of laws (legislative oversight)

Stage Four: Multiple Features
Response specifies two or three of the critical features or functions enumerated in Stage 3 above.

Stage Five: Textbook Description
Response specifies with reasonable completeness all of the critical features enumerated in Stage 3 above.

Stage Six: Self-Conscious Ideological Interpretation
Response must meet the criteria for Stage 5 above but must also acknowledge the possibility of varying interpretations based on differing value or ideological assumptions.

Criteria for Staging Responses to "What Is the Supreme Court?"

Stage One: Symbol Recognition
Stage 1 responses associate the term with government, politics, or an important public entity (including, for example, jail or army), but are extremely vague or inaccurate in describing the relationship.

Stage Two: Task Pooling
Response identifies the institution or process in a partially accurate way, but does not specify or imply a critical feature enumerated in the Stage 3 criteria listed below. Stage 2 responses may suggest handling big or important cases or making references to judicial processes, for example, judging guilt or innocence and determining punishment.

Stage Three: Critical Features
Responses specify one of the following critical features or functions:
a) highest authority in the court system

b) co-equal with the President and Congress
c) interpreter of Constitution
d) umpires relationship between the nation and states, the President and Congress, or the individual and government

Stage Four: Multiple Features
Response specifies two or three of the critical features or functions enumerated in Stage 3 above.

Stage Five: Textbook Description
Response specifies with reasonable completeness all of the critical features enumerated in Stage 3 above.

Stage Six: Self-Conscious Ideological Interpretation
Response must meet the criteria for Stage 5 above but must also acknowledge the possibility of varying interpretations based on differing value or ideological assumptions.

Criteria for Staging Responses to "What Is a Senator?"

Stage One: Symbol Recognition
Response associates the term with government, politics, or an important public function or official, but is extremely vague or inaccurate. Stage 1 responses may offer name of a particular senator or may identify office with judicial or executive functions.

Stage Two: Task Pooling
Response identifies the office in a partially accurate way, but does not specify or imply a critical feature or a distinctive function (see Stage 3 below). Stage 2 responses may specify aiding President or governor, working in Congress or Senate, or accurately places senator in the governmental hierarchy.

Stage Three: Critical Features
Responses specify one of the following critical features or functions:
a) representative of a state in Congress (or a district, if a state senator)
b) law or rule maker; interacts with or assists President (or governor, if state senator)
c) oversees administration of laws

d) responds to citizen appeals for assistance

Stage Four: Multiple Features
Response specifies two or three of the critical features or functions enumerated in Stage 3 above.

Stage Five: Textbook Description
Response specifies with reasonable completeness all of the critical features enumerated in Stage 3 above.

Stage Six: Self-Conscious Ideological Interpretation
Response must meet the criteria for Stage 5 above but must also acknowledge the possibility of varying interpretations based on differing value or ideological assumptions.

Criteria for Staging Responses to "Tell Me Something About a Political Party."

Stage One: Symbol Recognition
Response associates the term with government, politics, or an important public function or official, but is extremely vague or inaccurate. Responses that mention a group of people, meeting, or a notion of there being two parties are examples of a Stage 1 response.

Stage Two: Task Pooling
Response identifies the institution in a partially accurate way, but does not specify a critical feature enumerated in the Stage 3 criteria listed below. Specifying in name only one or more parties constitutes a Stage 2 response.

Stage Three: Critical Features
Responses specify one of the following critical features or functions:
   a) group supporting candidates for public office, helping them seek votes (political recruitment)
   b) group advocating policies or programs that may differ from those of a competing group (political education)
   c) group participating in the law- or rule-making process
   d) group helping to govern a political jurisdiction

Stage Four: Multiple Features
Response specifies two or three of the critical features or functions enumerated in Stage 3 above.

Stage Five: Textbook Description
Response specifies with reasonable completeness all of the critical features enumerated in Stage 3 above.

Stage Six: Self-Conscious Ideologial Interpretation
Response must meet the criteria for Stage 5 above but must also acknowledge the possibility of varying interpretations based on differing value or ideological assumptions.

Criteria for Staging Responses to "What Do Politicians Do?"

Stage One: Symbol Recognition
Responses associate the term with government, politics, or an important public function or official, but are extremely vague or inaccurate.

Stage Two: Task Pooling
Response identifies the role in a partially accurate way, but does not specify a critical feature enumerated in the Stage 3 criteria listed below.

Stage Three: Critical Features
Response specifies one of the following critical features or functions:
   a) running for public office or helping others to run as candidates
   b) serving as public opinion leaders by advocating policies or programs that may be in opposition to one another
   c) participating in law- or rule-making function (formulating laws or rules)
   d) helping to govern, administer, or run a political jurisdiction

Stage Four: Multiple Features
Response specifies two or three of the critical features or functions enumerated in Stage 3 above.

Stage Five: Textbook Description
Response specifies with reasonable completeness all of the critical features enumerated in Stage 3 above.

Stage Six: Self-Conscious Ideological Interpretation
Response must meet the criteria for Stage 5 above but must also acknowledge the possibility of varying interpretations based on differing value or ideological assumptions.

C

Comparison of Sample and Nonsample Students on Third Grade Posttest*

Questionnaire Item	Sample (N=53)	Nonsample (N=114)
Have seen President on television	100.0	94.7
Believe policeman is a friend	100.0	97.4
Feel government would want to help if help needed	69.8	54.4
Feel people running government care about people	79.2	62.3
Feel government listens to what mom and dad say	66.0	57.0
Feel people in government care about mom and dad	52.8	54.4
Feel people like us can do something when things in government are wrong	64.2	62.3
Believe a policeman works for government	90.6	92.1
Believe a judge works for government	88.7	82.5
Believe a soldier works for government	86.8	65.8
Believe a TV newsperson works for government	73.6	55.3
Believe a mailman works for government	73.6	53.5
Believe a teacher works for government	69.8	47.4
Believe a gas station man works for government	64.2	38.6
Believe a milkman works for government	56.6	36.8
Believe a candy store person works for government	34.0	21.9
Believe a judge more important than an athlete	86.8	92.1
Believe a police chief more important than TV star	96.2	97.4

Questionnaire Item	Sample (N=53)	Nonsample (N=114)
Assessment of how frequently the President makes mistakes		
Often	20.8	13.2
Sometimes	45.3	54.4
Rarely	32.1	28.1
Never	1.9	4.4
Frequency of TV news watching		
Often	18.9	21.1
Sometimes	43.4	37.7
Rarely	30.2	26.3
Never	7.5	14.9
Sex		
Male	41.5	36.0
Female	58.5	64.0
Famous person you want to be like		
Male political	3.8	3.5
Male movie or TV	11.3	8.8
Female movie or TV	9.4	18.4
Athlete or sports	39.6	17.5
Myself	9.4	3.5
Other	18.9	13.2
NA	7.5	35.1

*By percentages.

D

Selection of Cognitive Map Questions

The 20 questions used in this map were selected from the 38 cognitive questions asked all five years to represent the six areas of political knowledge contained in the questionnaire: the national community (3), the regime (7), political authorities (3), public issues (2), political geography (3), and public- and private-sector occupational roles (2). The three symbols of the national political community—recognition of pictures of George Washington, the national Capitol, and the Statue of Liberty—were selected from five such questions; those not included in the map were the pictures of Abraham Lincoln, whose recognition level was similar to that of Washington, and the Liberty Bell, which seemed so similar to the Statue of Liberty that only one should be selected. Washington, rather than Lincoln, was selected because of the former's identification as "the father of our country." The selection of the Statue of Liberty rather than the Liberty Bell was arbitrary; either one seemed suitable, but including both would have been unnecessary duplication. The seven regime items in the map were selected from 16 regime-related questions that had been asked all five years:

Regime Questions In Cognitive Map	Regime Questions Not In Cognitive Map
Do we have a king in our country?	Who is the boss of our country?
What is an election?	Who does the most to run country?
What do politicians do?	
What does a policeman do?	What do you think the President does when he goes to work?

Regime Questions In Cognitive Map	*Regime Questions Not In Cognitive Map*
What does a soldier do?	Who picks the President?
What are taxes?	Why do some people have to go to jail?
What is the law?	If your mom and dad were speeding in a car and a policeman stopped them, what would happen to them?
	If the President were speeding in his car and a policeman stopped him, what would happen to him?
	What does the government do?
	Who makes the laws?

Some of the nine regime questions not included in the map were omitted because they would have been duplicative of other map questions. "Do we have a king...," for example, was the second question asked in each interview and was designed to get a sense of whether the child could distinguish between a nonelected political authority and an elected one. It seemed unnecessary to include in the map any of the other three questions relating to the executive function: "Who is the boss of our country?" (the first interview question), "Who does the most to run our country?", and "What do you think the President does when he goes to work?" The latter question, in fact, is used as one of the threshold cognitive variables in this study. Likewise, the question "What is an election?" seemed to test a child's awareness of the electoral process, and there was no need to include the second such question, "Who picks the President?"

The question "What is a law?" is a fundamental measure of the child's comprehension of the legal realm and so three other law-related questions were not included in the map: "Why do some people have to go to jail?," "If your mom and dad were speeding in a car and a policeman stopped them, what would happen to them," and "If the President were speeding in his car and a policeman stopped him, what would happen to him?" The latter two were designed to assess the child's perception of the rule of law and not to measure a cognitive understanding of the law per se. "What does the government do?" and "Who makes the laws?" were two other regime-related questions not included in the map. The former is one of the earliest cognitive threshold variables to be identified and the latter is one of the six questions comprising the Law Understanding Index.

We selected the chief executives of the three levels of government to represent the authorities category in the cognitive map—using recognition of the incumbent President's picture and the names of the governor of California (Ronald Reagan and Jerry Brown) and the mayor of Los Angeles (Tom Bradley) as the measures of cognitive awareness. Recognition of the incumbent President's picture was the most conservative measure of that awareness, while recognition of the names of the incumbent governors of California and mayor of Los Angeles was the most accurate way of measuring a child's awareness of those authorities.

The inclusion of two of the three public issues asked all five years, "Tell me something about Watergate" and "Tell me about the energy crisis," was an appropriate way of measuring awareness of issue-related phenomena. The Watergate question referred to the presidency and to one of the major political traumas experienced by the U.S. polity during the twentieth century. The energy crisis was of paramount concern during the 1970s and is likely to be a major domestic issue at least through the end of the century. The question, "Tell me something about Vietnam," was not included, in part because it became evident that the children's awareness of Vietnam often centered on it as a geographic entity or the former residence of refugee classmates rather than on Vietnam as a divisive public issue. Their cognition, in short, was not a political one.

The inclusion of the three major levels of political geography, "What city (state, county) do you live in?", corresponds to the three principal levels of government in our political system. Milkman and judge were selected as the occupations used to measure the ability to distinguish between public- and private-sector roles. Milkman was selected because it was the private role employed by Easton and Dennis in their eight-city study, while judge was the most obvious public-sector role when policeman and soldier were eliminated because they were already in the map as measures of regime awareness ("What does a policeman [soldier] do?").

— Index

NAME INDEX

275

SUBJECT INDEX

— About the Authors————

STANLEY W. MOORE is Professor of Political Science at Pepperdine University, Malibu, California. He has served four years as president of the Southern California Political Science Association and for six years as president of the California Center for Education in Public Affairs—which sponsors an annual Sacramento Legislative Seminar as well as one or more conferences each year on current political issues.

Professor Moore, in addition to this continuing longitudinal study of political socialization, has published articles in five areas of political science, including political theory, public policy, future studies, and Christianity and politics. In the spring of 1984 he interviewed the students of this panel as tenth graders—the ninth individual interviews so conducted. After the twelfth grade interviews he plans a second book covering fifth through the twelfth grades.

Professor Moore received his B.A. from Wheaton College, Illinois, and his M.A. and Ph.D. in government from Claremont Graduate School. He has held faculty appointments at Fullerton State University, Stanislaus State, the Monterey Institute of Foreign Studies and the University of Redlands.

JAMES LARE is Professor of Political Science at Occidental College in Los Angeles. He developed the Urban Studies Program at Occidental and is currently a member of its Advisory Board.

Professor Lare is co-editor (with Clinton Rossiter) of *The Essential Lippmann* and edited a 1964 Regional American Assembly final report on *The Congress and America's Future*. He is currently developing a series of case studies that examine public policy issues facing state and local officials in California.

Dr. Lare received his B.A. from Occidental and his M.B.A. and Ph.D. degrees from Cornell University. He has held faculty appointments at Cornell, the University of California, Los Angeles, and California State University at Northridge.

KENNETH A. WAGNER is Professor of Political Science at California State University, Los Angeles. He has served as chairperson of the Department of Political Science and as Director of the Social Science Data Archive and Computer Laboratory.

Professor Wagner combines research interests in political socialization and constitutional law. He is currently one member of a NEH-funded leadership team that will train secondary school teachers of American History how to use the stage-related concepts of law that were developed in this longitudinal study in a way that is designed to assist and to accelerate learning about the United States Constitution.

Professor Wagner received his B.S. and M. Ed. degrees from South Dakota State University. After several years of teaching American History and Government in secondary schools, he enrolled at the University of Iowa and was awarded his Ph.D. in Political Science in 1970.

Professors Moore, Lare, and Wagner have co-authored a number of papers on early childhood political socialization which have been presented at professional meetings during the time period of this study. Their article, "The Civic Awareness of Five and Six Year Olds," appeared in the *Western Political Quarterly* and a piece on "Developing Notions of Law and Morality in Kindergarten Through Third Grade School Children" appeared in the *Proceedings of the Eighth Annual International Conference on Piagetian Theory*.